choosing sides

ALSO BY TARA MATARAZA DESMOND

Almost Meatless: Recipes That Are Better for Your Health and the Planet

choosing sides

From Holidays to Every Day,
130 Delicious Recipes to Make the Meal

✦

TARA MATARAZA DESMOND

PHOTOGRAPHY BY BEN PIEPER

**Andrews McMeel
Publishing, LLC**
Kansas City • Sydney • London

Andrews McMeel Publishing, LLC
an Andrews McMeel Universal company
1130 Walnut Street, Kansas City, Missouri 64106

www.andrewsmcmeel.com

13 14 15 16 17 SDB 10 9 8 7 6 5 4 3 2 1

ISBN: 978-1-4494-2711-5

Library of Congress Control Number: 2013937539

Design: Holly Ogden
Photography: Ben Pieper Photography
Digital/Photo Assistant: Anneka DeJong
Food Stylist: Trina Kahl
Food Stylist Assistant: Dan Trefz
Photo page 67 © StockFood/Jon Edwards

ATTENTION: SCHOOLS AND BUSINESSES
Andrews McMeel books are available at quantity discounts
with bulk purchase for educational, business, or sales
promotional use. For information, please e-mail the
Andrews McMeel Special Sales Department: specialsales@
amuniversal.com

For Topher,
the best side I've ever chosen

· ·

Contents

Acknowledgments viii
Introduction xi
how to use this book xii • how to choose your sides xii
main-course pairings xvi • recipe notes xxiv

Acknowledgments

In life, the good people who surround you make everything better the way side dishes can make a meal. I'm lucky and grateful for so many who were alongside me while I wrote this book.

Clare Pelino, my agent, who was enthusiastic about this concept from the minute I suggested it and who remains supportive, patient, and empathetic to the juggle of motherhood and career.

Jean Lucas and the staff at Andrews McMeel Publishing for choosing, polishing, and designing this book. The talented folks at Ben Pieper Photography, whose styling and pictures made for the perfect visual helpings of the featured recipes.

Kevin Downing, an endless source of creativity, who spurred the title for this book in a weekday email exchange that I'll keep forever. Maureen Petrosky, who has been unselfishly available throughout my career, especially when her moral support as a fellow mother of twins rallied me through the very rough first trimester of babies and book writing. Liz Pollitt Paisner, who commiserated and propped me up when the notion of working in the early days of a twin pregnancy felt impossible. Cheryl Sternman Rule for being a professional and personal confidante who makes me laugh in the most cathartic and medicinal way; Robin Asbell for good advice on keeping it real in this business; Monica Bhide for an unwavering optimism and commitment to seeing it through; Nancie McDermott, whose energy comes bounding through email in a way that brings the camaraderie so much closer; Sandra Gutierrez, an inspiring author, woman, and mom for her deeply personal advice and encouragement; Jill O'Connor, who should really have her own comedy show if it wouldn't interfere with her sharing her incredible culinary and writerly talents; Ivy Manning for her generous and immediate cracker consultation, which spared me sleuthing time and made for the crispy, crunchy snacks I set out to make; Jennifer Lindner McGlinn for calling me from the hospital in labor to talk about pastry dough; Holly Herrick for a blind-baking consultation; Andy Schloss for his one-of-a-kind view of the world and life that keeps me laughing and thinking. Colleagues and friends who are always on hand, however far away, for invaluable exchanges, especially those from the food writers Google group, the Facebook cookbook writers group, Facebook friends who weighed in on questions that fueled this book's content, the Food Writers Symposium, and the International Association of Culinary Professionals (IACP).

Friends who contributed recipes to *Choosing Sides*, including Allyson Evans for helping me create Herbed Biscuits (page 31) and always believing I can make anything happen; Lish Steiling, who lent her authentic, unfussy, and precise culinary sensibilities and her arm's beet tattoo to the development of Roasted Beets with Shaved Fennel and Marcona Almonds (page 145); Anna Marchini and her mother, Antonietta DeRenzo Marchini, for teaching this very American Italian-American the ways of Frittata di Pasta (page 160); Denise Downing for mastering a family heirloom recipe from her grandmother-in-law, Rosemary Foote, and sharing it with me to publish here as Vintage Potato Salad (page 114), and Carroll Downing for sharing details of her mother's life; Caoimhe O'Kelly, who schooled me in the ways of Irish Brown Bread (page 49), and her husband, Kurt Deil, who helped translate to "American" the intricacies of the recipe for this book; the Fell sisters, especially Grace Fell Regan and Martha Fell Desmond, for detailing their parents' (my husband's grandparents) treasured recipes to be shared here in the form of Heritage Cornbread (page 45) and Legacy Cornbread Dressing (page 199).

The cadre of recipe testers who tested, retested, offered feedback, and kicked around ideas, improvements, and alterations that made this book so much better than it would have been if I had written it without their input. Their involvement helped me anticipate questions that you, the reader and the cook, would ask; kept me on my toes; and kept me company in a quiet kitchen. They include Anthony Abbatiello, Robin Asbell, Soma and Audreesh Banerjee, Cathy Baglieri, Deacon and Erika Chapin, Denise and Kevin Downing, Allyson Evans, Matt Grande, Tara Hoey, Joy Manning, Jennifer and John Mataraza, Paula and John Mataraza, Caoimhe O'Kelly, Alyson Oswald, Chrissy Quisenberry, Cheryl Sternman Rule, Julie Solomon and Gregg Narod, Chris Soltis, Liz Tarpy.

My mother, Paula Mataraza, who taught herself how to cook so successfully that it made me want to do it for a living. She contributed some of my favorites to this book, especially Eggplant Feta Rollatini (page 158). And my dad, John Mataraza, who keeps convincing me that I'll only live once, so I might as well keep trying . . . and keep eating cheese and drinking wine.

My daughter, Abigail, now two years old, who pushes her stool up to the kitchen counter to cook with me. I hope she always will. And the twins, Timothy and Miles, who were literally with me every step of the way on the journey of writing this book.

My husband, Topher, without whom life would be as incomplete and unsatisfying as Thanksgiving dinner without mashed potatoes and gravy. I am endlessly thankful that he is by my side every day.

Introduction

Every Thanksgiving my sister-in-law and I square off over the mashed potatoes, competing with our forks for the last fluffy bites. My mother makes buttered turnips, which only she eats. My grandfather brings his orange cranberry relish and at least four varieties of stuffing. My aunt shows up with six loaves of bread and matching spreads. My father-in-law hogs the oven for the better part of the morning preparing his candied sweet potatoes. There are always the requisite green beans amandine, even if they've been overlooked until the last minute. Oh, and somewhere on that table there's a turkey. It's a given, but it's no one's priority.

Side dish has subordinate implications that misrepresent the true impact the food in this category has on a meal. Despite the moniker, side dishes end up being a major part of the main event. Plus, as animal protein moves away from the center of the plate, a spot it has dominated throughout history, other ingredients, especially vegetables and grains, once auxiliary, now garner more attention. Side dishes have been elevated by arrangements much more interesting than plain potatoes or buttered noodles. These days, the food on the side is as important, glamorous, and riveting as the ingredient intended to be the focal point, whether during a holiday feast, a weekday supper, or a restaurant meal.

Restaurateurs and chefs have taken to emphasizing the periphery in recent years too. They now reference accompaniments with colorful, descriptive prose in their menus, leaving only steak houses and diners among those to simply list the main protein or element without referencing accompaniments. This strategy plays right into my susceptibility to being swayed by embellishments. At a favorite restaurant recently, I was drawn to both the grilled pork chop and the Spanish octopus selections, but the accompanying sides made my decision for me. The octopus mingled with housemade chorizo and potato confit with lemon and pimiento. The pork showed up with wood-braised white beans, Tuscan black kale, and pickled mustard seeds. Beans woo me every time. The mustardy kale is the icing on the cake. And a cake without icing is like a burger without a side of fries.

Most meals come standard with time-honored sides whose roots are tied up with those of our family trees. But for all the history we bake into gratins for Christmas dinner or tote in Tupperware to Fourth of July picnics or spoon out for a simple supper on a Tuesday night, we are always on the hunt for new favorites. At least once a week I am solicited for suggestions for dishes to contribute to a dinner party, recipes that might match a theme, and options for filling out a weeknight supper plate. A Google search for *side dishes* returns nearly four million results. Cooks and eaters harbor an unwavering belief that accompaniments make the meal.

All of us who cook at home hungrily seek sides for simple dinners every day of the week and occasions all year long. *Choosing Sides* is devoted entirely to side dishes and offers a collection of recipes that honors the standards while making the case for fresh ideas and new favorites. It maximizes on the trend of emphasizing ingredients that have traditionally played a supporting role at the table. It capitalizes on our obsession as cooks with our ability to accessorize a meal with quality ingredients in inspired, varied, and memorable recipes.

I wrote this book for food enthusiasts on a quest to create beautifully complete meals for any day of the year, every holiday on the calendar, and each occasion spent around the table. I mean for it to be a compendium of time-honored favorite sides and new recipes that are destined to become classics themselves.

Few cookbooks on the market today serve as a singular source for answering the perpetual question "What should I serve *with* this?" I hope *Choosing Sides* does for you.

how to use this book

This book is intended to help you build a meal from wherever you want to start, so there are a few ways to approach choosing sides from its pages. First, flip through the chapters, which are arranged by specific categories of side dishes (breads, salads, etc.) and types of meals (weeknight, holiday, brunch, etc.). But don't get boxed in by those parameters. Cook recipes from each chapter for whatever occasion you like. It's your choice.

If you've picked a recipe you'd like to try but are unsure about what to serve with it, scan the suggestions for main dishes in the "Alongside" list included with each recipe. I've considered flavor, texture, cuisine, and seasonality of both the side dish and the main in making my suggestions. You can consult your cookbook collection or browse dependable Internet sources for recipes to make the same or similar main dishes. Or maybe the ideas will remind you of a favorite that would be just right.

When you already have your main dish in mind, but are struggling with options for sides, scan the "Main-Course Pairings" chart on page xvi for ideas based on popular main-course ingredients. If you have a chicken to roast, take a gander at the list of recipes under "Chicken" in the chart, then flip to those recipes throughout the book to decide.

Finally, use the index at the back of the book to find side-dish recipes for a specific ingredient (potatoes, beans, tomatoes, carrots, etc.).

Whichever way you refer to the book, use it to inspire you to plan complementary meals with the idea that side dishes play a critical role in making them satisfying, exciting, and memorable.

how to choose your sides

Some people get a thrill from throwing open their closet doors and choosing what to wear. Picking fabrics and colors, factoring in designers' signature lines, upgrading from casual to chic, and coordinating clothes and accessories makes their days. I hurry up with my wardrobe selection so I have more time to get the same thrill from throwing open the doors of my refrigerator and pantry to decide what to cook. For me, accessorizing a meal is as pleasantly complex as choosing a killer wardrobe ensemble is for fancy girls and a few men. Plus I find it much more satisfying. Matching ingredients by color and texture, considering flavors, and making a meal to match my mood or to wow dinner guests is more fun than a shopping spree for me.

Maybe you think picking a side dish is about as uncomplicated as life gets. You go to your kitchen, see what you've got, think about it for seven seconds, grab some rice and accoutrements, and carry on. Your lack of labored consideration about what to serve with your main dish might come from the fact that your kitchen mojo is exceptionally polished and putting it all together comes naturally to you. Or maybe you simply enjoy the mini-challenge of composing a meal, no matter how simple or sophisticated.

On the other hand, maybe you're the type to get overwhelmed by making dinner, so you just boil and butter some noodles to fill up the plate without much regard for the big picture. If this is the case, you might also admit to feeling underwhelmed by your meal in the end. Choosing side dishes to complement a meal is a creative endeavor that's easily prompted by plenty of cues. These could be as obvious as the urge to satisfy a craving for something in particular or as precise as the need to showcase family favorites on a holiday table. Meal planning always begins from wherever you are. In other words, your vantage point drives the menu and influences the choices. Most of the time, one or more of the following categories come into play when choosing sides.

INVENTORY

Especially when weeknight dinners are the task at hand, already stocked ingredients determine what we make. Sometimes inventory might be sparse, leaving few possibilities to ponder. Other times you're committed to clearing out before stocking up, and in an effort to "eat down the fridge" or pantry, you use what you've got. During farm share season, I wait to eyeball our week's bounty before making many decisions on main dishes and side dishes alike. Gardeners might operate similarly, cooking with whatever is ready on any given day. Many of the recipes in this book will show you how to put to good use the simplest ingredients—cornmeal (Parmigiano Polenta Two Ways, page 150), rice (Lime Rice, page 96), potatoes (Crisply Roasted Garlic Potatoes, page 90), canned or dried beans (Za'atar Chickpea Mash, page 132)—that might be mainstays in your kitchen.

FLAVORS, CUISINES, AND THEMES

Some foods are destined to be together, and challenging those classic pairings is a Sisyphean task. Instead, use them as easy aids for choosing sides to match a main. Tomatoes and basil. Meat and potatoes. Rice and beans. In cases like these, you don't need to deviate from proven success, though you might try adding a little riff on the basics to make them your own. For example, try Roasted Fingerlings with Warm Rosemary Vinaigrette (page 140) instead of plain baked potatoes with your porterhouse. Sometimes your choice of cuisine can lead the way. If you've already decided to pan-sear ginger-soy-marinated fish for a dinner party, you've narrowed your flavor options to Asian and can pick a side accordingly. Try Lemongrass Vermicelli (page 176) or Sesame Braised Bok Choy (page 97). A flavor-themed meal will help dictate accompaniments in the same way. Building a meal around apples? Head straight for ingredients that pal around with apples in any application. Try Bacon Cheddar Spoonbread (page 146) with a cider-braised fresh ham or Cinnamon Challah Muffins (page 7) with apple sweet potato pancakes and sage sausage.

TEXTURE

Texturally speaking, a menu of cream of mushroom soup, meat loaf with a side of mashed potatoes, and chocolate mousse for dessert is going to raise some skeptical eyebrows, unless you're cooking for people who just had oral surgery or who have no teeth at all. But cream of mushroom soup and Caraway Flatbread (page 28), followed by meat loaf with Potato Stracciatella (page 148) and Apple Cabbage Chopped Salad (page 62), rounded out by a silky, rich parfait of chocolate mousse, whipped cream, and candied hazelnuts will earn you appreciative (toothy) grins. Textural variety keeps things interesting and appealing and is a good gauge for evaluating your meal plans. Think about spanning the spectrum (crisp romaine, soft pears, smooth blue cheese), incorporating opposites (crusty toasted baguette, tender rib-eye slices, snappy endive, creamy Brie), or jumbling a mixture (thick yogurt, sticky pomegranate molasses, chewy oats and raisins, brittle toasted sliced almonds). If your main dish is texturally one-dimensional, your side dish is the perfect opportunity for variety. A simple pork loin (soft and tender) matches perfectly with Crunchy

Corn Tortilla Salad (page 60), which includes snappy lettuce, smooth avocado, juicy pineapple, velvety mango, and crunchy corn tortilla strips. By comparison, a heaping spoonful of entirely soft Smoked Gouda Grits (page 99) can't be beaten next to twice-fried buttermilk chicken, all crunchy on the outside and juicy tender on the inside.

BALANCE

The most literal interpretation of the age-old dinner plate standard, "protein, starch, vegetable," evokes an image of plain beef, flanked by mashed or a baked potato, next to a pile of boiled peas, broccoli, or carrots. That stodgy arrangement is slowly going out of style as cooks learn to use more ingredients in new ways and to opt for de-emphasizing meat. The intent to build a balance is alive and well, but things are becoming more interesting and appetizing. Increasingly, side dishes play a bigger role in balance than the main dish does, especially where meat as the main is concerned. Elaborate salads like Honey Balsamic Peaches and Burrata (page 55), grains with fruit and nuts like Bulgur with Apricots, Golden Raisins, and Pistachios (page 143), and extravagant potato dishes like Potato Stracciatella (page 148) are dressing things up and giving good reason to pay more attention and grant even more real estate to accompaniments. I'm content with a few strips of grilled steak alongside a heap of salad and a warm roll. No matter how it shakes out in your kitchen, the point of balance is to round out the meal so it feels and tastes like you've eaten more than simply three plain food items. You've enjoyed a bevy of tastes and textures and feel satisfied by the combination of ingredients, even if they are still counted as protein, starch, and vegetable.

COLOR

We eat with our eyes. While no one will deny that a monochromatic dark brown chocolate cake donning a thick, luscious cap of dark brown chocolate frosting captures as many gawking gazes as runway models in giant wings and sparkly things, bursts and blends of colors more assertively draw our eyes and entice our appetites even before we smell or taste a thing. The more colorful or color coordinated a plate, the more likely it will pique our interest. Side dishes are often the best opportunity to infuse color, especially if slices or hunks of meat play the leading role. The Panzanella Trifle (page 174) with its layers of vibrant green, yellow, red, golden, and white ingredients is spectacular next to a platter of grilled chicken or steak and is all you need to brighten the plate. However, the side dish doesn't have to be a rainbow to bring visual balance to the meal either. Chimichurri Green Beans (page 185) are consummately emerald, but a pile of them adds life to a plate of tan, beige, and golden cumin-crusted pork tenderloin and roasted potatoes. When you're drawing a blank on completing the plate, a color survey of the ingredients will inspire your instincts.

SEASONALITY AND AVAILABILITY

One of the best ways to stay out of a food rut is to follow the lead of the seasons. If you do, then recipes like Mixed Greens with Cherries, Berries, and Cheese (page 56) will become an annual treat that celebrates the fleeting cherry season and offers reprieve from some other overserved salad of which you've had your fill. You're also more likely to discover naturally harmonious combinations because of the truth told in the phrase "food that grows together goes together." Zucchini Melts with Garlic Breadcrumbs (page 19) put to use summer squash and tomatoes, which simultaneously reach their plentiful peaks every year. Flavors like butternut squash, pumpkin, cranberries, and blood oranges are easily associated with the late-in-the-year holidays for the same reason. If it's an ingredient's time to shine, go with it!

NUTRITION

Side dishes might be the best place to score nutritional bonus points for your meal. Marinated grilled vegetable wraps make a dashing lunch but could use a lift from protein. Red Quinoa with Cherries and Smoked Almonds (page 142) is brimming with protein from the grains and nuts, so it fills a nutritional void while adding texture and color. Lean flank steak contributes lots of iron, which the body absorbs more readily with a little help from vitamin C. Baby Spinach with Oranges and Manchego (page 68) pairs perfectly with steak and lends lots of C for iron absorption. Dinner is done. If your inventory (see previous category) already typically includes whole grains, fresh fruits and vegetables, and unprocessed ingredients (no boxed rice and noodle bits with a seasoning packet of unpronounceable powders), then you're ahead of the game.

VARIETY

When I talked to people about the concept for this book, so many confessed their abuse of the same old side-dish recipes. A lot of them noted that they might spend considerable time and energy on a special main course and then slap plain rice and a boring garden salad with bottled dressing on the table next to it and feel drained of the accomplishment of preparing something impressive. Even if you aim to keep it simple with a side of rice, the preparation can elevate it out of the lineup of usual suspects with dishes such as Spiced Rice Pilaf (page 98). Maybe your standby weeknight supper is soup with salad and bread. It's still the same convenient, nourishing meal if you substitute Butter Lettuce with Ribbons and Chives (page 66) for the pile of chopped romaine hearts and grape tomatoes you usually serve and plug in Parmigiano-Reggiano Crackers (page 40) for the baguette that's starting to bore you. You can even make the crackers ahead of time over the weekend. If you stop making accompaniments an afterthought, your entire meal will feel much more inspired.

TIME, SPACE, AND LOGISTICS

This category dictates most things in life, our side-dish selections included. On a weeknight after work, uncomplicated and relatively fast recipes trump any that require more energy than the little you have in reserve. Browse Chapter Four, "Weeknight Dinners," for good ideas. Plans for your contribution of a side dish for a family Thanksgiving feast might require a make-ahead recipe (take a look at Pumpkin Cozy Rolls, page 51) or a dish that can fit on another rack of the oven, and at the same temperature, while the turkey roasts (consider Legacy Cornbread Dressing, page 199). Your main dish for a back-deck dinner might be simple enough to free up time and space for a more elaborate side dish, like Layered Esquites Corn Salad (page 157) or Oven-Dried Tomato Tart Gratin (page 166). And a potluck invitation might mean you have to consider a crowd and the host's ability to accommodate your dish. Options abound in Chapter Seven, "Potlucks and Parties." Almost always, these factors will help you choose something perfect.

MOOD, PREFERENCES, AND OCCASION

Nothing, besides maybe psychotherapy, prompts you to explore your feelings more than food does. What do you *feel* like eating? What are you in the *mood* for? How about a big bowl of *comfort* food? This Bacon Cheddar Spoonbread (page 146) is so *satisfying*. You get the idea. Your own mood and preferences, or those for whom you're cooking, are honest gauges for choosing sides and an entire meal. Similarly, occasions dictate menus. An annual holiday buffet might warrant the time and energy it takes to make Caramelized Onion and Roasted Garlic Herb Stuffing (page 196). Your desire to add a little oomph to the neighborhood Sunday Soup Supper could inspire you to try your hand at Multigrain Pretzel Knots (page 42). A summertime family reunion that spans generations points to a time-honored classic like Vintage Potato Salad (page 114) to round out a menu of grilled goodies. Go with what your gut tells you. It's closest to your stomach, after all.

main-course pairings

If you're planning a meal based on what you have in mind for the main dish, use this chart to help you find good side-dish pairings from all eight chapters of the book. A vegetarian category with a lengthy list of options is included for building meat-free meals. If you're not sure of your cooking strategy for the main ingredient yet, take a look at some of the suggestions in the "Alongside" list included with each recipe that interests you from this index.

CHICKEN

FISH AND SEAFOOD

LAMB

PASTA

PORK

TURKEY AND OTHER POULTRY

VEGETARIAN

recipe notes

BLACK PEPPER: Freshly ground black pepper is more flavorful than packaged ground black pepper, so I prefer it. These recipes offer a teaspoon measure and an approximate number of grinds to spare you the arduous task of grinding the pepper and then attempting to scoop, stuff, or flick it into a measuring spoon. Generally, freshly ground pepper is coarser than packaged ground pepper, so use slightly less than the recipe calls for if using ground pepper from a jar. As is the case with salt, always adjust pepper seasoning to taste.

BUTTER: While I prefer salted butter melted into the crannies of my thick-cut toast, I use unsalted butter for baking and cooking to keep a tight rein on the salt content of the final dish. If you have only salted butter on hand, use a little less salt than called for in the recipe.

FLOUR: Other flours (bread, whole wheat, white whole wheat, oat, etc.) should not be substituted when unbleached all-purpose flour is called for since weight, flavor, and texture vary significantly. When measuring flour, always scoop it into a dry cup measure and level off with a straight edge. Dipping the cup measure into the container of flour and packing the flour into the cup adds more to your recipe and will adversely affect the outcome.

OLIVE OIL: The olive oil in the recipes is extra virgin, but feel free to substitute light olive oil for cooking and baking. When the olive oil's flavor is especially noticeable, as in dressings and vinaigrettes, or when added just before serving, I like to use a higher-quality extra virgin olive oil if I have it. Unless noted, do not substitute olive oil for other oils like vegetable or safflower, which are used for their mild flavor.

SALT: The recipes that follow call for kosher salt, unless otherwise noted. If you use sea salt in your kitchen, adjust the amounts based on the type of grain (fine or coarse). Use ½ teaspoon of fine sea salt in place of 1 teaspoon of kosher salt, for example. Coarse sea salt grains are generally larger than kosher salt grains (some are significantly larger), so use slightly more to equate to the kosher salt measure. Regardless of the type of salt, size and shape of the crystals should be considered per recipe. Finer, smaller salt crystals (like those of table salt or fine sea salt) dissolve faster and more uniformly, making them more popular in baking. Their saltiness is more potent by volume too, as noted above. Coarser crystals are a good choice for seasoning when a little bit of added texture is pleasant, as is the case in White Wine Focaccia (page 38), Multigrain Pretzel Knots (page 42), or Oven-Dried Tomatoes (page 166). Salt is a flavor enhancer and an important part of most recipes. But preferences vary. While the measures offered in each recipe are intended to be a good general gauge, always adjust seasoning to taste. The more you cook and season, the less you will depend on specific measurements for salt.

A guide to metric conversions and equivalents is available on page 209.

chapter one

Brunches and Luncheons

Midday meals tend toward lighter fare with bright flavors. They run at a leisurely pace, and the menus usually suggest that you dabble in a variety of tastes. This chapter offers recipes that tip a respectful nod toward the beverage of the hour, coffee, and offers plenty of savory options that commit to the second half of the day. Some recipes are intended to impress, but others are simple enough to arrange quickly for a relaxed, untailored gathering.

pear, gruyère, and ham puff pancake

banana oat waffle triangles

salmon caper cream pumpernickel tart

cinnamon challah muffins

roasted mushroom jumble with crème fraîche

roasted strawberry goat cheese

spinach shallot ricotta boursin

salted citrus olive oil spread

lemon sugar butter

maple cinnamon butter

honey orange butter

bloody mary shrimp salad

orecchiette verde

tortilla rancheros quiche

zucchini melts with garlic breadcrumbs

andouille frittata bites

chèvre, potato, and asparagus pie

sushi salad

pear, gruyère, and ham puff pancake

serves 6 to 8

You might abandon all other brunch menu plans when you pull this billowy puff out of the oven. In fact, you might abandon your brunch companions and hide away in the kitchen, hoarding it for yourself. Made in the likeness of a tarte tatin, the famous upside-down apple tart of French cuisine, a bottom layer of sweet and savory gets baked together by a neutral batter and ends up on top after a quick, careful flip. Sliced peaches, nectarines, or apples make happy substitutes for the pears.

. . . .

2 tablespoons plus 1 tablespoon unsalted butter

1 pear, halved, cored, and sliced about ⅛ inch thick

1 tablespoon plus 1 tablespoon brown sugar

3 large eggs

½ cup milk (preferably whole but low-fat is OK)

½ cup unbleached all-purpose flour

½ teaspoon kosher salt

2½ ounces sliced ham (3 or 4 slices), cut into ½-inch strips

2 ounces Gruyère cheese, grated (½ cup)

alongside

✦ MAPLE COCONUT GRANOLA PARFAITS
✦ CHAMPAGNE POACHED EGGS
✦ WHOLE ROASTED ROSEMARY CHICKEN AND POTATOES
✦ ROASTED PORK LOIN WITH GARLIC AND THYME

Preheat the oven to 425°F.

Melt 1 tablespoon of the butter in a 10-inch ovenproof skillet over medium heat. Add the pear slices and sweat them for 5 minutes, stirring once or twice, just to soften them.

While the pears cook, melt the remaining 2 tablespoons of butter in the microwave or on the stovetop in a small saucepan. Stir in 1 tablespoon of the brown sugar. In a medium mixing bowl, whisk together the eggs until foamy, about 1 minute. Then whisk in the milk, flour, salt, and the melted butter and sugar just until everything is combined and few lumps remain.

Nudge the pears into an even layer across the bottom of the skillet (or, if you're a perfectionist, take them out of the pan and then replace them in a decorative spiral arrangement). Sprinkle the remaining 1 tablespoon of brown sugar across the surface and then scatter the ham and cheese on the pears. Pour the batter on top.

Bake for 25 minutes, until the pancake puffs impressively around the edges and is speckled brown. Remove from the oven (the pancake will deflate).

Place a large round plate, a wooden cutting board, or a baking sheet over the top of the skillet (situate the board or pan so that the short top and bottom sides are perpendicular to you). Very carefully, using dry kitchen towels to hold the edges of the hot skillet, invert the pancake onto the plate so the pear layer is on top. Cut the pancake in half and each half into quarters and serve immediately.

banana oat waffle triangles makes 20 to 24 triangles

Belgian waffles are a perennial brunch item, especially popular at restaurant buffets where a made-to-order station draws crowds. At home, where you don't have the waffle station chef and his toque to man the batter and the maker while you tend to your guests, you can make these triangles ahead of time and add them to a bigger brunch buffet spread. Serve with softened Maple Cinnamon Butter (page 13) in lieu of a sticky drizzle of maple syrup.

. . . .

2 overripe bananas

1½ cups buttermilk

2 large eggs, beaten

¼ cup packed dark brown sugar

½ teaspoon vanilla extract

½ cup old-fashioned rolled oats
   (not quick or instant)

¼ cup raisins, coarsely chopped (optional)

2 cups unbleached all-purpose flour

1½ teaspoons kosher salt

1 teaspoon ground cinnamon

1 teaspoon baking powder

½ teaspoon baking soda

2 tablespoons turbinado sugar (optional)

alongside

+ FRESH BERRIES AND CANTALOUPE
+ GOAT CHEESE AND HAM QUICHE
+ BACON OR BREAKFAST SAUSAGE
+ YOGURT AND GRANOLA PARFAITS

Mash the bananas with a fork in a large mixing bowl. Add the buttermilk, eggs, brown sugar, and vanilla and whisk thoroughly to distribute the banana through the liquid as much as possible. Stir in the oats and raisins and set the mixture aside for 5 to 10 minutes while you prepare the other ingredients and heat the waffle iron.

Combine the flour, salt, cinnamon, baking powder, and baking soda in a sifter or a fine-mesh strainer and sift into a medium bowl. Once the oats have soaked in the liquid for several minutes, sprinkle half of the dry ingredients into the liquid and fold in with a large rubber spatula. Repeat with the remaining dry ingredients. Let the batter rest for about 5 minutes while you clean up.

Cook the waffles according to the waffle iron manufacturer's instructions. (You may need to brush the iron with oil to help prevent sticking.) For extra sweetness and a subtle crust, sprinkle about 1 teaspoon of the turbinado sugar across the batter just before closing the iron to cook the waffle. Transfer each finished waffle to a cooling rack. Once cooled, cut the waffle into 4 triangles (follow the lines of a circular Belgian waffle iron or cut each waffle into halves or quarters if your maker is square).

Just before serving, toast the waffles in a 375°F oven for about 10 minutes, until warm and lightly crisp on top. Tuck into a breadbasket lined with a clean kitchen towel to keep the waffles warm and serve.

tip: Make the waffles a day or two in advance, cool completely, wrap tightly with plastic wrap and foil, and refrigerate until ready to reheat and serve. You can also freeze them, tightly wrapped, for up to 2 months and warm them straight from the freezer, adding 5 minutes or so to be sure they are heated through and crisp.

salmon caper cream pumpernickel tart

serves 8 to 10

Thin slivers of this decadent savory tart add something special to your brunch menu. Use your favorite smoked salmon (lox, Nova, cold or hot smoked). If you opt out of poaching fresh salmon, look for a canned wild Alaskan variety, such as Copper River, which, while a dollar or two more than its Atlantic farmed salmon counterpart, is better-quality fish and more environmentally sound. The soft, sour pumpernickel bread crust is the perfect foil for the flavors in this mix.

- 8 ounces wild salmon fillet or 1 (6-ounce) can wild salmon in water, drained
- 6 ounces pumpernickel bread, cut into ½-inch cubes (about 3 cups)
- 2 tablespoons unsalted butter, melted
- 8 ounces cream cheese, softened
- 4 ounces smoked salmon (cold or hot smoked), sliced into 1-inch pieces or flaked (about 1 cup)
- 2 tablespoons drained capers
- ¼ cup loosely packed fresh dill
- ¼ teaspoon freshly ground black pepper (about 20 grinds)
- 2 tablespoons minced fresh chives
- 1 small cucumber, very thinly sliced

Preheat the oven to 375°F.

Bring 2 cups of water to a boil in a medium saucepan or deep sauté pan over medium-high heat (or use 1 cup of water and 1 cup of dry white wine for more flavor). When the water boils, lower the heat to medium-low and slide the salmon fillet skin down into the hot water. Cover the pan and poach the fish for 7 minutes, until firm and cooked through. Lift the salmon out of the water, set it on a plate, and cool completely in the refrigerator. Discard the water.

Put the bread in a food processor and process for about 30 seconds to make tiny crumbs. Drizzle the butter over the crumbs and then pulse again 5 or 6 times to distribute the butter. Dump the crumbs into a 9-inch fluted tart pan with a removable bottom and press them into an even layer across the bottom and partway up the sides. Set the tart pan on a baking sheet and bake for 15 minutes, until the crumb crust is toasty on top. Set aside to cool completely.

Wipe any stray crumbs out of the food processor. Add the cream cheese, smoked salmon, capers, dill, and pepper. Process until the ingredients come together into a smooth paste, about 20 seconds. Scrape down the sides and repeat if necessary. →

alongside

SHIRRED EGGS WITH FRESH HERBS ✦ CHERRY TOMATO FRITTATA ✦ CANTALOUPE AND HONEYDEW SALAD
ROASTED POTATOES AND BACON ✦ WARM POTATO AND BOILED EGG SALAD WITH CRÈME FRAÎCHE AND CAVIAR

Scoop the cream cheese mixture into a medium mixing bowl. Remove the skin from the cooled poached salmon and then crumble the fish into flakes and add to the bowl along with the chives. Fold the salmon and chives into the cream cheese using a large rubber spatula. Taste and adjust the seasoning to your preference (the smoked salmon and capers add quite a bit of salt).

Spread the salmon mixture in an even layer across the cooled crust. Cover and refrigerate for at least 2 hours or overnight. Before serving, top the tart with the cucumbers. Start in the middle and build a layered spiral all the way out to the edges.

Lift the tart out of the fluted edge and slice into thin wedges to serve. Replace the ring of the pan around any leftover tart and refrigerate, covered, for up to 2 days.

cinnamon challah muffins
makes 1 dozen muffins

Cross French toast, bread pudding, and a portable morning muffin and this recipe is the result. Sweet from maple syrup and brown sugar and spiced with cinnamon, these muffins account for all the expected breakfast flavor favorites at a brunch gathering. The primary recipe calls for an overnight soaking method that resembles the typical procedure for bread pudding, but if you're tight on time and can't prep the night before, see the tip for a quicker version.

. . . .

4 large eggs, beaten

1 cup heavy cream

1 teaspoon vanilla extract

¼ cup pure maple syrup
(grade B preferred)

½ cup plus 2 tablespoons packed
dark brown sugar

1 teaspoon plus ½ teaspoon ground
cinnamon

½ teaspoon kosher salt

6 cups ½-inch cubed challah
(about 8 ounces)

2 tablespoons cold unsalted butter,
cut into ¼-inch cubes

1 to 2 tablespoons confectioners' sugar

alongside

✦ BREAKFAST SAUSAGE QUICHE
✦ TOASTED COCONUT GRANOLA AND YOGURT
✦ MIXED FRESH BERRIES, PINEAPPLE CHUNKS,
   AND MELON SLICES
✦ BANANA ORANGE SMOOTHIES
✦ HAM AND SWISS OMELETS

In a large mixing bowl, whisk together the eggs, cream, vanilla, maple syrup, ½ cup of the brown sugar, 1 teaspoon of the cinnamon, and the salt. Add the bread cubes and gently fold them several times into the wet ingredients until all the cubes are moistened. Cover the bowl and refrigerate overnight (8 to 12 hours). The cubes will soak up most of the egg base, but some of the base may still pool a bit at the bottom.

In a small mixing bowl, combine the remaining 2 tablespoons of brown sugar and ½ teaspoon of cinnamon and stir together with a small whisk or a fork. Add the butter cubes and then mash the butter into the sugar and cinnamon with a fork. Cover and refrigerate until ready to use.

When you're ready to bake the muffins, preheat the oven to 350°F. Grease a 12-cup standard muffin tin with butter or vegetable shortening.

Scoop a level ¼-cup measure of the bread mixture (including any excess egg base at the bottom of the bowl) into each muffin cup. Flick two or three bits of the cinnamon sugar butter on top of each muffin. Transfer to the oven and bake for 35 minutes, until the tops are golden brown and there's no trace of wetness around the edges of the muffins.

Run a butter knife around the inner edges of the muffin cups to release the muffins and transfer them to a cooling rack. Use a sifter or a fine-mesh strainer to sprinkle the tops with confectioners' sugar and serve while still warm.

Reheat leftovers in a toaster oven or a warm (325°F) oven for 10 minutes.

tip: To make these muffins without the overnight soaking step, cut the challah into ¼-inch cubes and use only 3 eggs and ¾ cup of cream. Proceed with the directions, skipping the soak. The decrease in liquid and surface area of each cube allows for the custard to be absorbed quickly so you can proceed to baking immediately.

roasted mushroom jumble with crème fraîche

serves 4 to 6

At first glance, mushrooms offer every reason to overlook them. They're tan, the color of ordinary; they're spongy, not crunchy or snappy or juicy; and they're a fungus, one of the least appetizing descriptors there is. But mushrooms are meaty, deeply savory, and rich with flavors that vary by type. Here they are the focal point, and a heaping spoonful made brighter by flecks of chives and topped off with an indulgent dollop of crème fraîche will make you pity the poor fungi that lose their oomph in blander preparations.

- 2 pounds mixed fresh mushrooms (portobello, cremini, white button, shiitake, oyster)
- 1 large shallot, thinly sliced (about ¼ cup)
- ⅓ cup safflower or vegetable oil
- 1 teaspoon kosher salt
- ¼ teaspoon freshly ground black pepper (about 20 grinds)
- ¼ cup minced fresh chives
- ⅓ cup crème fraîche at room temperature

Place 2 baking sheets on separate racks and preheat the oven to 450°F.

Trim the mushrooms (plucking stems and scraping the gills from portobellos). Quarter the portobellos and cut them into ½-inch pieces. Quarter or halve the cremini, white button, and shiitake mushrooms and chop the oyster mushrooms into bite-sized pieces.

Combine all of the mushrooms and the shallot in a large mixing bowl. Drizzle with the oil and sprinkle with the salt and pepper. Toss several times to coat.

Take the hot pans out of the oven and spill the mushrooms and shallots evenly between them, spreading them out in a single layer.

Roast for 8 to 10 minutes. Toss them with a spatula, return the pans to the oven, switching racks for even roasting, and continue to roast for 8 to 10 minutes, until soft and tender.

Scrape the roasted mushrooms and shallots into a serving bowl and mix in the chives. Adjust the seasoning to taste. Serve immediately, passing the crème fraîche at the table for diners to add a dollop to each serving.

alongside

STEAK FRITES SALAD ✦ FLORENTINE QUICHE ✦ POACHED EGGS AND SMOKED GOUDA GRITS **8**
SIMPLE RISOTTO **128** ✦ CIDER-BRINED TURKEY BREAST ✦ FENNEL, ONION, AND WINE BRAISED CHICKEN THIGHS

bagel and bread spreads

Even the most effortless side dish—a basket of assorted store-bought breads—can be made memorable with an assortment of outstanding spreads. Here are six sweet and savory butters and cheeses that will transform a bag of bagels into something more impressive. Each recipe offers ideas that go beyond the breadbasket too.

roasted strawberry goat cheese   makes about 1⅓ cups

While this cheese is undeniably sweet and perfect for breakfast breads of all kinds, it holds its own on the savory side, spread on toast with herbs and balancing bitter greens in sandwiches.

1 tablespoon balsamic vinegar

2 tablespoons dark brown sugar

2 cups whole strawberries (about 8 ounces), hulled and quartered

8 ounces goat cheese (or 1½ cups crumbled) at room temperature

Preheat the oven to 375°F. Whisk the vinegar and brown sugar together in a medium mixing bowl to dissolve the brown sugar a bit. Add the strawberries to the bowl and fold them in to coat them with the vinegar and brown sugar. Dump the strawberries onto a baking sheet in a single layer but close together, scraping in any remaining vinegar mixture. Roast the strawberries for 15 minutes, until they are just starting to soften and their juices plus the vinegar and brown sugar are bubbling around them. Remove from the oven and let them cool at room temperature for about 20 minutes.

Use a large rubber spatula to scrape the strawberries into the bowl of a stand mixer fitted with the paddle attachment or use a mixing bowl and handheld electric beater. Add the goat cheese and mix on low for about a minute and a half until soft and smooth with chunks of strawberries.

Refrigerate for about an hour and up to 3 days to let the flavors come together and to firm up the cheese a little.

alongside

BAGELS, ESPECIALLY WHOLE WHEAT OR PUMPERNICKEL ✦ LEMON SCONES
BANANA BREAD ✦ PANCAKES AND WAFFLES ✦ TOASTED BAGUETTE WITH ARUGULA OR WATERCRESS

spinach shallot ricotta boursin *makes 2 cups*

Use this cheese spread as a dip for chips and crackers or slather thickly across grilled pizza dough and top with slices of fresh tomatoes and shreds of radicchio.

. . . .

1 cup loosely packed fresh baby spinach

5 large fresh basil leaves

2 tablespoons minced shallot (about 1 medium)

1 small clove garlic, minced

1 cup whole-milk ricotta

4 ounces (½ cup) cream cheese at room temperature

½ teaspoon kosher salt

Combine the spinach, basil, shallot, garlic, ricotta, cream cheese, and salt in the bowl of a food processor and process for about 30 seconds or until smooth and creamy. Season to taste with additional salt if needed.

alongside

PARMIGIANO-REGGIANO CRACKERS **40** ✦ CARAWAY FLATBREAD **28**
WHITE WINE FOCACCIA **38** ✦ BAGELS ✦ GRILLED PIZZA DOUGH

salted citrus olive oil spread makes ¾ cup

This butter and olive oil combo melts into nooks and crannies of warm hunks of ciabatta or focaccia. If there is any left after the loaf is gone, scoop a few teaspoons onto a hot steak and let it melt over the top as a sauce or toss some with hot fusilli pasta and sautéed summer veggies.

2 packed teaspoons finely grated
   lemon zest (about 2 small lemons)

¼ cup extra virgin olive oil

8 tablespoons (1 stick) salted butter
   at room temperature

⅛ teaspoon freshly ground black pepper
   (about 10 grinds)

Combine the lemon zest, olive oil, butter, and pepper in a medium mixing bowl and whip with a handheld electric whisk or beaters for about 30 seconds until ultra-smooth and creamy. Use immediately or refrigerate in an airtight container for up to 2 weeks and use a scoop at a time.

alongside

DINNER BREADS AND ROLLS ✦ SAVORY MUFFINS AND SCONES
LIGHT AND FLUFFY YUKON GOLD POTATOES **201** ✦ ROASTED, STEAMED, OR GRILLED VEGETABLES

lemon sugar butter makes about ⅔ cup

Just shy of as-sweet-as-cake-frosting, this butter will brighten any breakfast or breadbasket with a sunshiny lemon zing and smooth vanilla backdrop.

8 tablespoons (1 stick) unsalted butter at room temperature

2 tablespoons sugar

1 tablespoon finely grated lemon zest (about 2 small lemons)

¼ teaspoon vanilla extract

Combine the butter, sugar, lemon zest, and vanilla in a small mixing bowl. Mash the sugar and zest into the butter and vanilla by hand with a fork, a rubber spatula, or the back of a spoon. Stir and fold until the mixture is soft, smooth, and creamy. Scoop into a small ramekin to use or cover tightly with plastic wrap and store for up to 2 weeks. Alternatively, spoon the butter into a pile in the center of a small rectangle of plastic wrap or wax paper. Roll the wrap over the butter and squeeze it by hand into a log shape. Continue wrapping all the way around and pinch or knot the ends like a candy wrapper. Refrigerate until hardened. Slice pats of butter off as you use it or cut it into ¼-inch-thick coins for a butter dish. Freeze the butter tightly wrapped and stored in an airtight container or zip-top bag for up to 2 months.

alongside

BLUEBERRY MUFFINS ✦ SWEET SCONES ✦ RICOTTA PANCAKES ✦ THICK-SLICED TOASTED BAGUETTE

maple cinnamon butter makes ⅔ cup

Sweet enough to stand in as the icing atop cinnamon rolls, this butter almost overrides the need for syrup on a stack of pancakes. It will also complement roasted root vegetables as a stand-in for plain butter.

- 1 tablespoon pure maple syrup
- 1 teaspoon dark brown sugar
- 1 teaspoon ground cinnamon
- Pinch of kosher salt
- 8 tablespoons (1 stick) unsalted butter at room temperature

Combine the syrup, sugar, cinnamon, and salt in a small mixing bowl and stir to dissolve some of the sugar and salt. Add the butter and press it into the other ingredients with the back of a spoon or a rubber spatula. Continue stirring until the ingredients are evenly distributed in the smooth, creamy butter. Scoop into a small ramekin to use or cover tightly with plastic wrap and store for up to 2 weeks. Alternatively, spoon the butter into a pile in the center of a small rectangle of plastic wrap or wax paper. Roll the wrap over the butter and squeeze it by hand into a log shape. Continue wrapping all the way around and pinch or knot the ends like a candy wrapper. Refrigerate until hardened. Slice pats of butter off as you use it or cut it into ¼-inch-thick coins for a butter dish. Freeze the butter tightly wrapped and stored in an airtight container or zip-top bag for up to 2 months.

alongside

PUMPKIN COZY ROLLS **51** ✦ BANANA OAT WAFFLE TRIANGLES **3**
OATMEAL PANCAKES ✦ CHALLAH FRENCH TOAST ✦ ROASTED SWEET POTATOES ✦ BAKED APPLES

honey orange butter makes ⅔ cup

All three ingredients are in the title of this recipe, but the simple combination transforms ordinary butter into something special. Use it with flavors that typically pal around with orange or add a pat to play against savory spiciness anywhere butter might have a place.

8 tablespoons (1 stick) unsalted butter at room temperature

2 tablespoons mild honey, such as clover or orange blossom

1 tablespoon finely grated orange zest (about 1 medium orange)

Combine the butter, honey, and orange zest in a small mixing bowl. Mash the honey and zest into the butter by hand with a fork, a rubber spatula, or the back of a spoon. Stir and fold until the mixture is soft, smooth, and creamy. Scoop into a small ramekin to use, or cover tightly with plastic wrap and store for up to 2 weeks. Alternatively, spoon the butter into a pile in the center of a small rectangle of plastic wrap or wax paper. Roll the wrap over the butter and squeeze it by hand into a log shape. Continue wrapping all the way around and pinch or knot the ends like a candy wrapper. Refrigerate until hardened. Slice pats of butter off as you use it or cut it into ¼-inch-thick coins for a butter dish. Freeze the butter tightly wrapped and stored in an airtight container or zip-top bag for up to 2 months.

alongside

HERITAGE CORNBREAD **45** ✦ PUMPKIN COZY ROLLS **51**
TOASTED MULTIGRAIN BREAD ✦ ROASTED BUTTERNUT SQUASH ✦ SPICY BAKED YAMS

bloody mary shrimp salad serves 6 to 8 (makes about 5 cups)

This recipe has the signature flavors of the great brunch cocktail mix with cool shrimp and crunchy celery in a versatile salad. Serve it straight up in a chilled bowl as part of a bigger spread; dab some on top of toasted, buttered brioche squares; stuff wide celery hearts or perfectly cupped Bibb or romaine lettuce leaves with spoonfuls; tuck into mini pita pockets; or fill tiny cordial classes with it and serve with cocktail forks as an amuse-bouche. (You might opt to chop the shrimp and celery smaller if the salad is destined for two-bite portions to be stuffed, tucked, or piled high.) Consider grilling the shrimp to add a smoky flavor, which matches the rest of the ingredients perfectly.

2 pounds cooked large (31/35) shrimp, tail shell removed (see Tip for cooking raw shrimp)

3 stalks celery, halved lengthwise and sliced diagonally ¼ inch thick (about 1½ cups)

¼ cup loosely packed fresh parsley, chopped

½ cup canned crushed tomatoes

¼ cup prepared horseradish

2 tablespoons finely chopped fresh chives

2 tablespoons mayonnaise

2 tablespoons extra virgin olive oil

1 tablespoon fresh lemon juice (about ½ medium lemon)

1 teaspoon Worcestershire sauce

½ teaspoon hot sauce, such as Tabasco

½ teaspoon kosher salt

¼ teaspoon celery salt

⅛ teaspoon freshly ground black pepper (about 10 grinds)

alongside

+ GRILLED FILET MIGNON WITH HORSERADISH CREAM
+ JUMBO OLD BAY CRAB CAKES
+ ROMAINE WITH LEMON GARLIC CROUTONS AND PARMIGIANO-REGGIANO **69**
+ GRILLED WORCESTERSHIRE-MARINATED SKIRT STEAK AND LIME RICE **96**
+ IRISH BROWN BREAD **49**

Cut each shrimp into 4 small pieces and pile them into a large mixing bowl. Add the celery and parsley and toss to combine.

In a small mixing bowl or large spouted measuring cup, whisk together the tomatoes, horseradish, chives, mayonnaise, olive oil, lemon juice, Worcestershire sauce, hot sauce, kosher salt, celery salt, and pepper.

Pour the tomato mixture over the shrimp and stir everything together. Adjust the seasoning to taste. Cover and refrigerate for at least 1 hour and up to overnight. Stir well again before serving.

tip: Raw shrimp can be markedly less expensive per pound than cooked shrimp. To prepare it yourself, you'll need to peel and devein the shrimp first. Work your thumb beneath the thin shell where an opening is accessible at the head end. Lift the shell up away from the body of the shrimp and peel it away by hand. Depending on your purposes, you may choose to leave the tail shell intact (if you're making shrimp cocktail, for example). For this recipe, peel and discard it along with the rest of the shell. Next, hold the shrimp in one hand so the wider curved "back" is facing upward toward you and the shrimp is curled downward. You will be able to see a dark line beneath the surface of most of the shrimp. Run a sharp paring knife down the middle of the shrimp, along this line, cutting only about 1/16 of an inch deep. Pull out the dark vein and discard it. To cook the shrimp, bring a pot of water to a boil (size depending on the amount of shrimp you're cooking) over high heat. Lower the heat to low so the water is barely simmering and add the shrimp. Poach them for 2 to 3 minutes, until they are pink and white without any visible gray left. Drain the shrimp and run cold water over them until they are completely cool. Use them within a day or two.

orecchiette verde serves 8 to 10

Orecchiette ("little ears") cook into tiny disks perfect for catching pools of bright green herb sauce sharp with garlic and Pecorino Romano cheese. The pasta is most flavorful at room temperature, so if you make it ahead of time and refrigerate (it can be made the day before), leave it out on the counter to warm for about an hour before serving. Stir in a few extra tablespoons of olive oil or water to moisten the pasta if you prepare it in advance, as it will absorb liquid from the sauce and turn slightly sticky when refrigerated. Alternatively, cook the pasta and prepare the sauce ahead and assemble the dish just before serving.

1 pound orecchiette pasta

3 cups packed arugula

2 cups loosely packed fresh basil

1 cup loosely packed fresh flat-leaf parsley

1 small clove garlic

1 tablespoon red wine vinegar

½ cup extra virgin olive oil

½ cup finely grated Pecorino Romano cheese

Kosher salt and freshly ground black pepper

1 pint (about 2 cups) grape tomatoes, quartered

1½ cups pitted green olives (try cerignola or picholine), chopped

Cook the pasta al dente according to the package instructions. Drain and rinse it with cold water to prevent cooking it further. Leave the pasta to drain and dry a bit while you prepare the rest of the ingredients.

Put the arugula, basil, parsley, and garlic in the bowl of a food processor and pulse 10 to 20 times, until everything is very finely chopped (stop to push herbs back down against the blade with a wooden spoon or spatula if necessary). Add the vinegar. With the processor running, pour the olive oil through the food chute in a slow, steady stream and continue to process until a thick, mostly smooth sauce forms from the herbs and oil. Add the cheese and pulse the processor several times to incorporate it. Season the sauce to taste with salt and pepper.

Dump the cooled pasta into a large serving bowl. Scrape the sauce from the processor onto the pasta and add the tomatoes and olives. Use a large rubber spatula to mix everything well, coating the pasta with the sauce. Season to taste with salt and pepper.

alongside

ROASTED SALMON ✦ GRILLED CHICKEN PARMESAN WITH POMODORO SAUCE
EGGPLANT FETA ROLLATINI **158** ✦ ZUCCHINI MELTS WITH GARLIC BREADCRUMBS **19**
SHRIMP SCAMPI ✦ ROASTED VEGETABLES WITH FRESH MOZZARELLA ✦ CRAB CAKES WITH LEMON AÏOLI

tortilla rancheros quiche *serves 8 to 12*

Huevos rancheros is a dish that started as a quick and frill-free late-morning meal for farmers in Mexico. Today in America it's one of the most popular items on a Sunday brunch menu next to vodka-spiked Bloody Marys. At its simplest, huevos rancheros is a couple of fried eggs on top of crunchy corn tortillas and beneath a spicy tomato sauce. According to most restaurant brunch menus, the dish includes those originals plus beans, cheese, and often a fresh tomato salsa instead of a smoother sauce. This quiche takes its lead from the original, adds elements from derivatives, and bakes all of it into a quiche that serves the masses. The portion size of this recipe is intended as a contribution to a larger brunch spread. If your party is smaller, cut the quiche into larger squares.

- -

2 medium plum tomatoes (8 ounces), stem end trimmed and discarded, finely diced (about 1 cup)

1 cup cooked black beans (drained and rinsed if using canned)

⅓ cup packed fresh cilantro leaves, chopped

⅓ cup thinly sliced scallion (about 4 scallions)

1 chipotle pepper in adobo sauce, seeds scraped out, minced

1½ teaspoons kosher salt

2 cloves garlic, minced and mashed to a paste or pressed

6 large eggs

¼ cup whole or low-fat milk

1¼ cups plus ¼ cup shredded sharp Cheddar cheese (about 6 ounces)

6 (6-inch) soft corn tortillas at room temperature or warmed slightly in a microwave to soften

Preheat the oven to 375°F.

In a large mixing bowl, combine the tomatoes, black beans, cilantro, scallion, chipotle, salt, and garlic and stir well to distribute the chipotle throughout the ingredients.

In a separate medium mixing bowl, beat together the eggs, milk, and 1¼ cups of the cheese. Pour the eggs into the tomato mixture and stir to combine.

Brush the bottom and sides of an 8-inch square baking dish with a teaspoon of vegetable oil or coat with cooking spray and then line the dish with the corn tortillas. Start with one or two tortillas in the center of the dish and then overlap the remaining tortillas, pushing them into the edges and up against the sides of the dish as you would with pie dough. (If the tortillas are cold, they will crack during this process.) Pour the egg mixture into the tortilla-lined dish and sprinkle the reserved ¼ cheese on top. Set the dish on a baking sheet pan and transfer to the oven to bake for 35 to 40 minutes, until the quiche is set firmly around the sides and springy but not jiggly in the middle when you give the sides of the dish a shake.

Let the quiche sit for 5 to 10 minutes before slicing into 12 squares. Serve immediately or cover with foil, refrigerate, and reheat in a 350°F oven when ready to serve.

alongside

PINEAPPLE AND WATERMELON SALAD ✦ WARM BAGELS WITH SCALLION CREAM CHEESE ✦ SWEET CINNAMON TORTILLA CHIPS ✦ PANFRIED OR GRILLED BREAKFAST SAUSAGE OR CHORIZO ✦ CHILE-KISSED CHICKEN SALAD

zucchini melts with garlic breadcrumbs

serves 6 to 8

Your favorite zucchini bread recipe, which has been the answer to your summer zucchini surplus for years, is about to get bumped. These melts come together quickly and round out a meal with a ton of flavor from ripe veggies, herbs and spices, and salty sharp provolone cheese. You can make them ahead and reheat them just before serving (in a warm oven for 10 minutes or in the microwave for a minute or two), but wait to top off with the crunchy breadcrumbs until the minute they hit the table.

1 large zucchini (about 1 pound and 2½ inches in diameter), sliced diagonally ½ inch thick (about 18 slices)

¼ teaspoon plus ¼ teaspoon kosher salt

¼ teaspoon garlic powder

¼ teaspoon onion powder

¼ teaspoon dried oregano

2 tablespoons extra virgin olive oil

2 large plum tomatoes (about 8 ounces), sliced lengthwise ¼ inch thick

4 ounces thinly sliced provolone cheese (use a block of sharp imported or mild from the deli counter), cut into 2-inch pieces (if your slices are round, cut each into 8 triangles)

½ cup panko breadcrumbs or fine crumbs made from stale bread

1 tablespoon unsalted butter

1 clove garlic, minced

⅛ teaspoon freshly ground black pepper (about 10 grinds)

Place a baking sheet in the oven and preheat the oven to 475°F.

In a large mixing bowl, toss the zucchini with ¼ teaspoon of the salt, the garlic powder, onion powder, oregano, and olive oil. Use a large spatula or clean hands to make sure each slice is coated with the oil and seasonings.

Take the hot pan out of the oven and arrange the zucchini in a single layer across it. Roast the zucchini for 5 minutes. Remove the pan from the oven and flip each slice over using tongs. Top each slice with a piece of tomato and several pieces of provolone. Return the pan to the oven and roast for 10 minutes more, until the cheese is melted, bubbly, and just starting to brown.

While the zucchini roasts, toast the breadcrumbs. Heat a large sauté pan over medium heat. Add the breadcrumbs and toast for 2 to 3 minutes, tossing every 30 seconds or so, until very light brown. Set the breadcrumbs aside in a small mixing bowl. Return the pan to the heat, add the butter, and melt it. Add the garlic and sauté for 1 minute, until fragrant but not browning. Scrape the butter and garlic into the breadcrumbs along with the remaining ¼ teaspoon of salt and the pepper. Mix thoroughly with a spoon.

Remove the zucchini from the oven and transfer to a serving platter. Top each slice of zucchini with a few heaping teaspoons of the breadcrumbs and serve immediately.

alongside

FETA, SPINACH, AND KALAMATA QUICHE ✦ EGG AND SPICY SAUSAGE SANDWICHES ON TOASTED CIABATTA
CAPELLINI WITH SALTED CITRUS OLIVE OIL SPREAD 11 ✦ FRITTO MISTO (FRIED MIXED SEAFOOD)
WITH AÏOLI ✦ PASTA PUTTANESCA ✦ LEMON BASIL CHICKEN SCALOPPINE
SIMPLE RISOTTO 128 WITH GRILLED PORTOBELLOS OR SAUSAGES

andouille frittata bites makes 16 (1½-inch) bites

Spicy and savory, these little squares will balance out a brunch buffet table set with fresh fruit, bagels, and schmear. Smoky andouille sausage has a kick and an affinity for onions and bell peppers, all of which are fixtures in Cajun cuisine. Bake it and serve right away or make ahead and reheat just before the meal.

8 large eggs

¼ cup milk

1 teaspoon kosher salt

⅛ teaspoon freshly ground black pepper (about 10 grinds)

8 ounces andouille sausage, fresh or dried (see cooking variations in instructions)

1 medium Yukon Gold potato, cut into ¼-inch cubes (about 1¼ cups)

1 small yellow onion, cut into ¼-inch pieces (about 1 cup)

1 small red bell pepper, seeds and veins removed, cut into ¼-inch pieces (about 1 cup)

1 small green bell pepper, seeds and veins removed, cut into ¼-inch pieces (about 1 cup)

1 cup grated sharp Cheddar cheese (about 4 ounces)

Preheat the oven to 400°F. Butter an 8-inch square baking dish.

Beat the eggs together with the milk, salt, and pepper in a large mixing bowl and set aside.

If using fresh andouille sausage, squeeze the sausage out of the casings and discard the casing. Heat a large sauté pan over medium heat. When the pan is hot, add the sausage, breaking it up into small pieces as you flick it into the pan. Cook the meat for 5 to 7 minutes, stirring often with a wooden spoon, until it is cooked through and has started to brown. Use a slotted spoon to transfer it into a medium mixing bowl, leaving most of the liquid fat from the sausage in the pan. Set the sausage aside.

If using dried andouille sausage, cut the pieces into ¼-inch cubes and cook in the large sauté pan over medium heat for 3 to 5 minutes, to draw out some of the fat and brown them just a bit. Use a slotted spoon to transfer it to a medium mixing bowl, leaving most of the liquid fat from the sausage in the pan. Set the sausage aside.

alongside

BLOODY MARY SHRIMP SALAD **15** ✦ CAJUN SPICE-RUBBED SALMON

PEACHES, PECANS, AND ARUGULA ✦ HERBED BISCUITS **31** ✦ CRISPLY ROASTED GARLIC POTATOES **90**

Return the sauté pan to medium heat and add the potatoes. (If there doesn't seem to be enough fat in the pan, add 1 or 2 teaspoons of vegetable oil.) Cook for 5 minutes, stirring every 30 seconds or so until the potatoes start to soften a little. Add the onion and peppers and cook for 10 minutes longer, stirring often. As the vegetables release their water, scrape the brown crust that forms on the bottom of the pan from the sausage and potatoes. Toward the end of the 10 minutes, if the crust sticks stubbornly to the pan, add 2 tablespoons of water a little at a time and scrape the crust up as the water sizzles on the hot pan.

Scrape the cooked potatoes and vegetables into the reserved sausage. Take a taste and season with additional salt and pepper if needed. (The potatoes will be just slightly underdone at this point but will continue to soften as the frittata bakes.)

Add about ¼ cup (or a heaping spoonful) of the hot veggies and sausage to the eggs and stir. Repeat this 3 or 4 times until the temperature of the eggs warms enough so that you can scoop the rest of the hot ingredients in without cooking the eggs with the heat. Stir in the cheese.

Pour the egg mixture into the buttered dish and bake for about 30 minutes, until the top has begun to brown and the frittata is firm and set. (Test by tapping the center of it with your fingertips. If it wiggles, give it another 5 minutes and test again.) Remove from the oven and let it rest for 10 to 15 minutes.

Place a large plate or a baking sheet pan on top of the baking dish and carefully flip it over to invert the frittata on the pan. Cut the frittata into 16 (1½-inch) squares. (If you are serving a smaller crowd, cut larger squares accordingly.) Transfer the squares to a platter and serve immediately.

To make this ahead, bake, cool completely, and cut, and then refrigerate the squares under plastic wrap or in an airtight container. Just before serving, situate the squares on a baking sheet about ½ inch apart and warm in a 350°F oven for 10 minutes or until heated through.

chèvre, potato, and asparagus pie *serves 6 to 8*

Take a homemade piecrust, stuff it with mashed potatoes, add goat cheese and asparagus, and you have a new side dish that honors the perfection of the potato with a little more pizzazz. You can make and bake the piecrust a day ahead and proceed with the rest of the recipe shortly before serving. Like most potato dishes, this one pairs nicely with countless ingredients, from breakfast and brunch standards like eggs, bacon, and smoked salmon to dinner party specials like prime cuts of beef and big, bold red wines.

. . . .

1½ cups unbleached all-purpose flour

1 teaspoon kosher salt

4 tablespoons (½ stick) cold unsalted butter, cut into ½-inch cubes

½ cup plus 2 tablespoons (5 ounces) cold soft chèvre

2 teaspoons apple cider vinegar

3 to 4 tablespoons ice water

1 pound asparagus, tough ends snapped off

1 tablespoon vegetable oil

1½ pounds small to medium red potatoes (about 6), quartered

¼ cup milk

¼ teaspoon freshly ground black pepper (about 20 grinds)

Combine the flour and ½ teaspoon of the salt in a food processor and pulse 10 times to combine. Add the butter and ¼ cup of the chèvre a little at a time, processing for about 5 seconds after each addition until tiny bits of both are dispersed throughout the flour. Add the vinegar and water and process again for about 10 seconds. Remove the processor lid and squeeze some of the flour together in your fingertips to test that it stays together in a little bunch. If it crumbles apart, add another tablespoon of ice water and pulse the mixture a few more times.

Dump the crumbly dough out onto a clean work surface. Push it into a heap and then squeeze it together into a ball. Knead it gently 4 or 5 times, just enough to smooth it out a little. Press and shape the ball into a disk about 1 inch thick. Wrap tightly in plastic wrap and refrigerate for at least 20 minutes and up to 1 day.

Roll the dough out into a 12-inch round. Set it in a 9-inch pie pan, fold the ends in to create an edge that stands about ½ inch from the top of the pie pan, and then flute the crust with your fingers. Put the crust in the freezer for 15 minutes (or refrigerate for 30 minutes).

Preheat oven to 375°F while the crust chills.

alongside

POACHED SALMON WITH CAPER DILL RELISH ✦ FRIED EGGS WITH CHIVES AND BACON ✦ POACHED EGGS WITH GREEN PEPPERCORNS AND MALDON SALT FLAKES ✦ ROAST BEEF WITH HORSERADISH CREAM SAUCE ✦ FILET MIGNON WITH BORDELAISE OR PEPPER CREAM SAUCE ✦ SLICED HONEY HAM ✦ ROASTED CHICKEN WITH ONION GARLIC GRAVY

Put the asparagus on a baking sheet pan, drizzle with the oil and ¼ teaspoon of the remaining salt, and toss to coat the asparagus. Arrange the asparagus in a single layer across the pan.

Remove the piecrust from the freezer and poke the bottom and sides all over with a fork. Cut a piece of parchment paper or aluminum foil and fit it inside the pie plate to cover the bottom of the crust and sit flush against its sides. Fill the plate with an even layer of pie weights or dried beans that will keep the parchment in place and the dough flat while baking. Set the pie plate on a baking sheet.

Transfer the asparagus and crust to the oven on separate racks (piecrust on the top rack). Roast the asparagus for 15 minutes, until bright green and just tender. Remove from the oven and set aside. Also take the piecrust out after 15 minutes and carefully lift the weighted parchment out. Return the crust to the oven for an additional 15 to 20 minutes, until the edges and bottom are light golden.

While the asparagus and crust are in the oven, cook the potatoes. Put the potatoes in a medium saucepan and cover them by about an inch of cold water. Cover the pot and bring the water to a boil. Once it boils, decrease the heat to low and simmer the potatoes for 15 minutes or until tender when poked with a fork. Drain the potatoes, return them to the pot, and add the milk, the remaining ¼ teaspoon of salt (or to taste), and ¼ cup of the remaining chèvre. Mash with

a handheld potato masher or a fork (the mashed potatoes won't be completely smooth, just smashed with some chunks remaining).

Arrange half of the asparagus in a single layer across the crust. Scoop the potatoes on top of the asparagus and spread out evenly with a spatula. Arrange the remaining asparagus on top of the potatoes in a single layer (to make slicing wedges easiest, situate the spears like the spokes of a wagon wheel, with the tips meeting in the center). Sprinkle bits of the last 2 tablespoons of chèvre across the top. Bake for 20 minutes, until heated through.

Let the pie rest for about 10 minutes before slicing into wedges with a sharp knife and serving.

Refrigerate any leftovers in the pie plate covered with aluminum foil or plastic wrap for up to 5 days. To reheat leftovers, slice into wedges and warm in a 375°F oven for about 15 minutes, until hot through the middle of the pie.

sushi salad serves 8 to 10

This cold rice salad unravels a sushi roll and tosses the famous flavors together. Make it with or without fish, depending on the accompanying spread or your company. The rice is sticky, just as it is in sushi, rather than the loose grains of other cold rice salads. If you love the punch of wasabi, add more to taste to the dressing, at the end or on the side. Stir in minced pickled ginger or serve a condiment bowl of it next to the salad for people who wouldn't think of eating sushi without it. The salad can be made up to a day in advance.

- 2 cups short-grain white sushi rice
- 2 cups water
- 3 tablespoons low-sodium soy sauce
- ½ cup rice vinegar
- 1 tablespoon prepared wasabi paste or 1 tablespoon all-natural wasabi powder whisked with 1 tablespoon water
- 2 teaspoons sugar
- 2 teaspoons sesame oil (light or dark)
- 4 sheets nori, quartered and cut into ⅛-inch-wide strips (see Tip)
- 2½ cups ¼-inch diced English cucumber (about 1 cucumber)
- 1 large carrot, coarsely grated (1 cup grated)
- ½ cup thinly sliced scallion (2 or 3 large scallions)
- 2 tablespoons plus 2 tablespoons toasted sesame seeds
- 2 avocados, peeled, pitted, and thinly sliced
- 1 pound cold cooked shrimp, tail shell removed, or 1 pound claw or lump crabmeat (optional)

Pour the rice into a large bowl situated in the sink. Run cold water over it and then strain it through a mesh strainer or a colander with very small holes 3 or 4 times, until the water is mostly clear.

Scrape the rice into a medium saucepan and add the water. Cover the pot, bring the water to a boil, and then turn the heat down to low. Simmer the rice for 15 minutes. Turn off the heat and let the rice sit, covered, for 10 minutes.

In a small bowl or spouted measuring cup, whisk together the soy sauce, vinegar, wasabi, sugar, and sesame oil.

Uncover the rice and fluff it a bit with a fork. Use a large flat wooden spoon or a rubber spatula to push the sticky cooked rice into a large wide serving bowl. (If you are presenting this salad on a big platter instead, do the mixing of ingredients in a big bowl first and then transfer to the platter.) Drizzle a third of the soy sauce mixture over the rice and fold to coat the grains. Repeat two more times with the dressing. Sprinkle the nori strips across the rice a little at a time and fold them in, taking care to mix well. Be sure to add the nori while the rice is still warm so that the seaweed relaxes as it absorbs the steam and heat of the grains, which will also prevent it from clumping together.

Let the rice cool to room temperature before folding in the cucumber, carrot, scallion, and 2 tablespoons of the sesame seeds. →

alongside

SEARED TUNA ✦ TERIYAKI CHICKEN ✦ SESAME-CRUSTED TOFU
VEGETABLE TEMPURA ✦ SOY-MARINATED GRILLED STRIP STEAKS

Arrange the avocados and the shrimp or crab decoratively on top of the salad and sprinkle the remaining 2 tablespoons of sesame seeds all over the surface.

If you make the salad ahead, cover it without the toppings and refrigerate. Add the avocados, shrimp, and remaining sesame seeds shortly before serving.

tip: Kitchen shears, rather than the blade of a knife, make lighter work of cutting the nori into strips. Cut the sheets into quarters or eighths and stack the pieces. Then cut each stack into skinny strips.

chapter two

Breads for Any Occasion

Bread alone can make a meal, a fact that fuels a borderline overuse of the suggestion "Serve with crusty bread for a complete dinner!" Its versatility makes any variety of bread a staple side dish. These recipes are created with stews, sauces, and entrée salads especially in mind. Whether to round out one's own homemade meal or as a contribution to a small gathering or communal feast, freshly baked bread is the ultimate complement.

caraway flatbread makes 8 flatbreads

In a lineup, this flatbread would slip itself right between pizza dough and naan. As a base (without the caraway seeds), it's as versatile as a basic pizza crust and will happily wear any toppings you choose. As bread, its crumb is made rich by milk and tender by a splash of vinegar, like naan, which is often made with acidic yogurt. The flatbread puffs just slightly in the oven, and its insides stay soft between a crisp top and bottom. Caraway seeds lend their unmistakable flavor, but feel free to substitute sesame or poppy seeds, coarse salt, or herbs painted on with a little oil.

1 cup whole milk

1 teaspoon sugar

1 envelope (2¼ teaspoons) active dry yeast

2½ cups bread flour, plus more for kneading

1½ teaspoons kosher salt

2 tablespoons vegetable oil, plus oil for the bowl

1 teaspoon distilled white or white wine vinegar

1½ tablespoons caraway seeds

Combine the milk and sugar in a small saucepan or a small glass mixing bowl and warm to 110°F (measure with an instant-read thermometer) over medium heat or in the microwave. Sprinkle the yeast across the surface of the milk and stir a bit. Let the mixture sit for 5 to 10 minutes, until foamy. Meanwhile, whisk the flour and salt together in a large mixing bowl.

Once the milk is foamy, add the oil and vinegar to it and stir to combine. (The milk will curdle a little when the vinegar meets it, which is normal, but work quickly and don't let the mixture sit around.) Pour the liquid ingredients into the flour and stir with a wooden spoon until the flour is moistened and a very shaggy dough forms.

Turn the dough out onto a lightly floured surface and squeeze the loose bits into the mass. Now knead the dough for 8 minutes, until the surface of the dough is smooth and soft. Add flour sparingly as needed to the board and your hands if the dough begins to stick.

Brush a large bowl with a teaspoon or so of oil and add the dough. Turn the dough over once or twice to coat with some of the oil. Cover it and set it in a warm place to rise for 1 hour, until doubled in size.

Preheat the oven to 500°F.

alongside

ROOT VEGETABLE STEW ✦ BEEF CARBONNADE ✦ ROASTED SALMON WITH DILL CREAM SAUCE
CREAM OF MUSHROOM AND POTATO SOUP ✦ PAN-ROASTED PORK CHOPS WITH FENNEL AND BEETS

Put 2 ungreased baking sheets in the hot oven on separate racks while you work with the dough. Pull the dough out of the bowl onto a work surface. Cut it into 8 even pieces. Working with one at a time, roll each piece flat, thin, and about 8 inches long with a rolling pin. Don't worry much about the shape of each piece, which might be best described as a rather rustic rectangle with rounded edges. Sprinkle a heaping ½ teaspoon of caraway seeds across the surface. Fold the short ends of the dough inward to meet in the middle and run the rolling pin across the dough again to encase the seeds in the dough.

Pull the hot baking sheets out of the oven and situate 4 pieces of dough on each. Bake for 5 to 7 minutes, rotating the pans and swapping racks halfway through, until golden brown and slightly puffed. Take the flatbreads from the oven and let them cool slightly before serving. If making ahead, let the flatbreads cool completely before wrapping tightly in aluminum foil. Reheat in a toaster oven or 325°F oven for 5 minutes.

Northern Girl Herbed Biscuits

I'm about as southern as the North Pole despite the fact that some of my roots are tied up in Dixie on account of my paternal grandmother, Dagmar or "Sid" (the nickname that exposed her southernness like a lace slip peeking out from the hem of a Sunday church skirt). I never had much of a relationship with Mom Mom, though she lived nearby. We came together the same way holiday Catholics do: on the days of obligation for the ceremony of a celebratory meal. So I never stood beside her apron strings learning to cook southerly things. I don't even know if she knew how to make biscuits from scratch and by heart the way girls from down south are supposed to. Even if she could make them with the best of the belles, she probably rarely did because she was under so much pressure to cook Italian food. Sid was the only non-Italian married into a 100 percent Italian-American clan living in New York's Hudson Valley.

I grew up there in the Hudson Valley, too, but my mother's New England lineage was most prominent in my childhood. Her people were from Massachusetts and ate baked beans, potatoes, haddock, and London broil. There was bread and butter, but not really ever any biscuits.

So like the rest of Americans north and west of southern, I've always perched safely as an admiring fan of biscuits without claiming I could execute a batch worth a bet on a pitcher of sweet tea. I resigned to my insecurities that mine would be fraudulent attempts at emulating the tender puffs pierced by generations-old biscuit cutters in a hot kitchen with a screen door whose hinges twanged like the folks who swept through it.

But on a cold March day in a Vermont kitchen warmed by a wood-burning stove, I changed my mind about biscuits belonging to the southern states and their cooks. Bundled in a wool sweater and ski socks, the day's uniform for collecting maple sugaring sap in the snow, I cupped a mug of hot tea with my bone-chilled hands and watched my friend, a pastry chef, use hers to fold and press the dough of biscuits that may have been the best I'd tasted to date. She talked while she rotated the mass of butter and flour and gave away no relation to the South in her diction, just an occasional long o that revealed formative years spent in Minnesota.

There was no buttermilk or lard or White Lily flour. But the warm results that nestled into a cozy towel-lined basket on the dinner table in a dark dining room lit up by candles and the moonlight bouncing off settled snowflakes could put up a fight with a rebel biscuit any day.

After our visit, phone consultations with my friend taught me better than any southern primer how to make buttery, multilayered, soft, and tall biscuits. I don't own an antique biscuit cutter from a place and time below the Mason-Dixon line, so I slice mine square with a long, sharp chef's knife and don't have to fiddle with the scraps made by rounds.

These are the ones I'll teach my grandchildren to make. If my grandmother were still alive, I'd ask her to bake them with me and invite her to tell me about her Dixie roots after all these years.

herbed biscuits makes 1 dozen

The crux of this recipe is the folding technique, which accounts for the height and layering of the final product. For years I struggled with achieving structural biscuit nirvana. I mastered crumbly biscuits that were tasty enough but functionally inept for sandwiching anything clever. I also served my share of stiff pucks whose layers were fused by overworking or cutting mishaps. I know I'm not alone. These folded, pressed, and single-cut biscuits, however, have crunchy tops and bottoms and soft middles. Slice them in half and stack them with fried eggs and sliced ham, or turkey and cheese. Or just eat them intact, warm from the cooling rack.

2½ cups unbleached all-purpose flour, plus more for work surface

1 tablespoon plus ½ teaspoon baking powder

1 tablespoon sugar

2 teaspoons kosher salt

8 tablespoons (1 stick) cold unsalted butter, cut into ¼-inch cubes

1 cup cold whole milk

2 tablespoons finely chopped fresh chives

1 teaspoon fresh thyme leaves

Preheat the oven to 425°F.

Sift the flour, baking powder, sugar, and salt into a large mixing bowl. Add the butter and cut it into the dry ingredients using a pastry blender or 2 knives until the butter pieces are pea-sized and distributed throughout. In lieu of a pastry blender or knives, use your fingers: squeeze the butter cubes between your fingers as if you're snapping to crush it into small bits. Work quickly to avoid warming the butter with the heat of your hands.

Dig a little well in the center of the butter-flour mixture and pour in half of the milk. Gently fold the ingredients together with a large rubber spatula, wetting the dry with the milk. Drizzle the remaining milk across the mixture and continue to fold the milk into the dry ingredients until a shaggy dough starts to form and none of the liquid remains at the bottom of the bowl.

Scrape the dough out onto a lightly floured surface and squeeze it slightly into a mound. Press the dough into a ½-inch-thick rectangle, about 8 inches by 6 inches, with the shorter sides at the top and bottom (like a sheet of paper situated vertically). Tuck any loose dough pieces onto the mound. Combine the chives and thyme and then sprinkle 1 tablespoon of the herbs across the surface of the dough and press them in lightly. ➡

alongside

Classic Fried or Oven-Fried Chicken ✦ Baked Spiral Ham ✦ Tomato and Fontina Frittata
Grilled Vegetables with Fresh Ricotta and Marinated Mozzarella
Potato Corn Chowder ✦ Buttermilk Garlic Marinated Turkey Tenderloin

Fold the dough in half onto itself, pulling from the top short side of the rectangle to the bottom. Press any escapee herbs back into the dough. Shift the dough clockwise a quarter-turn, using a pastry scraper or offset spatula to dislodge any stuck pieces from the work surface. Press the dough back into a rectangle, about 6½ inches by 5½ inches. Fold and turn this way 3 more times, pressing the dough out into a rectangle with the same dimensions each time. Go easy on the dough: Don't knead it vigorously as you would bread dough. Be much more casual about it, because the less you press it, the lighter and flakier the resulting layers will be.

Sprinkle the remaining herbs across the surface of the bread. Fold the dough in half, rotate again, and press into a rectangle one last time, 8 inches by 6½ inches and ½ inch thick. A rolling pin helps produce this size rectangle more evenly and quickly.

Use a sharp chef's knife (not serrated) to cut the biscuits into 12 squares (cut 3 rows by 4 rows). Avoid using a sawing motion or dragging the knife through the dough, both of which will inhibit the rise of the biscuits when they bake.

Set the biscuits on an ungreased baking sheet, snuggly situated next to each other with no space between, back into the rectangle shape. Bake for 20 to 25 minutes, turning the pan halfway through, until the tops are golden brown.

Remove from the oven and transfer to a cooling rack to cool slightly before serving.

panfried chapatis makes 12

I learned how to make this East African staple when we hosted elite Kenyan runners at our home for the Philadelphia marathon and half-marathon. Everyone at our house was running the next morning, and I made our traditional prerace pasta dinner with light tomato sauce, a simple salad, and good crusty bread for the Americans in the bunch. But Joseph and Kiptu used our kitchen to prepare the fuel that does them good: food from home. Beef with greens simmered in a pot, cornmeal ugali, and these chapatis. Simple rounds of unleavened bread, similar in appearance, taste, and texture to a flour tortilla, though slightly thicker, chapatis are just the tool for scooping up stews and curries. Joseph rolled a batch big enough for all of us, and none remained by the end of dinner. We all ran a little faster the next day.

3 cups unbleached all-purpose flour, plus more for kneading

1 teaspoon kosher salt

¼ cup vegetable oil, plus oil for brushing

½ cup plus ½ cup water

Whisk together the flour and salt in a large mixing bowl. Drizzle the oil across the surface. Mix the oil into the flour until shaggy clumps start to form. Pour ½ cup water across the flour and mix it in until no more pools of liquid are visible. Add another ½ cup water and use clean hands to continue mixing it together, sort of folding and kneading it onto itself as it begins to cling into a ball of dough. Use a bowl scraper or the dull side of a butter knife to flick off the dough that sticks to your fingers.

Pull the dough plus any loose bits and flour onto a lightly floured surface. Work the pile into a single mass, squeezing it and pushing it at first. Once it comes together, knead it for 5 minutes, sprinkling additional flour on the board and your hands as needed, until the dough is smooth and soft, not at all lumpy.

Use a rolling pin to roll the dough into a vague square, about 14 inches long. Cut the dough into 12 (1-inch thick) strips (a pizza cutter makes quick and relatively straight work of this job). Starting at the top end of the dough farthest from you, roll each strip downward onto itself into a coiled spool.

alongside

BEEF AND CHARD STEW ✦ PORK POSOLE ✦ ROASTED ROLLED LEG OF LAMB WITH ROOT VEGETABLES AND MERLOT GLAZE ✦ CURRIED COD AND VEGETABLES WITH RICE ✦ SPICED SQUASH AND BEAN STEW

Heat a large skillet over medium-high heat. If you have a long griddle pan that can accommodate one or two chapatis at a time, use it.

Set the dough coils off the board and cover them with a clean kitchen towel. Working with one at a time, pat each coil flat with your hands and then use a rolling pin to roll it out to about 5 or 6 inches in diameter. Brush one side of the dough with a bit of oil and place it oiled side down in the hot pan. Fry it for 1 minute or until you can see light brown spots speckling the surface when you use a spatula to peek underneath. Flip the chapati over and cook the other side for another minute.

Transfer the hot chapati to a plate or a basket lined with a clean kitchen towel. Cover the chapatis to keep them warm while you fry the remaining dough.

tip: While these are most scrumptious hot out of the pan, you can make the batch ahead of time, cool completely, and refrigerate stacked on a plate and wrapped tightly with plastic or in an airtight container. Warm them in a 350°F oven for about 10 minutes before serving. Leftovers are also irresistible toasted and doctored up with melted butter, sugar, and cinnamon for breakfast.

cheddar pepper scones makes 16 scones

Background heat from freshly ground black peppercorns and bits of sharp Cheddar make for deeply savory scones. Set your pepper mill to grind coarse flecks of pepper for the most flavor rather than the much finer grind that's fit for a pepper shaker. Both textures of extra-sharp Cheddar serve a purpose: The grated cheese joins the butter in making the dough tender and flaky; the cubes melt into studs of sharp, cheesy bites throughout the scone.

1½ cups unbleached all-purpose flour

½ cup whole wheat pastry flour

2 teaspoons baking powder

1 teaspoon coarsely ground black pepper (about 40 grinds)

½ teaspoon kosher salt

4 tablespoons (½ stick) very cold unsalted butter, cut into ¼-inch cubes

½ cup shredded extra-sharp Cheddar cheese (about 2 ounces)

½ cup ⅛-inch-cubed extra-sharp Cheddar cheese (about 2 ounces)

¾ cup cold buttermilk

Preheat the oven to 400°F. Line a baking sheet with parchment paper or a silicone mat.

In a large mixing bowl, whisk both flours thoroughly with the baking powder, pepper, and salt.

Cut the butter into the dry ingredients with a pastry blender or use your fingers, pinching the butter cubes between your middle fingers and thumbs like you're snapping. The resulting butter bits should be very small and well distributed throughout the flour, which will be shaggy and bumpy. Handle the butter quickly and with a light touch so the heat from your own hands doesn't soften it too much. Dump the cheese in and toss it into the buttery flour with your hands to distribute it evenly.

Pour about a third of the buttermilk over the flour mixture and use a large rubber spatula to gently fold everything together. Repeat this two more times until a crumbly dough ball starts to form. Use your clean hands to pat everything together tenderly. Gather in as many crumbs and butter bits as you can.

alongside

CRACKED CRAB ✦ MAPLE AND SPICE BRINED FRESH HAM ✦ BUTTER AND SAGE BRUSHED CHICKEN AND GRAVY
GRILLED VEGETABLE AND SHRIMP SALAD ✦ BROCCOLI AND RED PEPPER OMELETS OR FRITTATA ✦ CORN CHOWDER
SPLIT PEA SOUP ✦ ROAST BEEF AU JUS

Transfer the dough ball to a clean surface like a cutting board or butcher block or your countertop. Pat any stray pieces into the dough and then nudge it into a circle about ½ inch thick. Cut the circle in half and then cut each half into 4 wedges for a total of 8 triangular scones. To make 16 mini-scones, divide the dough into 2 smaller circles first, about ½ inch thick, and cut each of those circles into 8 wedges.

Arrange the scones evenly spaced on the baking sheet. Put the pan in the freezer for 15 minutes.

Transfer the scones to the oven and bake for 25 to 30 minutes (20 to 25 minutes for the mini-scones), until the tops are blond with browned bits of cheese poking through and browned on the bottom. Some of the Cheddar cubes will bake out into crispy pieces on the edges of each scone.

Cool slightly on a wire rack before serving.

Store completely cooled scones in an airtight container at room temperature for up to 3 days. Toast or reheat in a warm oven.

tip: Whole wheat pastry flour is different from regular whole wheat flour and produces completely different results in baked goods. Pastry flour has a much lower protein content than whole wheat flour, which makes it great for tender pastries, cakes, muffins, and scones like these. Substituting regular whole wheat flour will result in borderline leaden and dry scones. Pastry flour (regular and whole wheat varieties) is available in the baking section of grocery stores.

white wine focaccia

makes 1 large loaf (serves 6 to 8)

Focaccia has become my favorite homemade all-purpose bread. Required ingredients are few, and the method is straightforward and flexible. (Don't have a food processor? Knead by hand as directed below.) The white wine in this recipe brings natural sugars and extra yeastiness, contributing to the softness and aroma of the finished crumb. While these instructions make for an unadorned table bread, this thick, chewy focaccia stands up beautifully as a base for the addition of toppings like thinly sliced and marinated onions, Oven Tomatoes (page 121), or chopped herbs. I prefer the way the dough bakes tall and crisp in a cast-iron skillet, but you can also press the dough into a free-form rectangle on a baking sheet (it will not fill an entire pan) or substitute a cake pan, as noted.

¾ cup warm (115°F) water

½ cup dry white wine at room temperature

1 envelope (2¼ teaspoons) active dry yeast

3 cups bread flour, plus more for kneading

2 teaspoons kosher salt

¼ cup extra virgin olive oil, plus oil for coating the bowl

2 teaspoons finishing salt (coarse sea salt, Maldon flakes, or any specialty salt you prefer)

Combine the water and wine in a large spouted liquid measuring cup. Sprinkle the yeast across the surface of the liquid, stir it gently, and let sit for 5 minutes, until it swells and foams.

In a food processor, combine the flour and kosher salt and pulse the ingredients several times to mix thoroughly.

Stir 2 tablespoons of the olive oil into the yeasty water. With the food processor running, slowly pour the liquid ingredients through the chute into the dry ingredients in a steady stream. Process just until the dough comes together and spins around the bowl on the blade. The dough will be very moist and sticky.

Scrape the dough onto a lightly floured surface and knead it for 2 minutes, using a bench scraper to help you lift the sticky dough and sprinkling the surface very sparingly with flour as needed. Resist the urge to add too much flour, despite the dough's incessant sticking. It requires minimal kneading, so don't try to force it to be manageable by drying it out.

alongside

LINGUINE AND CLAMS OREGANATA ✦ TOMATO-BRAISED BEEF BRACIOLE ✦ CHICKEN OR VEAL SALTIMBOCCA
PASTA E FAGIOLI ✦ CAULIFLOWER AND SQUASH CHOWDER ✦ EGGPLANT PARMESAN

Coat a large glass or metal bowl with a little olive oil (about 1 teaspoon). Transfer the dough to the bowl and turn it over once or twice to coat it with oil. Cover the bowl with plastic wrap. Let the dough rise in a warm place (75° to 80°F) for 2 hours, until doubled in size.

Preheat the oven to 425°F.

Coat the surface of a 12-inch cast-iron skillet with 1 tablespoon of the remaining olive oil. Pull the dough out of the bowl and set it in the skillet. Gently press and push the dough out toward the edges of the skillet with the length of your fingers. Drizzle the last tablespoon of oil on the dough and use your hands to distribute it across the surface. Dimple the dough by sinking your fingers about halfway down into it so there are dimples all over the entire surface, about 1 inch apart. Let the dough rise again for 30 minutes. (If you do not have a cast-iron skillet, use a 9-, 10-, or 12-inch cake pan instead. It will produce a taller, thicker bread.)

Dimple the dough with your fingertips again. Sprinkle the finishing salt over the dough.

Bake in the center of the oven for 25 to 30 minutes, until the top is crisp and golden brown and a thermometer inserted into the center of the bread registers 190°F.

Let the focaccia cool slightly before slicing.

TO MAKE BY HAND: Combine the water and wine in a large mixing bowl. Sprinkle the yeast across the surface of the liquid, stir it gently, and let it sit for 5 minutes, until it swells and foams.

In a medium bowl, thoroughly whisk the flour and kosher salt together.

Stir 2 tablespoons of the olive oil into the yeasty water. Sprinkle 1 cup of the flour across the surface of the liquid and mix it in using a wooden spoon. Continue adding and mixing in the flour ½ cup at a time until the mixture goes from a lumpy, very wet pancake batter consistency to a soft, scraggly ball of dough that becomes difficult to stir with the spoon. At this point, turn the dough and any scraps, crumbs, and loose flour out onto a lightly floured surface. Push and pat everything into a mound and then knead the dough very casually for 3 minutes, sprinkling the surface very sparingly with flour as needed and using a pastry scraper to help you lift and fold the sticky dough. Resist the urge to add too much flour, despite the dough's incessant sticking. It requires minimal kneading, so don't try to force it to be manageable by drying it out.

Coat a large glass or metal bowl with a little olive oil (about 1 teaspoon). Transfer the dough to the bowl and turn it over once or twice to coat it with oil. Cover the bowl with plastic wrap. Let the dough rise in a warm place (75° to 80°F) for 1 hour, until doubled in size.

Bake as directed.

tip: Gauging the temperature of water is important when baking yeast breads. If the water is too cool, the yeast won't wake up and go to work the way it's supposed to. If the water is too hot, it will kill the yeast, rendering it useless in the leavening process. Measuring the temperature with an instant-read thermometer solves these potential pitfalls. The typical target temp for bread making is 110°F. In this focaccia recipe, I suggest a slightly higher 115°F because the room temperature wine will drop the water's temperature a little bit. By touch, water in this range feels comfortably hot, like bath water, but not as hot as water for a cup of tea.

parmigiano-reggiano crackers

makes about 1 pound of dough, about 8 dozen (1-inch) square crackers

I love this intensely cheesy dough for its simplicity and versatility. Just like fresh pasta, you can roll it by hand or with a pasta roller and cut it into any shape you prefer, using a sharp knife, pizza cutter, ravioli roller, fluted pastry wheel, or cookie cutters. When rolling the dough by hand, take the time to work it as thinly as you can so you don't end up with partially soft, chewy crackers. The thinner the dough, the crisper the cracker. If you have a pasta roller, use it to make ultra-thin, wide wisps of crackers for a breadbasket or crisp shards instead of croutons for salads or soups.

1 cup unbleached all-purpose flour, plus more for rolling

½ cup semolina flour

½ teaspoon kosher salt

1 cup freshly grated Parmigiano-Reggiano (lightly piled, not packed) or ¾ cup of the coarser store-grated version (see Tip)

3 tablespoons extra virgin olive oil

6 tablespoons ice water

Put the flours, salt, and cheese in a food processor and pulse about 20 times to combine. Add the olive oil and pulse again about 20 times, until the flours start to resemble clumpy sand from the moisture of the oil. With the processor running, drizzle the water through the food chute and process for about 30 seconds, until the flour starts to cluster up away from the walls of the processor. Despite little masses of dough, much of it will still look sandy and crumbly. If you pinch some of it together, it should stay put in the squeezed lump of dough.

Scrape the dough out of the processor and onto a lightly floured surface. Use your hands to pack it all together into one big mass, as you would with pie dough. Knead the dough, folding it onto itself, about 20 times, until it is a cohesive ball. Press it into a round disk about 1 inch thick and cover it with plastic wrap. Refrigerate the dough for at least 20 minutes and up to 24 hours.

Preheat the oven to 400°F. Line 2 baking sheets with parchment paper.

alongside

SPAGHETTI AND MEATBALLS WITH CAESAR SALAD ✦ TOMATO BASIL SOUP
PASTA E FAGIOLI ✦ CLAM CHOWDER ✦ ANTIPASTO ✦ MUSSELS IN SPICY MARINARA

Cut the dough into 4 equal pieces. Working with one piece at a time on a lightly floured surface (cover the other pieces with the plastic wrap or a clean kitchen towel), roll the dough out into a rough rectangle or oval as thinly as possible, flipping and rotating it as you go, sprinkling flour sparingly only if the dough starts to stick to the surface or roller. When you think it's as thin as you can get it, drape it over your hand and look for the silhouette of your fingers through it. If the dough is still too thick, keep rolling. Be patient.

Transfer the dough to the parchment-paper-lined baking sheet. Using a pizza wheel or a sharp chef's knife, score the dough into long ½-inch strips, 1-inch squares, or shapes of your choice, without cutting the dough all the way through. Leave room for another piece or two of dough on the baking sheet. (You can also cut completely through the dough and line the baking sheet with the individual crackers.)

Continue the process with the other pieces of dough, transferring them to the baking sheets and scoring them into shapes.

Bake until very lightly browned and crisp, about 10 to 12 minutes. Remove from the oven and cool completely on a cooling rack before breaking the crackers apart along the score lines. The crackers will get crispier as they cool.

TO MAKE THE DOUGH USING A PASTA ROLLER: After removing the dough from the refrigerator, cut it into 6 equal pieces. Shape each piece into a small rectangle. Work with one piece at a time, covering the others with the plastic wrap or a clean kitchen towel. Situate a piece of dough lengthwise with a short side down toward the roller. With the roller at the widest setting (1), send the dough through 3 times, folding the ends of the dough to the center to create a shorter rectangle after each roll. Next roll the piece through each of the smaller settings (2 through 5), until the dough is too thin to send through again or to send through the smallest setting. If the dough starts to stretch too long to manage, cut it in half and work with shorter pieces. Transfer the rolled dough to the baking sheet. Continue the process with the remaining dough. Leave as long sheets or cut it into shapes as you wish. Bake these ultra-thin sheets of cracker dough for about 8 to 10 minutes, until very lightly browned and crisp. These will darken and crisp faster than the thicker, hand-rolled crackers. Transfer to a cooling rack to cool completely before using.

Store in an airtight container for up to 3 days.

tip: It's important to measure the cheese according to the textural variety you're working with. If you buy a block of Parmigiano-Reggiano and grate it by hand, use the medium holes on a box grater instead of the large holes, which make strips of cheese that won't blend well with the dough. If you buy pregrated Parmigiano-Reggiano that is machine ground and packed at the store (usually sold in plastic containers by weight from the specialty cheese section or deli), the recipe requires less by volume (¾ cup instead of 1 cup) because the same cup measure actually weighs more than hand-grated cheese. The difference is significant enough to affect the results of the cracker.

multigrain pretzel knots makes 1 dozen

In Philadelphia, where I live, soft pretzels are as omnipresent as cheesesteaks. People buy them from food trucks and eat them at their office desks for breakfast. The trouble is, they are dense and stiff and generally unappealing. I'm never sure why the likes of the doughier, more flavorful pretzels of neighboring Pennsylvania Dutch Country don't override their popularity. Tradition dies hard. But these multigrain pretzel knots are soft and pay no mind to the dominant twist in these parts. Rich and tender from butter, the knots are perfect for a breadbasket. Leftovers make excellent mini-sandwiches with fillings like egg and cheese, ham and mustard, or cream cheese and jam.

2 tablespoons dark brown sugar

1 cup warm water (110° to 115°F on an instant-read thermometer)

1 envelope (2¼ teaspoons) active dry yeast

2 cups unbleached all-purpose flour, plus more for kneading

¾ cup white whole wheat flour (see Tip)

½ cup oat flour

2 teaspoons kosher salt

8 tablespoons (1 stick) unsalted butter, melted

1 teaspoon vegetable oil

½ cup baking soda

1 egg, lightly beaten

½ teaspoon or more coarse sea salt, pretzel salt, or other finishing salt

Dissolve the brown sugar in the water in a large spouted measuring cup. Sprinkle the yeast on top of the water, mix it casually, and let it sit for 5 minutes, until it swells and foams.

Meanwhile, in the bowl of a stand mixer, whisk all three flours and the kosher salt together thoroughly.

Pour the melted butter into the dry ingredients. Fit the mixer with the dough hook and mix on low for about 30 seconds, just to combine. Stop the machine and scrape the flour that has been pushed to the side into the moist mound in the middle. Then, with the mixer running on its lowest speed, pour the foamy yeast mixture into the flour. Once the majority of the flour is wet, increase the speed to 3 and knead the dough for 7 minutes, stopping to scrape the sides with a rubber spatula if necessary, incorporating any dry flour hiding at the bottom of the bowl. The dough will be sticky.

Scrape the dough onto a lightly floured surface with a bowl scraper or spatula and knead by hand for about 2 minutes, sprinkling the board just a little with extra flour every few turns, only if necessary.

Transfer the dough to a large clean bowl coated with the oil, cover with plastic wrap, and let the dough rise in a warm place until it nearly doubles in size, about 1 hour. ➡

alongside

BAKED HAM WITH A MUSTARD GLAZE ✦ KIELBASA AND CABBAGE ✦ BREADED PORK CUTLETS WITH APPLES AND MUSTARD CREAM ✦ SMOKED-SALT POTATO CHOWDER ✦ EGGS BENEDICT (USE THE PRETZELS IN PLACE OF MUFFINS) HONEY THYME TURKEY OR CHICKEN BREAST

Preheat the oven to 425°F. Line 2 baking sheets with parchment paper.

Bring 6 cups of water to a boil in a large, wide saucepan.

Pull the risen dough out of the bowl and onto a lightly floured surface. Cut it into 12 even pieces (about 2.3 ounces each, if using a scale). Working with one piece at a time and keeping the others covered with a kitchen towel, roll each piece into a 12-inch rope of even thickness. Hold the ends of the rope in each hand. Cross the end in your right hand behind the end in your left hand so that you are holding a horseshoe with crossed legs. Now switch the hands holding each end. Take the end in your right hand and tuck it around the dough behind it and through the loophole. Now take the end in your left hand and fold it down over the dough in front of it and into the loophole, filling up some of the space. Now fold the end in your right hand down onto itself to fill the remaining space in the loophole to complete the knot of the roll. Repeat the process with each rope, setting the finished knots (knot side up) onto the parchment-lined sheet pans, 6 per pan.

Sprinkle the baking soda into the boiling water a little at a time. The water will foam and bubble vigorously. Using a slotted spoon, gently lower the knots into the water, 3 at a time. Boil for 30 to 45 seconds, nudging them over to their other sides in the water halfway through. Using the slotted spoon, lift each knot, jiggle the spoon to shake off excess water, and then tap the bottom of the spoon on a dry kitchen towel to catch additional moisture. Transfer the knot back to the baking sheet. Repeat for all 12 knots.

Using a pastry brush, paint each knot with a little of the egg. Sprinkle the knots with a pinch of the coarse salt. Bake for 15 to 20 minutes, until the pretzel knots are medium brown and an instant-read thermometer inserted into the center registers 190° to 200°F.

Let the knots cool slightly before serving. Or cool completely and store in an airtight container for several days. To prevent mold from moisture during extended storage, refrigerate and reheat in a toaster or low oven for 10 minutes before serving.

tip: White whole wheat is a whole grain product and is different from both whole wheat flour and refined all-purpose flour. It is made from white wheat rather than the red wheat that yields regular whole wheat flour and is lighter in flavor and texture than its red wheat counterpart. Unlike all-purpose flour, white whole wheat is processed in a way that retains the bran, germ, and endosperm. King Arthur and Bob's Red Mill are just two brand options. White whole wheat flour is widely available, including in major grocery chains.

heritage cornbread *serves 8 to 10*

My husband's grandmother Milly made cornbread the way southerners do: straight cornmeal, several knobs of bacon grease from the can that stored drippings, a few other ingredients, and a cast-iron pan. No white flour or sugar, both of which were signs of northern tampering that made cake, not bread. The resulting slices were thin and dense with crisp edges, devoid of sweetness, and the perfect sponge for red beans and rice or gumbo. This is that bread and can hardly settle in the same category as the thick squares of soft, fluffy, light yellow cornbread that's tender from creamed butter, sugar, and eggs. I added a touch of sugar for textural and flavor balance and can only hope my in-laws will forgive me for tampering with the original. Use this recipe to make Legacy Cornbread Dressing (page 199).

2 cups stone-ground yellow or white cornmeal

¼ cup sugar

1 teaspoon kosher salt

½ teaspoon baking powder

1 large egg

1½ cups buttermilk (whole-fat if you can find it)

2 tablespoons plus 2 tablespoons melted bacon grease or butter

Place a 10- or 12-inch cast-iron skillet or cake pan in the oven and preheat the oven to 400°F.

In a large mixing bowl, whisk together the cornmeal, sugar, salt, and baking powder.

In a spouted measuring cup or small mixing bowl, beat the egg lightly and then add the buttermilk. Whisk together to combine.

Dig a little well in the center of the cornmeal and pour in the egg and buttermilk. Use a large rubber spatula or wooden spoon to fold the wet ingredients into the dry ingredients until just combined. Drizzle 2 tablespoons of the bacon grease or butter into the batter and gently fold it in.

Remove the hot skillet from the oven, add the remaining 2 tablespoons of bacon grease or butter, and brush the entire inside of the pan to coat with the fat. Pour the batter into the pan and bake for 25 to 35 minutes (longer for the smaller pan, shorter for the larger), until the bread feels completely set when tapped lightly with your fingers and the top is just starting to speckle brown.

Cool slightly before slicing.

To store leftovers, lift the bread out of the pan and wrap tightly in foil or plastic wrap. Leave at room temperature or refrigerate in warmer weather.

alongside

PANFRIED CHICKEN CUTLETS WITH PEPPER GRAVY ✦ DEEP-FRIED TURKEY ✦ SHRIMP OR CRAWFISH ÉTOUFFÉE
SPICY BEAN CHILI, WITH OR WITHOUT BEEF ✦ HAM-STUFFED PORK CHOPS WITH BOURBON SAUCE

buttermilk stew bread makes 1 large loaf

Irish soda bread as Americans know it is actually not authentically Irish, but rather an amalgamation of traditional Irish recipes for bread leavened with baking soda and recipes more reflective of American tastes and ingredients, including extravagant things like white flour, eggs, butter, dried fruit, and seeds. This stew bread is a closer replica of more historically accurate and utterly simple white Irish soda bread without raisins or caraway seeds. It's not sweet or cakey like most Americanized Irish soda breads. The bread's tight crumb is perfect for sopping up sauces, especially thick, rich ones like the velvety liquid background of beef stew.

4 cups unbleached all-purpose flour, plus more for kneading and the baking sheet

1¼ teaspoon baking soda

3 tablespoons sugar

1¼ teaspoon kosher salt

1¾ cups buttermilk, plus 1 teaspoon for glazing the bread

Preheat the oven to 400°F. Sprinkle about 1 teaspoon of flour across the center of the baking sheet to cover about 8 inches by 4 inches.

In a large mixing bowl, combine the flour, baking soda, sugar, and salt. Whisk thoroughly to blend and aerate the ingredients.

Dig a little well in the center of the flour mixture with a large rubber spatula. Pour half of the buttermilk into the well and then gently fold the liquid into the dry ingredients, forming a lumpy pile of flour. Add the remaining buttermilk and repeat the folding process until a very shaggy dough forms. Take care not to overwork the mixture. Just lift and fold several times.

Turn out the dough onto a lightly floured surface. Dip your hands in a little flour and brush it on your palms and fingers. Then sort of halfheartedly knead the dough, folding it over onto itself and tucking in the sticky, scraggly bits as you go (stop to scrape the buildup from your fingertips now and then too). A bench scraper helps to keep the dough from repeatedly sticking to the board or countertop and to itself.

alongside

BEEF BARLEY STEW ✦ SPICED LENTIL SOUP ✦ SMOKY HAM AND SPLIT PEA SOUP
BAKED ORANGE MARMALADE HAM ✦ BEEF BURGUNDY ✦ CHICKEN MULLIGATAWNY
NEW ENGLAND OR MANHATTAN CLAM CHOWDER ✦ IRISH LAMB STEW

Shape the dough into an oblong/rectangle loaf, about 8 inches long, 4 inches wide at the center, and 1½ inches thick. Transfer the loaf to the baking sheet. Cut a shallow (about ½ inch deep), narrow X lengthwise from corner to corner. Then cut a shallow line across the center of the X. Brush the remaining teaspoon of buttermilk across the surface of the loaf. Transfer to the oven and bake for 35 to 40 minutes, until much of the surface is light golden brown and an instant-read thermometer registers 190°F when inserted into the center of the loaf.

Let the bread rest for about 10 minutes before slicing or cool completely and wrap tightly in plastic wrap or foil to store at room temperature. (Refrigerate the bread in warmer weather or in an environment prone to moisture.)

In Edenderry

In Edenderry, Ireland, in the mid-1980s, Caoimhe O'Kelly and her sister Aisling would walk from St. Mary's Primary School to their grandmother's house for lunch, where warm brown bread with a thick spread of melting butter and a cup of milky tea were almost always on the menu. In those days, clear across the Atlantic at a cafeteria table in New York's Hudson Valley, I sat surrounded by classmates and our white bread sandwiches packed from home alongside juice boxes with tiny bendable straws.

Today at a preschool in Philadelphia, Caoimhe's daughter and mine sit next to each other, giggling over insulated lunch bags stuffed with finger foods and sippy cups of milk.

Over the couple years since we met soon after our daughters were born, Caoimhe and I have gotten to know each other over lots of conversations, many of which revolved around food. I learned early on about her brown bread, which she makes regularly in her American kitchen as a convenient staple and a symbol of home all this way from there.

We started talking recipes so I could understand this Irish mainstay that doesn't exist in America, and Caoimhe produced notes from every which way. A handwritten recipe that yields a loaf closer in spirit to what we know in America as Irish soda bread; links to the Irish company Odlums for details about whole meal flour; an original recipe written by Caoimhe's aunt, scattered with sprightly directives about ingredients, funny notations on methods, and exclamation points throughout; and an email from her cousin recounting their granny's brown bread (titled "Bown Bown Bead" for her mother's toddler-aged pronunciation of the stuff) with notes about additions of grains and substitutions of olive oil for margarine.

Brown bread is as much a utilitarian recipe in Ireland as it is a favorite heirloom baked good. Its constitution is basic, its preparation quick, and its uses countless. Most of all, its impact is lasting, because its fibrous bulk is stick-to-the ribs energy fodder of the hardiest kind. It toasts beautifully for breakfast, dons a cap of butter and salmon for lunch, and rounds out braised lamb or a boiled dinner.

In time, Caoimhe, like her grandmothers, has taken to making her "cakes" of brown bread by heart, sight, and touch. "I just take fistfuls of what I have on hand and add enough buttermilk till it looks right, scraping the dough into a loaf pan or two if there's enough to split it up," she explained during a visit where I tried to mine as much detail as I could to attempt an American's respectable replica of her loaf.

Soon the outcome of our informal chatter that schooled me in Irish cuisine became as much about learning to make an authentic cake of brown bread for inclusion in this book as it did about extracting a clearer semblance of a documented recipe from Caoimhe for her to pass down to her own daughter. For all the lunch tables Maeve will huddle around with friends in years to come, few if any will include edible ties to her roots. But eventually, armed with a recipe that tells her how, she'll find her way right back to Edenderry, where her mother and aunts and grandmothers ate brown bread for lunch nearly every day.

irish brown bread makes 1 loaf

Authentic, un-Americanized Irish brown bread is all about the wheat. Its aroma, flavor, and texture are heady with the grain's unrefined earthiness, making for a staunchly firm, hearty crumb with barely a trace of sweetness. In Ireland, it's a constant at the table as a versatile accompaniment to everything from daytime tea and marmalade to evening Cheddar, stew, and beer, including cocktail-hour canapés with butter, smoked salmon, and capers. A fail-safe preparation is a thin slice, toasted warm and crisp, wearing a generous smear of salted butter that melts into the heat of the bread. Add a drizzle of honey to brighten it if you like.

2 cups stone-ground whole wheat flour

1½ cups unbleached all-purpose flour

½ cup wheat bran

½ cup wheat germ

2 teaspoons baking soda

2 teaspoons kosher salt

1¾ cups buttermilk (whole-fat if you can find it)

1 large egg, beaten

2 tablespoons molasses

1 tablespoon extra virgin olive oil

Preheat the oven to 375°F. Butter or grease a 2-quart loaf pan (9 by 5 by 3 inches).

In a large mixing bowl, whisk together the flours, wheat bran, wheat germ, baking soda, and salt.

In a large spouted measuring cup, whisk together the buttermilk, egg, molasses, and olive oil.

Dig a little well in the center of the dry ingredients and pour in half of the liquid ingredients. Using a large rubber spatula, fold the dry ingredients into the wet, dampening the flours and forming a shaggy pile in the bowl. Drizzle half of what's left of the liquid ingredients into the dry and fold again. Now pour the remaining liquid ingredients into the bowl and, using wet hands, fold the wet, sticky dough onto itself, making sure that all loose flour has been incorporated and the entire ball is damp. (The dough will handle like meatball or meat loaf mix, heavy and dense, but unkneadable and unpourable.)

Lift the dough into the buttered pan and press it out to fill the loaf as evenly as possible. Transfer to the oven and bake for 45 to 50 minutes, until the top is brown and a toothpick inserted in the center of the loaf comes out clean.

Let the bread cool slightly before slicing and serving. Wrap tightly to store and toast slices on subsequent days. The loaf will keep at room temperature for up to 5 days.

alongside

MUSTARD-GLAZED ROAST SALMON ✦ BAKED HONEY HAM WITH BRAISED CABBAGE
POTATO CHOWDER AND MIXED GREENS ✦ POACHED EGGS AND SAGE SAUSAGE ✦ GUINNESS-GLAZED LAMB

pumpkin cozy rolls makes 1 dozen

A dozen big, soft, buttery rolls bake together into a snug crown fit for the center of a holiday table. Pumpkin lends its hue, plus sweetness and moisture, to the crumb, which is redolent with the squash's favorite spices. The lengthy rise time is a trademark for the rich brioche family of bread, but the investment guarantees a very special addition to the menu. You'll have to decide whether to unveil the rolls at the dinner table or at breakfast, warmed, spread with butter, and drizzled with maple syrup.

. . . .

3½ cups unbleached all-purpose flour

2 teaspoons kosher salt

1 teaspoon ground cinnamon or pumpkin
   pie spice

1 envelope (2¼ teaspoons) active dry yeast

1 cup pumpkin puree at room temperature

¼ cup buttermilk at room temperature

2 tablespoons pure maple syrup

2 large eggs at room temperature, plus
   1 large egg for egg wash

8 tablespoons (1 stick) butter, cut into
   ¼-inch cubes, at room temperature,
   plus 1 or 2 teaspoons for the pan

In the bowl of a stand mixer fitted with the dough hook, whisk together the flour, salt, cinnamon, and yeast. Add the pumpkin, buttermilk, and maple syrup and mix on medium-low speed (2 on a KitchenAid mixer) until a lumpy, floury mixture begins to form. Stop the machine and scrape the flour that builds up to the sides into the damp mix below it. Start the mixer again at the same speed and mix for about a minute.

Add the eggs, one at a time, and mix at medium speed (4 on a KitchenAid) after each addition. Continue mixing for about 3 minutes, until the eggs are completely incorporated, making the dough and the sides of the bowl less visibly wet than when the eggs were first added.

With the mixer running on medium-high (setting 5), add the butter cubes 2 or 3 at a time, pausing to let them blend into the dough until barely visible before adding more. It will take about 5 minutes to work in all the butter. Don't rush it.

Now let the mixer knead the dough on medium-high speed for a full 10 minutes. The dough will be very tacky at first, sticking to the walls and bottom of the bowl as it slaps against it for the first 7 or 8 minutes. Toward the end of kneading, the bottom and sides of the bowl will be mostly clear of the dough, which will work up into a mass stretched between the hook and the bottom of the bowl. ➡

alongside

ROASTED TURKEY AND GIBLET GRAVY ✦ HONEY-BAKED HAM AND FRIED EGGS
PORK SHOULDER SLOW ROASTED WITH APPLES, BOURBON, AND BACON ✦ DUCK CONFIT SALAD
MUSHROOM AND SAGE CANNELLONI ✦ MAPLE BACON QUICHE OR FRITTATA

Butter the bottom and sides of a 9-inch springform pan. Scrape the dough into the pan, pulling it down off the hook and using a big rubber spatula to release it from the bowl. The dough will feel soft and buttery and will look like shiny, stretchy taffy when it's being pulled on the machine in a beach boardwalk storefront.

Cover the pan with plastic wrap and let the dough rise in a warm place for 1½ to 2 hours, until doubled in size.

Push the dough out of the pan and onto a very lightly floured surface. Knead it lightly 5 or 6 times to work some of the air out of it and then let it rest for 15 minutes. Cut the dough into 12 equal pieces (about 3 ounces each, if using a scale). Rebutter the springform pan.

Push each piece of dough into a small round boule by shaping it as follows. Make a tight C shape with one of your hands so that only about ½ inch of space remains open between your index finger and your thumb and so your palm curves slightly into a cupped shape behind the outline of the C. Stuff one of the 12 pieces of dough through the middle of the C shape and into the palm of your hand behind it. Now, using all of the fingers of your free hand, push the dough back up through the "C" to create a smooth, round roll shape. Open your hand and pinch the bottom of the dough boule to close up the space where your fingers pushed upward. Put the boules into the springform as you finish them, repeating the process with all 12 pieces of dough.

Situate the rolls inside the springform so they fit snuggly next to one another. Start by setting 3 in the center and then arrange the remaining 9 around them along the perimeter of the pan. Cover the pan with the plastic wrap and refrigerate overnight (at least 8 hours and up to 12).

After the refrigerator rise, let the rolls rest, still covered, at warm room temperature for 45 minutes to 1 hour. The rolls will puff up just slightly. Meanwhile, preheat the oven to 400°F.

Beat the remaining egg with 1 teaspoon of water. Brush the egg wash across the tops of the rolls. Set the springform pan on a baking pan and transfer to the oven. Bake the rolls for 40 minutes, until the tops are dark brown and an instant-read thermometer registers 190° to 200°F when inserted into the center of a roll.

Let the bread cool in the pan to just warm, about 30 minutes. Release the springform and then separate the rolls by cutting them with a serrated knife along the visible dividing lines. Serve immediately.

tip: Make the rolls 1 or 2 days in advance, cool completely, and reheat, covered with foil, in a 350°F oven for 10 to 15 minutes.

tip: KitchenAid stand mixer users will note that once the machine is set to a speed of 5 or more, it will shimmy and shake . . . and move across the countertop as it works. Take care not to wander too far away and keep an eye on it if you are busy with other tasks during the kneading step, or you'll be reminded when it crashes to the floor!

chapter three

Salads and Dressings

Today's salads are consummately creative, often stealing the spotlight from main dishes and departing far from tosses of iceberg strewn on a plate under a glob of "house dressing" and named "side salad." Salad can enrich nearly every homemade meal, either simple or embellished. Fresh and interesting ingredients, varied textures, and vibrant colors will wave a flourish onto the most unadorned dinner table. And even a straightforward mix of greens can be remarkable with a drizzle of distinctive dressing. From basic lettuce salads and vinaigrettes to inspired tangles of garden greens and toppings, this chapter is dedicated to one of the most popular accompaniments of all. Its contents are versatile enough to match every type of meal covered in the book. While each salad doesn't have its own designated dressing, I offer a few good options that you can mix and match from the vinaigrettes and dressing recipes.

honey balsamic peaches and burrata serves 4 to 6

Naming this salad "peaches and cream" would aptly describe the indulgence of burrata. The ultra-soft bundle of fresh mozzarella cheese is filled with cream, which spills out when the cheese is cut down the middle. It's a decadent topping for bitter greens and sweet, ripe peaches marinated in tart balsamic. If you can't find burrata in a grocery or cheese shop in your area, substitute fresh mozzarella, thinly slicing it and fanning it out across the top of the salad.

¼ cup balsamic vinegar

2 tablespoons honey

Pinch of kosher salt

5 grinds black pepper, plus more for garnish

4 ripe peaches, pitted and thinly sliced

5 cups packed baby arugula

1 small head of radicchio, halved, cored and thinly sliced (about 4 cups)

10 basil leaves, torn into small pieces

1 bundle of burrata

2 tablespoons extra virgin olive oil

In a medium bowl, whisk together the vinegar, honey, salt, and pepper. Add the peaches and toss to coat. Let them marinate for 10 to 15 minutes while you prepare the rest of the salad.

Toss the arugula, radicchio, and basil together and spread them out across a small serving platter. Scatter the peaches and balsamic across the lettuces.

Set the burrata in the center of the platter and slice it into 4 or 6 pieces, letting the cream spill out into the salad below. Drizzle the olive oil over the salad and season with extra freshly ground black pepper.

alongside

FRESH LINGUINE WITH HEIRLOOM TOMATOES AND BASIL ✦ ZUCCHINI AND HERB RISOTTO
LEMON CAPER CHICKEN OR VEAL SCALOPPINE ✦ GRILLED GARLIC BUTTERMILK-MARINATED PORK TENDERLOIN
PAN-SEARED SCALLOPS AND SHRIMP WITH OLIVE TAPENADE

mixed greens with cherries, berries, and cheese serves 4 to 6

Cherry season whizzes by every year at a pace that sends me into a frenzy of invention, trying to come up with as many uses for the sweet gems as I can before they're gone. While making my way through one summer boon of dark sweets and bright yellow sours, I realized that while I would never decline a sugar-crusted cherry crumble, I prefer cherries of all kinds in savory applications, and in recipes that don't bury the ruby rounds beneath other flavors and textures. I like the way blackberries look and taste alongside cherries in this simple salad, which lets the fruits' sugars shine among tart, creamy goat cheese and mild, tender greens; but substitute blueberries or raspberries if you prefer.

6 ounces mixed greens (about 6 packed cups)

8 ounces cherries, pitted and halved (about 2 cups)

1½ cups blackberries (about 6 ounces)

2 tablespoons chopped fresh chives

3 ounces crumbled goat cheese (about ½ cup)

In a large, wide mixing bowl, toss the greens with the cherries, blackberries, and chives. Sprinkle the goat cheese on top and toss once or twice to combine. Drizzle with the dressing of your choice and serve.

try with

SHERRY SHALLOT VINAIGRETTE 75 ✦ SWEET BALSAMIC VINAIGRETTE 74 ✦ LEMON HONEY VINAIGRETTE 70

alongside

GRILLED TURKEY TENDERLOIN WITH THYME AND YOGURT SAUCE ✦ PAN-SEARED PORK TENDERLOIN WITH BALSAMIC SAUCE ✦ BASIL-BREADCRUMB-CRUSTED VEAL CUTLETS ✦ GRILLED CHICKEN LEGS AND THIGHS WITH CHERRY BOURBON SAUCE ✦ LAMB CHOPS WITH ZA'ATAR AND POMEGRANATE SAUCE ✦ ROASTED EGGPLANT, ZUCCHINI, AND RED ONION PANINI ✦ BASIL RICOTTA RAVIOLI WITH LEMON CREAM

Mastering the Art of Salads

I learned how to do a lot of memorable things in culinary school. I ground my own sausage blends and stuffed them into their sheer, slippery casings; mastered fish mousseline and consommé, neither of which I'll ever make again unless I mistake a time machine for a taxi and end up a servant in Downton Abbey; kneaded, shaped, and baked fresh bread and ate torn chunks of the hot loaves with a thick spread of cold, rich-with-fat Plugrá (I gained a few pounds that semester); rolled out fresh pasta and stuffed it with dreamed-up fillings; competed against classmates to whip a huge bowl of egg whites to stiff peaks by hand (this is more exhausting than it sounds); raced myself to butcher a chicken, filet a fish, and clean a rack of lamb faster than the time before.

But one of my favorite and most valuable classes was a single-session basic-skills lesson on salads and vinaigrettes. My classmates and I huddled around a table piled with a jungle of greens, munching and comparing. We tasted spoonfuls of a dizzying display of oils and vinegars. Most of us reveled, wide-eyed in discovery, urging one another to try this or that. A few of the class shifted their boredom between their feet, longing to do something more hard-core, like break down a side of beef or flambé something, anything, with a heavy-handed pour of booze.

For me, though, this class was a game changer. It freed salads from their ancillary place and repositioned them as an opportunity to really showcase the skill of featuring and matching ingredients.

Our assignment was to make a salad and a dressing. When it came time to turn out our plates, none were the same. A parade of artfully arranged composed salads lined up next to tangled medleys of mixed greens with embellishments like fruit, candied nuts, shreds of vegetables, and cheese. The vinaigrettes and dressings further emphasized the individuality of each plate. Everyone had started with the rules of the standard vinaigrette (see page 76) and modified it to an original mixture using flavored oils, vinegars, fruit juices, dairy, herbs, and more.

Mastering the art of salad making will change the way you eat. Since that class, even the simplest salads, like baby arugula with shaved Parmigiano-Reggiano, have personality, and bottled dressings are a thing of the past. Salads are the most obvious way to bulk up and balance a meal, and the easiest way to add more plant food to your life. If you can wow yourself with raw vegetables and a quick-mix potion of oil and vinegar, culinary feats like a high-rising flambé are just silly smoke and mirrors.

persimmon, pomegranate, and pistachio salad serves 4 to 6

Sweet, ripe, and vibrant orange persimmons are a soft, satiny bed for a colorful tangle of greens adorned with shiny ruby pomegranate and peridot-hued pistachio bits. Fennel's earthy anise notes weave through all the flavors, which are perfect accompaniments to the most popular tastes and textures on a holiday buffet.

. . . .

2 medium ripe Fuyu persimmons

1 small pomegranate

½ cup shelled roasted and salted pistachios, chopped

1 small fennel bulb, very thinly sliced or finely shaved on a mandoline

6 packed cups (about 6 ounces) mixed greens or arugula

Use a sharp paring knife to cut the skins off the persimmons and then slice the fruit into very thin rounds (if you have a mandoline, use it set at smaller than ⅛ inch). Line a large platter with the slices.

Cut the pomegranate into quarters and tap out the arils, or juicy, edible seeds, from within. You'll have to do some work with your fingers to separate the arils from the peel and white membranes, which you can discard.

Toss the pomegranate seeds, pistachios, and fennel with the greens and pile the mixture on top of the persimmons. Drizzle with the vinaigrette of your choice and serve.

try with

POMEGRANATE MOLASSES VINAIGRETTE **77** ✦ SHERRY SHALLOT VINAIGRETTE **75**
SWEET BALSAMIC VINAIGRETTE **74** ✦ SOY BALSAMIC VINAIGRETTE **73** ✦ LEMON HONEY VINAIGRETTE **70**

alongside

HERB-CRUSTED ROASTED TURKEY BREAST ✦ MAPLE MUSTARD BAKED HAM ✦ GARLIC-STUDDED CROWN ROAST
OF PORK ✦ SEARED SCALLOPS WITH BROWN BUTTER ✦ ROASTED HALIBUT WITH OLIVE OIL AND THYME

crunchy corn tortilla salad *serves 4 to 6*

This salad is so full of color, flavor, and texture it can easily steal the show from the main dish. Use whatever tomato variety you prefer, but this mix is a perfect place for those little red, orange, and yellow cherry, grape, and pear varieties that look like gumballs and candies tucked into pint containers on farmstand tables all through the summer.

6 (6-inch) corn tortillas, quartered and cut into ½-inch-wide strips

1 tablespoon vegetable oil

Pinch of kosher salt

Pinch of ground cumin

Pinch of chipotle chile powder

2 cups quartered heirloom rainbow cherry and grape tomatoes (about 12 ounces)

1 medium mango, peeled and diced into small cubes (about ¾ cup)

1 cup fresh pineapple diced into small cubes

2 medium avocados, peeled, pitted, and diced (about 1 cup)

½ cup cooked black beans (drained and rinsed if canned)

½ cup cooked pinto beans (drained and rinsed if canned)

¼ cup fresh cilantro leaves, chopped

¼ cup thinly sliced scallion

1 clove garlic, minced and smashed into a paste (see Tip)

½ small head of iceberg lettuce, cored and cut across the leaves into ½-inch-wide pieces

½ small head of romaine lettuce, cored and cut across the leaves into ½-inch-wide pieces

1 cup crumbled queso fresco, feta, or coarsely grated ricotta salata

try with

LIME VINAIGRETTE (SEE TIP IN LEMON HONEY VINAIGRETTE) **70** ✦ LIME CUMIN KEFIR DRESSING **82**
BUTTERMILK CHIVE DRESSING **79** ✦ SMOKY TOMATO DRESSING **80**

alongside

GRILLED CHIPOTLE-MARINATED BONE-IN CHICKEN BREASTS ✦ SHRIMP, ZUCCHINI, AND BELL PEPPER KEBABS
MAHI MAHI FISH TACOS ✦ CARNE ASADA ✦ COCONUT PINEAPPLE MARINATED PORK TENDERLOIN

Preheat the oven to 400°F.

Put the tortilla pieces in a large mixing bowl, drizzle them with the oil, and sprinkle with the salt, cumin, and chile powder. Toss, using clean hands or tongs to coat the tortilla pieces with the oil and seasonings. Spread the tortilla pieces across a baking sheet and bake for 15 to 20 minutes on the middle rack, until they are crisp and lightly toasted. Keep a close eye on them as they bake to prevent burning if your oven tends to run high. Transfer the hot tortilla strips to a cooling rack to cool completely. (These can be prepared up to a day ahead, cooled completely, and stored in an airtight container or resealable plastic bag.)

In a large, wide serving bowl, combine the tomatoes, mango, pineapple, avocados, beans, cilantro, scallion, and garlic. Gently toss everything together. (This can be prepared up to a day ahead and stored, covered, in the refrigerator.)

Just before serving, add the lettuces and cheese to the tomato mixture and toss to combine thoroughly. Top with the toasted tortilla strips.

tip: Fresh garlic paste takes some of the bite out of raw garlic, which can be overpowering and unpleasant. To make a paste, mince the garlic as finely as you can. Then turn the blade of your chef's knife flat and press it firmly into the pile of minced garlic, holding the knife with one hand and pushing down on the top of the blade with the other. Now pull the knife toward you while pressing down on the garlic. Continue this motion, stopping a few times to gather the garlic into a pile again and mince further, until most of the minced pieces have given way into a paste.

apple cabbage chopped salad serves 4 to 6

This is no wallflower of a salad. It keeps your attention from the first forkful as an active toss of crunchy, earthy ingredients, not one of those quiet, wispy grazing piles that sits over on the salad plate, waiting to be a palate cleanser. With so much happening in one mix—sweet, snappy apples; audibly crisp cabbage; slightly bitter, deep purple radicchio; sticky, chewy dates; and coating, creamy, pungent cheese—you might expect discord. Instead, it's a symphony—or maybe more like a rock concert—of texture and flavor.

2 small crisp, sweet apples, such as Honeycrisp or Gala, cored and finely diced (about 2 cups diced)

½ small head napa cabbage, shredded or cut into 14-inch strips (about 8 ounces, 4 cups)

3 medium radishes, thinly sliced (about ⅔ cup)

6 to 8 Medjool dates, pitted and finely diced

½ small head of radicchio, shredded or cut into ¼-inch strips (about 3 cups)

3 medium stalks celery, thinly sliced (about 1 cup)

½ cup crumbled or cubed blue cheese

In a large, wide serving bowl, combine the apples, cabbage, radishes, dates, radicchio, celery, and cheese and toss well. Drizzle with your choice of vinaigrette or dressing just before serving or cover and refrigerate the salad until ready to serve.

try with

HERB VINAIGRETTE **72** ✦ SWEET BALSAMIC VINAIGRETTE **74** ✦ SMOKY TOMATO DRESSING **80**
BUTTERMILK CHIVE DRESSING **79** ✦ SOY BALSAMIC VINAIGRETTE **73** ✦ SHERRY SHALLOT VINAIGRETTE **75**

alongside

RICH PASTA DISHES LIKE FETTUCCINE ALFREDO OR SPAGHETTI CARBONARA ✦ COFFEE-RUBBED OR SALT-CRUSTED
RIB-EYE STEAKS ✦ BONE-IN PORK CHOPS WITH CIDER MUSTARD BRINE OR RUB ✦ TURKEY LONDON BROIL
OR ROASTED BREAST ROLLED WITH HAM AND DRIED CRANBERRIES ✦ BACON-WRAPPED FILET MIGNON
BUTTERNUT SQUASH SOUP

red grape and bacon salad serves 4 to 6

Lovers of the sweet and salty combo will mark this salad as a favorite (and if you're having them over for dinner, make more so they can indulge in seconds). Microgreens add their tiny, potent punch and look pretty to boot, but if you can't find any, just substitute an extra fistful of arugula or greens instead.

- -

4 ounces thick-cut bacon, cut into ½-inch pieces

6 packed cups (about 6 ounces) baby arugula or mixed greens

2 packed cups (about 2 ounces) microgreens

2 cups red grapes, halved

¼ cup thinly sliced scallion

Heat a large sauté pan over medium heat. When the pan is hot, add the bacon pieces and cook until crisp, 5 to 7 minutes, stirring every minute or so. Turn off the heat, lift the bacon bits from the fat in the pan with a slotted spoon, and set them on a paper-towel-lined plate to cool.

In a large serving bowl, toss the arugula with the bacon bits, microgreens, grapes, and scallion. Dress with the vinaigrette of your choice and toss to coat the salad.

tip: Prewashed packaged greens have become a staple convenience for their promise of instant gratification and more plant food on the table with less effort. Most are washed in chlorinated water, bagged, and then pumped with a blast of gas before the bag is sealed, which delays spoilage. All of these measures can affect flavor, overriding the ease of tearing open the bag for some. If you do use packaged salad greens often, consider reading a little bit about their processing to help you decide whether or not you'll bother with an extra rinse at home.

try with

SHERRY SHALLOT VINAIGRETTE **75** ✦ SWEET BALSAMIC VINAIGRETTE **74**
SOY BALSAMIC VINAIGRETTE **73** ✦ LEMON HONEY VINAIGRETTE **70**

alongside

PEPPER-CRUSTED RACK OF LAMB ✦ BRIE-STUFFED ROASTED CHICKEN BREASTS WITH WILD RICE
PAN-SEARED SCALLOPS WITH PORT SAUCE AND LENTILS ✦ GRILLED FENNEL SAUSAGES AND POLENTA
PAN-ROASTED PORK CHOPS AND PLUMS ✦ FUSILLI WITH SWEET PEAS, MINT, AND RICOTTA

arugula with sugar cranberries and pancetta

serves 4 to 6

This salad sparkles and bursts with color and sweet, tart bites; pops with arugula's peppery assertiveness; and surprises with the richness of tiny crisp and chewy bits of salty Italian bacon. The simple combination's hues and freshness are perfect for a fall or winter table laden with heavy, full-bodied dishes that could benefit from an invigorating forkful of lighter, brighter flavor.

1 cup plus 3 tablespoons sugar

1 cup water

1 cup fresh cranberries, rinsed and sorted

½ pound pancetta, cut into ¼-inch cubes

8 cups (5 to 6 ounces) baby arugula

try with

✦ SWEET BALSAMIC VINAIGRETTE **74**
✦ LEMON HONEY VINAIGRETTE **70**
✦ POMEGRANATE MOLASSES VINAIGRETTE **77**
✦ SHERRY SHALLOT VINAIGRETTE **75**
✦ SOY BALSAMIC VINAIGRETTE **73**

Combine 1 cup of the sugar with the water in a small saucepan over medium-high heat. Bring the water to a simmer and then lower the heat just slightly to medium to maintain a simmer but prevent a boil. Simmer until the sugar is completely dissolved, 5 to 7 minutes, to make a simple syrup. Remove from the heat.

Put the cranberries in a medium heatproof mixing bowl. Pour the hot simple syrup over them. Cover the bowl and refrigerate for at least 4 and up to 24 hours.

Strain the cranberries from the simple syrup (reserve the syrup for cocktails or homemade sodas if you like) and spread them out on a baking sheet. Sprinkle the remaining 3 tablespoons of sugar over the berries, creating a shimmering crust. Let them dry at room temperature, about 1 hour.

Heat a large sauté pan over medium heat. Add the pancetta and cook it until the fat melts from the pieces as they shrink and crisp, 10 to 15 minutes. Transfer the pancetta with a slotted spoon to a plate lined with paper towels.

In a large serving bowl or on a large, wide platter, toss the arugula with the cranberries and pancetta bits. Drizzle with the dressing of your choice and serve immediately.

alongside

RIGATONI WITH SHORT RIB RAGU ✦ ROAST TURKEY WITH SAGE
CROWN ROAST OF PORK WITH PEPPER CRUST ✦ BAKED HAM WITH MAPLE AND CLOVES
MIXED MUSHROOM AND MASCARPONE STUFFED SHELLS ✦ CHICKEN MARSALA

strawberry feta salad serves 4 to 6

Strawberries tucked into their usual uses—shortcakes, fruit salads, jams—are there for good reason. They're unquestionably the blushing sweetheart of their kind and a natural for showing off their sugars in pretty applications that err on the sweeter side of the menu. But that sassy berry in her red dress has some serious chemistry with savory big shots like red meat, onions, or sharp, salty cheeses. This salad boosts the berry to a place where it really shines and makes you promise yourself not to relegate it exclusively to the dessert table again.

2 cups thinly sliced strawberries (about 10 large strawberries)

3 packed cups (about 3 ounces) mixed greens or spring mix

3 packed cups (about 3 ounces) baby arugula

¼ cup thinly sliced scallion, white and green parts (2 or 3 scallions)

½ cup (about 3 ounces) cubed or crumbled feta

¼ cup sliced almonds, toasted (see Tip, page 181)

Toss the strawberries, mixed greens, arugula, scallion, feta, and almonds together in a wide serving bowl. Drizzle with the dressing of your choice and serve immediately.

tip: If you anticipate leftovers, add the almonds per serving instead of tossing them all with the entire salad, to ensure crunchy nuts later. Don't dress the salad entirely either, lest you're left with soggy greens for your second helping the next day. Drizzle a tablespoon or two of dressing over each helping.

try with

SHERRY SHALLOT VINAIGRETTE **75** ✦ SWEET BALSAMIC VINAIGRETTE **74** ✦ LEMON HONEY VINAIGRETTE **70**
POMEGRANATE MOLASSES VINAIGRETTE **77** ✦ BUTTERMILK CHIVE DRESSING **79**

alongside

SPRING VEGETABLE PRIMAVERA WITH GARLIC AND WHITE WINE
GRILLED BONE-IN RIB-EYE OR STRIP STEAK ✦ ROASTED LAMB CHOPS WITH MINT PESTO
PAN-SEARED SCALLOPS AND SHRIMP WITH LEMON AND PEAS ✦ GRILLED HALIBUT WITH CITRUS RELISH

butter lettuce with ribbons and chives serves 4 to 6

Crisp cups of butter lettuce score high on my list of favorite greens. Also called Boston or Bibb, this variety is cool and crunchy like iceberg or romaine hearts, but more textured and herbaceous than both. Its lemon-lime-colored leaves are tender and snappy at once, and its natural curved shape envelops other ingredients and catches little pools of dressings and vinaigrettes, arranging an ideal forkful of salad. Butter lettuce takes to most any kind of mix-ins and dressings, standing up to weightier ingredients or letting more delicate ones shine.

. . . .

1 head of butter lettuce (about ¾ pound)

1 large English cucumber

3 medium carrots

¼ cup minced fresh chives

try with

+ LEMON HONEY VINAIGRETTE **70**
+ BUTTERMILK CHIVE DRESSING **79**
+ SWEET BALSAMIC VINAIGRETTE **74**
+ HERB VINAIGRETTE **72**
+ SESAME GINGER VINAIGRETTE **71**
+ SMOKY TOMATO DRESSING **80**
+ LIME CUMIN KEFIR DRESSING **82**

alongside

+ CRISPY HAM AND CHEESE STUFFED CHICKEN BREASTS
+ BUTTER-BASTED BONE-IN TURKEY BREAST
+ BURGERS ON BRIOCHE BUNS
+ SLOW-ROASTED PORK RIBS
+ GRAPE TOMATO AND BASIL GEMELLI PASTA
+ FISH AND CHIPS WITH RÉMOULADE
+ VEGETABLE POTPIE

Peel off any loose, shaggy, or bruised outer leaves of lettuce to expose the more tightly bound shipshape layer. Pull the leaves apart, wash and spin or pat them dry, and then tear them into large bite-sized pieces. Pile them into a large serving bowl.

Peel the cucumber and trim the top and bottom ends. Then continue to peel the cucumber flesh, running down its length with the peeler and rotating it in your palm after each length to create long ribbons of vegetable. If the cucumber is extra long, simply run half the length and then turn it over to peel the other half. Continue peeling until the remaining cucumber becomes cumbersome to hold or is mostly the seedy core. (Eat the remaining stump as a snack, save it for another purpose, or discard it.) Add the cucumber ribbons to the lettuce.

Peel the carrots and trim them of their stem end. Repeat the ribbon-peeling process, flipping the vegetable throughout the peeling for consistent thickness. Add the carrot ribbons to the lettuce and cucumber.

Sprinkle the chives in with the other vegetables and toss and fold everything together to distribute evenly. Serve with the dressing of your choice.

tip: As with shaving cheese (page 84) a Y-peeler allows you to pull through the cucumber and carrot to create wide, thin strips. You could simply chop the vegetables into rounds, but veggie ribbons like these match the tenderness of the butter lettuce and adorn the leaves in a gracefully different way than do typically sliced salad accoutrements.

baby spinach with oranges and manchego

serves 4 to 6

If this salad could talk, it would have a Spanish accent that makes you want to slide into a flamenco dance. It's effortless but exotic and a wonderful use of oranges beyond their usual portable fruit capacity. Use your favorite variety, including seasonal blood oranges and Cara Caras, whose garnet pulp and juices decorate dishes. Manchego is a creamy, slightly salty semihard Spanish sheep's milk cheese that partners perfectly with the sweet ting of the citrus.

2 large navel oranges (or your favorite variety), segmented (see Tip, page 185)

6 packed cups (about 6 ounces) baby spinach

½ small red onion, very thinly sliced

4 ounces aged (6 months or more) manchego cheese, sliced into very thin triangles or strips (rind removed and discarded)

Collect the orange segments and any additional juice you can squeeze from the remaining membranes in a large serving bowl. Add the spinach, onion, and cheese to the oranges and toss to combine. Dress with the vinaigrette of your choice and serve immediately.

try with

LEMON HONEY VINAIGRETTE **70** ✦ HERB VINAIGRETTE **72** ✦ LIME CUMIN KEFIR DRESSING **82**
SWEET BALSAMIC VINAIGRETTE **74** ✦ SOY BALSAMIC VINAIGRETTE **73**

alongside

PAN-SEARED AND ROASTED ORANGE GARLIC MARINATED CHICKEN THIGHS ✦ CHILE-RUBBED STRIP STEAKS
GRILLED HALIBUT WITH CAYENNE AND PEPPER ✦ PLANK-ROASTED CITRUS SALMON
PAN-SEARED CHIPOTLE SCALLOPS ✦ CHICKEN MOLE ENCHILADAS ✦ RIGATONI WITH SPARE RIB RAGU

romaine with lemon garlic croutons and parmigiano-reggiano serves 4 to 6

Texture is the defining factor in this salad. Sturdy romaine leaves are audibly crisp; toasted, seasoned, and buttery bread cubes add big crunch; and wisps of Parmigiano-Reggiano go crumbly in each bite. This mix stands up to thick Creamy Garlic Dressing (page 78) and will make die-hard fans of Caesar salad wish they'd always known about these croutons.

2 tablespoons extra virgin olive oil

1 tablespoon unsalted butter

2 cloves garlic, minced

Finely grated zest of 1 large lemon

⅛ teaspoon freshly ground black pepper (about 10 grinds)

8 ounces Italian bread, sliced into 1-inch cubes (about 4 cups)

1 small head of romaine or 3 romaine hearts

2 ounces Parmigiano-Reggiano cheese, peeled into thin, wide ribbons (page 84) or coarsely grated

Preheat the oven to 375°F.

Heat the olive oil and butter in a large skillet over medium-low heat. Once the butter is melted, add the garlic and sauté for 2 minutes, until fragrant but not browning. Remove from the heat and stir in the lemon zest and pepper.

If your pan is big enough to hold all of the bread cubes, scrape them into it and toss them with a large spatula to coat them with the other ingredients. (Otherwise put the bread cubes in a large mixing bowl and pour the other ingredients all over them, tossing to coat.)

Spread the cubes in one layer across a baking sheet. Bake for 15 to 20 minutes, stirring once halfway through, until the cubes are just barely turning golden and feel toasty and firm when you squeeze one.

Remove from the oven and let the cubes cool completely before using.

While the croutons cool, core the lettuce, wash the leaves, spin or pat dry, and tear them into bite-sized pieces. Add them to a large serving bowl and toss to coat with the dressing of your choice.

Scatter the cheese and cooled croutons on top of the salad along with the dressing of your choice just before serving.

try with

CREAMY GARLIC DRESSING **78** ✦ SWEET BALSAMIC VINAIGRETTE **74** ✦ SOY BALSAMIC VINAIGRETTE **73**
LEMON HONEY VINAIGRETTE **70** ✦ HERB VINAIGRETTE **72** ✦ SMOKY TOMATO DRESSING **80**

alongside

BAKED ZITI ✦ PEPPERONI OR VEGETABLE STROMBOLI ✦ GRILLED SAUSAGE AND VEGETABLE PIZZAS ✦ MINESTRONE
BROILED COD OR SCALLOPS WITH LEMON AND OLIVE OIL ✦ SHRIMP SCAMPI ✦ CHICKEN OR VEAL PARMESAN

lemon honey vinaigrette makes ⅔ cup

When life gives you lemons, make this light, fresh, and adaptable vinaigrette. Bright, unmistakable citrus is distinct yet entirely complementary to so many vegetables and fruits, making it the perfect player for an all-purpose salad dressing. While olive oil and lemon are a perfect pair, this particular blend calls for a milder, less flavorful oil that lets the lemon and honey stand as the focal points.

¼ cup fresh lemon juice (about 2 small lemons)

1 tablespoon white wine vinegar

2 teaspoons honey

⅓ cup safflower oil (or another mild-flavored oil like vegetable or grapeseed)

Pinch of kosher salt

Finely grated zest of 2 small lemons

Whisk the lemon juice, vinegar, and honey together. Drizzle the oil into the juice in a slow, steady stream while whisking rapidly and constantly until the vinaigrette thickens slightly. Add the salt and lemon zest and whisk again to incorporate. Serve immediately or refrigerate in an airtight container for up to 3 days until ready to use. Whisk again to re-emulsify the vinaigrette before using.

tip: Make the same blend with any citrus fruit. Substitute the zest and juice of limes, oranges (including blood oranges), or grapefruit.

try on

BUTTER LETTUCE WITH RIBBONS AND CHIVES **66** ✦ PERSIMMON, POMEGRANATE, AND PISTACHIO SALAD **59**
ARUGULA WITH SUGAR CRANBERRIES AND PANCETTA **64** ✦ STRAWBERRY FETA SALAD **65**
MIXED GREENS WITH CHERRIES, BERRIES, AND CHEESE **56**

alongside

FLOUNDER FRANCESE WITH CAPERS ✦ CHICKEN, SPINACH, AND FONTINA SPIRALS
SUN-DRIED TOMATO AND ROASTED RED PEPPER RISOTTO ✦ TUNA AND WHITE BEAN TARTINE
TURKEY, GRAPE, AND PECAN SALAD ON CROISSANTS

sesame ginger vinaigrette makes ¾ cup

Here, all in a drizzle, are the flavors that whiz us right around the globe to Asian cuisine. A taste of an usual favorite salad tossed with the sweet and savory ginger-infused liquid is like dreaming in another language that you don't actually speak in your waking hours. It's so familiar and obvious, but redefining all at once. Try this, too, as a sauce for stir-fry, a marinade for fish, or a dressing for chicken salad studded with oranges and cashews, translated into Chinese.

1 teaspoon grated fresh ginger

1 tablespoon low-sodium soy sauce

1 teaspoon brown sugar

¼ cup rice wine vinegar

2 to 3 drops sriracha (optional)

2 teaspoons sesame oil (light or dark)

⅓ cup vegetable oil

In a small mixing bowl, whisk together the ginger, soy sauce, brown sugar, vinegar, and sriracha, if using, until most of the sugar is dissolved. Combine the sesame oil and vegetable oil in a spouted measuring cup. Slowly pour the oil into the other ingredients in a steady stream, whisking quickly and constantly to combine everything and thicken the dressing. Serve immediately or refrigerate until ready to use. Whisk again to combine before using.

try on

Butter lettuce with ribbons and chives **66** ✦ Apple cabbage chopped salad **62**
Baby spinach with oranges and manchego **68**

alongside

Spicy szechwan chicken, beef, pork, or vegetables ✦ Garlic and ginger stir-fried shrimp
Peanut beef satay ✦ Sweet and sour tofu ✦ Grilled, roasted, or fried chicken
Roasted salmon with lime rice **96**

herb vinaigrette makes about 1 cup

This blender batch is vibrantly green in color and flavor. It's a wonderful use of the fresh herbs that decorate your patio garden containers or that you carry away from farmers' markets in bouquets bigger than a bride's. Use it on simple salads or as a drizzle to brighten grilled seafood, shellfish, and meat.

2 tablespoons chopped fresh chives

¼ cup dill fronds

¼ cup fresh parsley leaves

5 fresh basil leaves

1 clove garlic

1 tablespoon finely grated lemon zest
   (1 large lemon)

3 to 4 tablespoons fresh lemon juice
   (1 large or 2 small lemons)

2 tablespoons white wine vinegar

½ teaspoon sugar

Pinch of kosher salt

5 grinds black pepper

Pinch of cayenne

½ cup extra virgin olive oil

Pile the chives, dill, parsley, basil, garlic, and lemon zest into a blender. Add the lemon juice and vinegar, cover, and blend for 20 to 30 seconds, until liquidy. Scrape down the sides of the blender and blend for another 10 to 20 seconds.

Add the sugar, salt, pepper, cayenne, and olive oil. Cover and blend again for 30 seconds, until the vinaigrette emulsifies, becoming thicker and uniform.

Serve immediately or refrigerate until ready to use. Whisk thoroughly before serving. Keeps well in the refrigerator for up to 3 days.

try on

BUTTER LETTUCE WITH RIBBONS AND CHIVES **66** ✦ STRAWBERRY FETA SALAD **65** ✦ RED GRAPE AND BACON SALAD **63**
ROMAINE WITH LEMON GARLIC CROUTONS AND PARMIGIANO-REGGIANO **69**
HONEY BALSAMIC PEACHES AND BURRATA **55**

alongside

SUMMERTIME PASTA PRIMAVERA ✦ BACON, LETTUCE, AND TOMATO SANDWICHES
GRILLED HALIBUT ✦ BUTTERMILK-MARINATED GRILLED PORK TENDERLOIN
PAN-SEARED SCALLOPS AND RISOTTO ✦ BAKED HAM AND SCALLOPED POTATOES

soy balsamic vinaigrette makes about ¾ cup

Soy sauce, an Asian cuisine staple, can get stuck in that category and miss out on its potential for so many other applications. Soy is intensely savory and a conduit of the coveted, hard-to-define umami flavor mystery that brings the satisfying richness of meat to nonmeat foods. Garlic and onion powders instead of the fresh alliums contribute to this depth. Brown sugar rounds out bold flavors of balsamic and the soy with background sweetness. This vinaigrette will make a statement in most salads with substantial ingredients (try with the Apple Cabbage Chopped Salad, page 62) but is especially destined for steak salads, since it could double as a riff on steak sauce or a marinade. Any leftovers can be stored covered in the refrigerator for several weeks.

3 tablespoons low-sodium soy sauce

⅓ cup balsamic vinegar

1½ teaspoons dark brown sugar

⅛ teaspoon freshly ground black pepper (about 10 grinds)

¼ teaspoon garlic powder

¼ teaspoon onion powder

⅓ cup safflower oil

In a small mixing bowl, whisk together the soy sauce, vinegar, and brown sugar until the sugar is mostly dissolved. Add the pepper, garlic powder, and onion powder and whisk to combine.

Drizzle the safflower oil into the bowl in a slow, steady stream, whisking briskly to emulsify the dressing. Serve immediately or cover and refrigerate until ready to use. Let the oil come to room temperature (solid to liquid state) before whisking again.

try on

APPLE CABBAGE CHOPPED SALAD 62 ✦ ARUGULA WITH SUGAR CRANBERRIES AND PANCETTA 64
BABY SPINACH WITH ORANGES AND MANCHEGO 68 ✦ MIXED GREENS WITH CHERRIES, BERRIES, AND CHEESE 56
RED GRAPE AND BACON SALAD 63 ✦ STRAWBERRY FETA SALAD 65

alongside

CHAR-GRILLED STRIP STEAKS AND T-BONE STEAKS ✦ BEEF, PORK, AND TURKEY BURGERS
MARINATED-SWORDFISH (Make a double batch of dressing and marinate the fish in half of it for 30 minutes or more, discarding the remaining marinade after grilling. Use the other half for an accompanying salad.)

sweet balsamic vinaigrette makes about ⅔ cup

Balsamic vinaigrette is ubiquitous, matching almost any salad. This one is sweet from a good, long squeeze of honey, which quiets balsamic's emphatic acidity and flavor just enough to balance the mixture and make way for the long-held note of garlic sung by a single clove that floats in the liquid but never physically becomes part of the dressing itself—only in spirit. Make a jar of this versatile vinaigrette and keep it in the fridge for a week or two to brighten weeknight salads.

1 tablespoon honey

¼ teaspoon Dijon mustard

¼ cup balsamic vinegar

¼ teaspoon kosher salt

⅛ teaspoon freshly ground black pepper (about 10 grinds)

⅓ cup extra virgin olive oil

1 clove garlic, halved

In a small mixing bowl, whisk together the honey, mustard, vinegar, salt, and pepper, taking care to incorporate all of the honey, which will stick to the bottom of the bowl otherwise.

Slowly drizzle in the olive oil, whisking rapidly. The olive oil and vinegar will emulsify, uniting into a more viscous liquid. Drop the garlic clove into the vinaigrette and let the flavors meld for at least 15 minutes. Whisk again before serving.

tip: Store leftover vinaigrette for up to 1 week in the refrigerator to prevent mold growth. Never store garlic in oil alone since this partnership affords the perfect environment for the potentially deadly botulism bacteria to grow.

try on

APPLE CABBAGE CHOPPED SALAD 62 ✦ STRAWBERRY FETA SALAD 65 ✦ RED GRAPE AND BACON SALAD 63
MIXED GREENS WITH CHERRIES, BERRIES, AND CHEESE 56 ✦ ARUGULA WITH SUGAR CRANBERRIES AND PANCETTA 64

alongside

SPAGHETTI AND BROCCOLI WITH QUICK MARINARA ✦ LONDON BROIL WITH ROASTED POTATOES
CHERRY TOMATO AND MOZZARELLA FRITTATA ✦ PENNE WITH GROUND PORK AND PEARS

sherry shallot vinaigrette *makes ¾ cup*

This dressing harmonizes two pitches—sweet high notes of sherry and sugar-thick maple and deep, savory tones of melted shallots and Dijon mustard. It's bold enough to turn a simple forkful of unadorned mixed greens into a memorable salad, but it will politely blend into the background of a more complex combination without stealing the show.

1 teaspoon plus ⅓ cup safflower oil or other mild-flavored oil

2 tablespoons finely chopped shallot (about 1 medium shallot)

2 tablespoons pure maple syrup (preferably grade B)

¼ cup sherry vinegar

½ teaspoon Dijon mustard

Pinch of kosher salt

5 grinds freshly ground black pepper

Heat 1 teaspoon of the oil in a small sauté pan over medium heat. Add the shallot and sauté, stirring often, until soft and fragrant but not browned, about 1 minute and 30 seconds. Transfer the shallot and any residual oil to a small mixing bowl.

Add the maple syrup, vinegar, mustard, salt, and pepper to the shallot and whisk together.

Pour in the oil in a slow, steady stream, whisking constantly to combine all ingredients.

Cover and refrigerate for at least 1 hour before serving to allow the flavors to meld together.

try on

BUTTER LETTUCE WITH RIBBONS AND CHIVES **66** ✦ ARUGULA WITH SUGAR CRANBERRIES AND PANCETTA **64**
APPLE CABBAGE CHOPPED SALAD **62** ✦ STRAWBERRY FETA SALAD **65** ✦ RED GRAPE AND BACON SALAD **63**
MIXED GREENS WITH CHERRIES, BERRIES, AND CHEESE **56**

alongside

ROASTED HERB-CRUSTED HALIBUT ✦ PAN-SEARED SALT-AND-PEPPER SCALLOPS ✦ CORNMEAL AND PISTACHIO
CRUSTED TROUT ✦ PORK TENDERLOIN WITH BLACK PEPPER AND PLUMS ✦ ROASTED THYME TURKEY BREAST

The Standard Vinaigrette

There are only two things standing in the way of your never buying another bottle of salad dressing again: a ratio and a quick tutorial on what makes a great vinaigrette every time.

The first step in making a simple vinaigrette is embracing the ratio 3:1, which is three parts oil to one part vinegar. So 3 tablespoons of oil whisked with 1 tablespoon of vinegar, or 6 tablespoons of oil to 2 tablespoons of vinegar, and so on. Though your tastes may warrant minor fiddling for your preferences (more vinegar, for example, if you like things particularly tart), this combination falls into an indisputable sweet spot—not too acidic and not too heavy with oil. The first few times you try your hand at homemade vinaigrette, use measuring tools to get the ratio right. Eventually, though, as per usual with kitchen work, you will perfect the balance with your eyes and taste buds.

There are a few other details to factor into a spot-on vinaigrette. Emulsification happens when two liquids mix together to become one. I know, who invited Mr. Wizard to dinner? This is important, though, because an emulsion gives body to a vinaigrette, thickening it into one substance and promising an even distribution of the combined liquids among the salad ingredients. When restaurants offer a set of oil and vinegar bottles in those cute little chrome caddies, you end up with an unbalanced salad dressing because some of the lettuce gets doused with oil while some of it gets spattered with vinegar. It makes for slick bites of flat oil and forkfuls of sharp acid, rather than a smooth combo of both. Even if you mix straight oil and vinegar together before dressing the salad, the emulsification is fleeting because the two liquids don't jibe without a little help. Lots of ingredients act as emulsifiers, but the most popular for vinaigrettes is mustard, typically Dijon. A naturally occurring substance in mustard seeds is purported to be the yenta of oil and vinegar. Just a bit of it, and hardly enough to affect flavor, coats the liquid molecules enough to hold the emulsification, making a more stable vinaigrette than oil and vinegar alone. Whisk ¼ teaspoon of Dijon mustard into 1 tablespoon of vinegar before whisking in 3 tablespoons of oil.

I always add a sprinkle or squeeze of sweetness to my vinaigrettes, usually in the form of honey or sugar, to brighten and balance the equation. If you taste your emulsion and feel like the tang of vinegar is too strong, a smidgen of sweet will likely pull it back down to even. Maple syrup, brown sugar, molasses, pomegranate molasses, fruit jams, syrups, and purees are excellent alternatives to honey and sugar. For every 1 tablespoon of vinegar, add ½ teaspoon of sweetener and adjust to taste from there.

With the base of your vinaigrette settled, you can flavor it further if you like. Add herbs and spices, fruit zest, chopped nuts, soy sauce, miso paste, or whatever suits your salad.

Once you've mastered the standard vinaigrette, you can riff a little, letting your preferences be your pilot. Substitutions for oil include mayonnaise, yogurt, sour cream, silken tofu, pureed fruit or vegetables, and nut butters. Alternatives to vinegar are citrus juice and acidic veggies like tomatoes.

With all the money you save not buying bottled dressings, treat yourself to some interesting ingredients for making great dressings at home. Consult the list of oils and vinegars on page 89 for vinaigrette inspiration when you're ready to start creating your own.

pomegranate molasses vinaigrette

makes about ½ cup

Pomegranate molasses is a reduction of pomegranate juice and is available bottled in Middle Eastern groceries, gourmet markets, and some supermarket ethnic food aisles. It is supremely tart with a sweet finish. It's used widely in desserts, but it really shines on the savory side of the menu.

2 teaspoons pomegranate molasses

3 tablespoons sherry vinegar

¼ teaspoon kosher salt

3 grinds black pepper

2 tablespoons safflower or vegetable oil

2 tablespoons extra virgin olive oil

In a small mixing bowl, whisk together the pomegranate molasses, vinegar, salt, and pepper. Add the oils and then whisk briskly until the liquids emulsify into a slightly thickened vinaigrette.

Use immediately or store in an airtight container for 2 weeks.

try on

MIXED GREENS WITH CHERRIES, BERRIES, AND CHEESE 56 ✦ RED GRAPE AND BACON SALAD 63
PERSIMMON, POMEGRANATE, AND PISTACHIO SALAD 59 ✦ APPLE CABBAGE CHOPPED SALAD 62
ARUGULA WITH SUGAR CRANBERRIES AND PANCETTA 64

alongside

ROASTED LEG OF LAMB WITH ROSEMARY AND POTATOES ✦ PAN-SEARED PORK TENDERLOIN AND PLUMS
LENTIL AND EGGPLANT STEW ✦ CHICKEN, MUSHROOM, AND ONION KEBABS

creamy garlic dressing makes ½ cup

Caesar dressing isn't going anywhere. It's a mainstay in the salad realm for its assertively salty, savory tang that plays against mild-mannered veggies. This is a lighter, brighter take on the blend, which traditionally relies on raw egg yolks and lots of oil for body. Smashed garlic paste, which is simple to make by hand, lends the telltale flavor without the unpleasant edge raw garlic can leave behind. Grated Parmesan cheese thickens and seasons. Like its inspiring predecessor, this blend is best on heartier lettuces like romaine, iceberg, butter lettuce, radicchio, and cabbage.

2 tablespoons mayonnaise

3 tablespoons plain yogurt

2 tablespoons extra virgin olive oil

1 teaspoon Dijon mustard

½ teaspoon garlic paste (1 medium garlic clove, minced and smashed into a paste; see Tip, page 60)

¼ teaspoon kosher salt

2 tablespoons freshly grated Parmesan cheese

5 grinds freshly ground black pepper

In a small mixing bowl, whisk together the mayonnaise, yogurt, olive oil, and mustard until completely smooth. Add the garlic, salt, cheese, and pepper and whisk again until smooth. Cover and refrigerate for at least 30 minutes and up to 5 days.

try on

ROMAINE WITH LEMON GARLIC CROUTONS AND PARMIGIANO-REGGIANO 69
BUTTER LETTUCE WITH RIBBONS AND CHIVES 66 ✦ APPLE CABBAGE CHOPPED SALAD 62

alongside

GRILLED, SAUTÉED, OR BREADED SEAFOOD WITH LEMONY NOTES ✦ CHICKEN OR VEAL PARMESAN
RIGATONI WITH SAUSAGE AND PEPPERS ✦ LASAGNE ✦ MEATBALL SANDWICHES

buttermilk chive dressing *makes about 1 cup*

This smooth, creamy blend studded with emerald flecks of herbs has the down-home air of ranch dressing in flavor but is a little bit more sophisticated at the heart of its makeup. Mayonnaise and sour cream give a boost to the body of tangy, smooth buttermilk, and fresh chives infuse their young oniony aura without being bumptious to the palate. There's nothing gloppy about this dressing; it coats the salads it's meant to escort without weighing heavy on the ingredients.

½ cup buttermilk

2 tablespoons mayonnaise

2 tablespoons sour cream

3 tablespoons finely chopped fresh chives

¼ teaspoon kosher salt

¼ teaspoon freshly ground black pepper
(about 20 grinds)

In a small mixing bowl, whisk the buttermilk, mayonnaise, and sour cream together until completely smooth. Fold in the chives, salt, and pepper. Cover and refrigerate for at least 30 minutes and up to 5 days.

try on

BUTTER LETTUCE WITH RIBBONS AND CHIVES **66** ✦ STRAWBERRY FETA SALAD **65**
APPLE CABBAGE CHOPPED SALAD **62** ✦ CRUNCHY CORN TORTILLA SALAD **60**

alongside

GRILLED STRIP STEAKS AND BAKED POTATOES ✦ SWEET HONEY CHILE BAKED CHICKEN
CRUNCHY BREADED PORK CHOPS ✦ SPRING VEGETABLE RISOTTO ✦ TURKEY BACON AND AVOCADO WRAPS

smoky tomato dressing makes 1½ cups

The juice and pulp of ripe summer tomatoes make this dressing voluptuous in savory roundness and viscosity. Blended into thick, tangy yogurt with balancing splashes of vinegar and oil, tomatoes that usually adorn lettuce in chunks or slices drape across greens in a saucy manner instead. Smoked paprika adds the unmistakable sultry flavor that suggests the same trademark tastes shared with bacon. All told, this smoked creamy tomato dressing captures the famed BLT. Try it tossed with pasta, spread on sandwiches, or mixed into chicken or tuna salad.

½ cup plain whole-milk or low-fat yogurt

1 medium tomato (about 7 ounces), cored and quartered

2 tablespoons extra virgin olive oil

2 tablespoons red wine vinegar

½ teaspoon smoked paprika

¼ teaspoon sugar

¼ teaspoon kosher salt

⅛ teaspoon freshly ground black pepper (about 10 grinds)

Add the yogurt, tomato, olive oil, vinegar, paprika, sugar, salt, and pepper to a blender and puree until completely smooth and creamy, 20 to 30 seconds. Adjust the seasoning to taste. Drizzle on salad immediately or cover and refrigerate for up to 1 week.

try on

BUTTER LETTUCE WITH RIBBONS AND CHIVES **66** ✦ CRUNCHY CORN TORTILLA SALAD **60**
ROMAINE WITH LEMON GARLIC CROUTONS AND PARMIGIANO-REGGIANO **69**

alongside

BURGERS AND OVEN FRIES (TRY CRISPLY ROASTED GARLIC POTATOES **90** ✦ GRILLED STRIP STEAKS AND BAKED POTATOES ✦ TURKEY CLUB SANDWICHES ✦ MINESTRONE ✦ PENNE WITH BACON AND BASIL

lime cumin kefir dressing makes 1 cup

Unsweetened kefir, a tangy, creamy cultured milk, is an excellent base for dressings. While kefir is pourable, it's still thick enough to coat salad ingredients without weighing them down. This dressing pairs well with lots of different flavors, including Asian, Mediterranean, Mexican, or Indian dishes, and especially any meals that have a kick of heat from spices or chiles, as kefir's cooling effect smothers the burn and refreshes the palate. It doubles as an excellent sauce for curries and grilled meats too.

⅔ cup plain unsweetened kefir

Finely grated zest of 1 lime (about 1½ teaspoons)

2 tablespoons fresh lime juice (about 1 lime)

1 teaspoon honey

½ teaspoon ground cumin

2 tablespoons extra virgin olive oil

¼ teaspoon kosher salt

5 grinds freshly ground black pepper

Whisk together the kefir, lime zest, lime juice, honey, cumin, olive oil, salt, and pepper in a medium mixing bowl. Let the dressing sit for at least 30 minutes before using or cover and refrigerate up to 5 days until ready to serve.

try on

BUTTER LETTUCE WITH RIBBONS AND CHIVES **66** ✦ CRUNCHY CORN TORTILLA SALAD **60**
BABY SPINACH WITH ORANGES AND MANCHEGO **68**

alongside

SPICY PAD THAI ✦ CHICKEN OR LAMB GYROS ✦ CARNITAS TACOS WITH RED ONION RELISH ✦ CHICKEN ENCHILADAS
BLACK BEAN BURRITOS ✦ TANDOORI CHICKEN WITH SAFFRON RICE AND NAAN

chapter four

Weeknight Dinners

For most of us, weekdays require more energy than we've got in reserve. Flitting, fluttering, and panting from one of life's demands to the next, we confess to being on a first-name basis with pizza delivery boys, or pouring the day's second bowl of easy-cleanup cereal, or resorting to a freezer-to-microwave stash between other versions of fast food. The creativity and energy required to come up with a complete meal seems laughably dismissible. These side dishes promise simplicity and the reward of fresh, nourishing fuel at the end of a long day. Each recipe calls for only a few ingredients, transformed by uncomplicated cooking methods. After a single foray, these will become staples of fussless homemade meals that keep takeout at bay Monday through Friday.

charred asparagus with shaved parmesan

serves 4 to 6

The simplest preparations of asparagus are the best, allowing the shoots to show off its own flavor without much fuss. Poaching and blanching are the most common methods, but this high-heat treatment deepens asparagus's natural earthy and unique flavor and adds a smoky, crunchy char. Seasoning with smoked salt complements the preparation, but if you don't have any on hand, regular kosher or sea salt is fine.

. . . .

1½ pounds asparagus, tough ends snapped off

2 tablespoons extra virgin olive oil

½ teaspoon coarse smoked salt (substitute kosher salt if necessary)

⅛ teaspoon freshly ground black pepper (about 10 grinds)

1 tablespoon fresh lemon juice (about ½ small lemon)

¼ cup shaved Parmesan cheese (about 1 ounce) (see Tip)

Preheat the oven to 425°F. Put a baking sheet on the middle rack of the oven for at least 5 minutes to get good and hot.

For asparagus spears that are ½ inch thick, cut in half lengthwise, then in half crosswise. For thin spears, just cut in half horizontally.

Put the asparagus in a large, wide mixing bowl or a rectangular baking dish. Drizzle the olive oil all over it and toss several times to coat.

When the baking sheet is very hot, remove it from the oven and immediately scrape the asparagus onto it, spreading it out in a single layer as much as possible to avoid steaming instead of roasting.

Roast for 15 to 20 minutes, tossing with a spatula once or twice, until the spears are very tender and are starting to blacken at the tip and in spots through the spear.

Transfer to a serving platter, season with the salt and pepper, and drizzle the lemon juice on top. Gently fold the spears to coat with the seasoning and juice. Scatter the shaved cheese over the top and serve immediately.

tip: To shave Parmesan cheese (including Parmigiano-Reggiano), hold the block of cheese in one hand with one of the flat sides facing up. Use a Y-peeler or a traditional vegetable peeler to create long, wide, thin wisps of cheese by running the blade down the length of the cheese.

alongside

SALT-AND-PEPPER LONDON BROIL ✦ CHICKEN AND DUMPLINGS ✦ ROAST COD WITH PISTACHIO PESTO
FUSILLI WITH TOMATO CREAM SAUCE ✦ TORTELLINI WITH HAM AND PEAS

chimichurri green beans serves 4 to 6

This version of fresh, snappy green beans brightens up the dependable standby. Chimichurri is the signature marinade and sauce used on Argentinean steaks and one of those condiments you taste and wonder what else you can slather it on. Parsley and cilantro mingle with garlic and some heat from jalapeño and pucker up with a kiss from lime juice and vinegar. A quick whir of the vibrant herbs in the blender and a bean dunk in a steam bath makes this a fast weeknight dinner side.

1 cup loosely packed fresh parsley leaves

1 cup loosely packed fresh cilantro leaves

1 small jalapeño pepper, seeds and veins removed, coarsely chopped

1 clove garlic

½ teaspoon cumin seeds

½ teaspoon plus ½ teaspoon kosher salt

Finely grated zest and juice of 1 lime (2 tablespoons juice) (see Tip)

2 teaspoons red wine vinegar

2 tablespoons extra virgin olive oil

2 cups water

1½ pounds green beans, stem ends trimmed

alongside

+ GRILLED OR PAN-SEARED STRIP STEAK
+ CUMIN-CRUSTED PORK TENDERLOIN
+ BROILED SCALLOPS WITH CHILE BREADCRUMBS
+ GRILLED GARLIC MARINATED JUMBO SHRIMP
+ VEGETABLE AND BLACK BEAN FAJITAS
+ CHICKEN OR MUSHROOM ENCHILADAS

Combine the parsley, cilantro, jalapeño, garlic, cumin seeds, ½ teaspoon of the salt, the lime zest and juice, vinegar, and olive oil in a blender. Process until a textured sauce forms, stopping 2 or 3 times to scrape down the sides of the blender and to give the mixture a stir with a wooden spoon to help the blending along. Set aside. (The chimichurri can be made ahead and refrigerated in an airtight container for up to 5 days. If you make the chimichurri in advance and refrigerate, bring it to room temperature before adding to the hot beans.)

Fill a large deep skillet with the water; add the remaining ½ teaspoon of salt to the skillet, cover with a lid, and bring the water to a boil over high heat. Add the beans, cover the skillet, and lower the heat to medium. Let the beans simmer and steam for about 8 minutes, until they are tender with the slightest bite. Drain the water from the beans and transfer them to a serving bowl. Scrape the chimichurri over the beans and toss them to coat evenly with the sauce. Serve immediately.

tip: If you're making green beans for a smaller crowd (say two or three), cook fewer beans but make the same amount of chimichurri. This recipe yields nearly 1 cup. Use leftovers as a sauce for beef, pork, chicken, turkey, or fish; mix into tuna salad; toss with cooked pasta or add to potato salad; use as salsa with chips or quesadillas.

tip: Juiciness of limes varies greatly, so if the lime you're using doesn't quite yield 2 tablespoons of juice, supplement with juice from an additional lime or make up the difference with water. The chimichurri sauce will be difficult to blend without enough liquid.

chorizo chard *serves 4*

One of the most nutritious leafy green varieties, chard is excellent in soups and stews, tangled with pasta, or strewn across pizza. But it is also superb on its very own. Here studs of spicy, smoky chorizo add meaty bites to silky, soft ribbons of chard, which boasts the slightest resemblance to its beet cousin. Brimming with flavor, a humble forkful will add something special to simple weeknight meals.

. . . .

1 large bunch (about 12 ounces) chard (any variety), raggedy ends trimmed

1 tablespoon extra virgin olive oil

4 ounces dry chorizo, cut into ¼-inch cubes (about ½ cup)

½ cup water

½ teaspoon dried oregano

Kosher salt and freshly ground black pepper

Cut the chard stems into ¼-inch pieces and then slice horizontally across the leaves into 1-inch ribbons. Set aside.

Heat the olive oil in a large deep sauté pan that can be fitted with a lid over medium heat. Add the chorizo and sauté for 5 minutes, stirring often as the sausage releases some of its fat.

Pour the water into the pan and scrape any bits from the bottom as it sizzles and steams. Add the chard and oregano and stir a bit to distribute the chorizo among the greens. Let the chard shrink in volume as it wilts and releases some of its water, nudging it around the pan occasionally for about 2 minutes.

Cover the pan, lower the heat to medium-low, and braise for 10 minutes, until the chard is silky and tender. Uncover the pan and increase the heat to high to cook off most of the liquid, about 2 minutes.

Season to taste with salt and pepper and serve immediately.

tip: There are several types of chorizo, including fresh links, which are sausages made of ground pork and spices stuffed into casing. Fresh chorizo is excellent browned in bits for meat sauces, tacos, chili, and more. But for this recipe, hard chorizo—dried, cured, smoked, or fully cooked—is best. You can find it in specialty shops, importer delis, bodegas, in the grocery store with the butcher, or in the meat case near the bacon. Try Wellshire Farms all-natural chorizo, which is free of nitrates, nitrites, and preservatives.

alongside

GRILLED OR BROILED STRIP STEAK ✦ BUTTERMILK FRIED CHICKEN ✦ PULLED PORK OR SHREDDED BRISKET
BRAISED MUSHROOMS AND LENTILS WITH RICE ✦ MUSSELS AND FINGERLING POTATOES IN HAM BROTH

chipotle black beans serves 4 to 6

A ubiquitous side dish in Mexican and Tex-Mex cuisine, black beans are usually satisfying, but sometimes a little bland. These are brimming with flavor from a quick sauce spiked with heat from chipotle peppers. Whether you use chipotle packed in adobo or chipotle powder, know that it's spicy indeed, so temper the heat with less if you or guests are heat-averse . . . or add more if you prefer to feel the burn over dinner.

2 tablespoons tomato paste

½ cup water

1 chipotle en adobo, seeded and minced to a paste (see Tip) or ½ teaspoon chipotle chile powder

1 teaspoon ground cumin

1 teaspoon plus 1 teaspoon apple cider vinegar

¼ teaspoon kosher salt, plus salt to taste

2 teaspoons vegetable oil

3 cloves garlic, minced

2 scallions, white and green parts thinly sliced separately

3 cups cooked black beans or 2 (15-ounce) cans, drained and rinsed

alongside

✦ CHILE AND GARLIC MARINATED GRILLED FLANK STEAK, PEPPERS, AND ONIONS
✦ CARNITAS TACOS WITH LIME RICE **96**
✦ SAUTÉED SALSA CHICKEN
✦ GROUND TURKEY TACOS
✦ HUEVOS RANCHEROS
✦ CHIPOTLE SHRIMP CHILE RELLENOS

In a small mixing bowl, whisk together the tomato paste and water until smooth. Add the chipotle, cumin, 1 teaspoon of the vinegar, and the salt. Stir to combine and set aside.

Heat the oil in a medium saucepan over medium-high heat. Add the garlic and white parts of the scallions and sauté for 30 seconds, until both are fragrant and starting to soften. Add the beans and the tomato paste mixture and stir to coat.

Cover the pot, lower the heat to medium-low, and simmer for 10 minutes, stirring once, until the liquid thickens as the beans release starch.

Stir in the remaining teaspoon of vinegar and season to taste with additional salt. Sprinkle with the green parts of the scallions and serve immediately.

tip: While canned beans are convenient and inexpensive, cooked dried beans are even more so. One cup of dried black beans yields 3 cups cooked and is a fraction of the cost of canned beans. The texture and flavor of cooked dried beans are more assertive than canned, which are often packed with quite a bit of salt (unless you seek out no-salt-added varieties). Best of all, you can prepare a big pot of beans and freeze portions in resealable plastic bags for future use, cooking right from frozen or thawing with a quick rinse of running water.

tip: To mash chipotle en adobo to a paste, trim its stem and scrape out the seeds (discard both). Mince the chipotle as finely as possible, running your knife blade over the little pile again and again until it resembles more of a paste than tiny bits of the chipotle. Wash your fingers well after handling chipotle, or you'll be reminded later if you take out your contacts or rub your eyes!

Side-Dish Upgrades

A cookbook full of recipes for great side dishes will certainly encourage meal upgrades, but so will some basic kitchen staples. A splash of vinegar, a drizzle of oil, a sprinkle of salt, or a shower of zest can transform an afterthought of a side dish into an integral part of a meal.

You're staring, unimpressed, at a bowl of steamed broccoli. Whisk a splash of sesame oil into a pour of soy sauce and drizzle it over the top.

You barely mustered the energy to make a pot of white rice. Lemon zest, almond oil, and fleur de sel make it taste like something special.

There's a bumper crop of tomatoes and cucumbers from a summer farm share on your kitchen counter. Good-quality extra virgin olive oil, tart white balsamic vinegar, and a sprinkle of dried oregano and smoked salt make a quick fresh side.

A well-stocked kitchen will spare you another night of boring side dishes without robbing you of precious time. Here's a short list of items to consider keeping in your kitchen for side-dish upgrades.

Oils

Olive oil, including light, extra virgin, and higher-end extra virgin reserved for drizzling and dipping
Grapeseed oil
Coconut oil
Walnut oil
Almond oil
Sesame oil
Peanut oil
Hemp oil
Hazelnut oil
Pumpkin seed oil

Vinegars

Distilled white vinegar
Apple cider vinegar
Red wine vinegar
Balsamic vinegar (including thick, rich aged balsamic)
White balsamic vinegar
Champagne vinegar
Unseasoned rice vinegar
Sherry vinegar
Infused vinegars like chive blossom, blackberry, apricot, plum, and yuzu vinegar
Chinese black vinegar
Malt vinegar

Condiments and Refrigerator Staples

Soy sauce and tamari
Anchovy paste
Dijon mustard
Tomato paste
Miso paste
Sour cream
Buttermilk
Citrus for juice and zest, especially lemons, limes, and oranges
Fresh ginger
Hard grating cheeses like Parmigiano-Reggiano, Grana Padano, and Locatelli

Salt

Flavored and specialty salts like smoked, truffle, Maldon, fleur de sel
Sea salt, fine or coarse
Kosher

Basic Spice Collection

Cinnamon
Ground cumin
Dried oregano
Peppercorns (black, green, red)
Garlic powder
Onion powder

crisply roasted garlic potatoes *serves 4*

A hot pan and a high oven make for crisp cubes of roasted potatoes with soft, creamy insides. Start these ahead of whatever you're making with them so they have time to brown perfectly while you forget about them to prepare everything else. Fresh garlic dries into an unpleasant chew in this preparation, so garlic powder promises the flavor without the borderline-burned slivers of cloves.

2 pounds russet potatoes, unpeeled and cut into 1-inch cubes

2 tablespoons safflower or vegetable oil

1 teaspoon garlic powder

½ teaspoon smoked salt or kosher salt, plus salt to taste

⅛ teaspoon freshly ground black pepper (about 10 grinds), plus pepper to taste

Preheat the oven to 425°F. Place a baking sheet on the middle rack of the hot oven for 5 minutes.

Toss the potatoes with the oil, garlic powder, salt, and pepper in a large mixing bowl.

Remove the hot pan from the oven and spill the potatoes out onto it. Spread them out across the entire pan, giving the pieces plenty of space. Crowding hinders crisping!

Roast the potatoes for 35 to 40 minutes, until golden brown and crisp, shuffling the potatoes around with a spatula about halfway through to promote even browning.

Sprinkle with additional salt and pepper to taste and serve immediately.

alongside

HERB-CRUSTED LAMB CHOPS ✦ SPINACH AND SWISS QUICHE ✦ CHEDDAR BURGERS WITH SMOKY BARBECUE SAUCE
ROASTED PORK AND PROVOLONE SANDWICHES WITH HOT PEPPER SAUTÉED GREENS
BLACK BEAN BURRITOS ✦ PANFRIED TROUT

cumin-dusted fried plantains serves 4 to 6

The sweetness of blackened plantains shines through in panfrying, but a sprinkle of savory spices keeps the dish planted on the other side of dessert. Cook these just before serving or they'll soak up oil as they wait to be unveiled at the table.

½ teaspoon kosher salt

½ teaspoon ground cumin

¼ teaspoon cayenne or chile powder

⅛ teaspoon freshly ground black pepper (about 10 grinds)

⅓ cup peanut oil

3 large very ripe plantains (about 1½ pounds), peeled and sliced on a sharp diagonal ½ inch thick

In a small mixing bowl, whisk together the salt, cumin, cayenne, and pepper. Set aside. Line a large plate or platter with a layer of paper towels.

Heat the oil in a large cast-iron skillet or deep sauté pan over medium-high heat until it shimmers on the surface. Place the handle end of a wooden spoon in the oil: If bubbles gather quickly around the handle, the oil is ready for cooking.

Gently slip the plantain slices into the oil and fry on each side for about 2 minutes, until a golden brown crust forms. Lift the fried plantains from the oil with a slotted spoon and transfer to the paper-towel-lined plate in a single layer. Sprinkle with the cumin mixture.

Cook and season in batches to avoid steaming, which results from overcrowding the pan. Serve immediately.

alongside

BLACK BEANS WITH TOMATILLOS, RICE, AND QUESO FRESCO ✦ PORK AND HOMINY STEW
FISH AND GRILLED VEGETABLE TACOS WITH PINEAPPLE SALSA ✦ TORTILLA RANCHEROS QUICHE **18**
COCONUT-CRUSTED CHICKEN BREAST WITH MANGO SALAD

hot buttered snow peas and shallots *serves 4*

Flat, thin-skinned snow peas stay crisp and sweet in a quick sauté or stir-fry. These peas are adorned with nothing more than fragrant shallots and melted butter. Brighter and lighter notes of green peppercorns mingle with salt to season a simple side with staying power.

2 tablespoons unsalted butter

1 large shallot, minced

1 pound snow peas, ends pinched off

½ teaspoon kosher salt

⅛ teaspoon freshly ground green or black peppercorns (about 10 grinds)

Melt the butter in a large sauté pan over medium heat. Add the shallot and sweat the bits for 2 minutes, stirring occasionally, until they start to soften in both color and texture.

Add the snow peas, turn the heat up to medium-high, and stir-fry, tossing almost constantly for 5 minutes, until the peas are bright green and just tender with a bit of a snap. Season with the salt and pepper and serve immediately.

alongside

TURKEY OR BEEF MEAT LOAF AND MASHED POTATOES ✦ ROASTED HALIBUT WITH LEMON BUTTER SAUCE
PLANK-GRILLED SALMON ✦ BROILED SHRIMP AND SCALLOPS WITH WHITE WINE GARLIC SAUCE AND RICE
SOY-MARINATED STRIP STEAKS ✦ TOFU AND SPRING PEA FRIED RICE ✦ LEMON GARLIC ANGEL HAIR PASTA

hot pepper broccoli rabe *serves 4 to 6*

Broccoli rabe's dark green stalks, leaves, and florets are pungent and sturdy. It is particularly fit for pastas and roasted beef or pork because its assertive flavor and texture balances milder counterparts. If you love a fiery air to your greens, add a little more crushed red pepper flakes. Use any leftovers of the rabe on sandwiches or chopped and mixed in with simple garlic, oil, and white wine spaghetti.

2 teaspoons kosher salt plus more
   for seasoning

1 pound broccoli rabe, ends trimmed and
   discarded, chopped into 2-inch pieces

2 tablespoons extra virgin olive oil

¼ teaspoon hot red pepper flakes

2 cloves garlic, thinly sliced

½ teaspoon anchovy paste

1 pound cherry tomatoes (about 1 pint),
   halved

Freshly ground black pepper

Fill a large saucepan with water, add the 2 teaspoons of kosher salt, and bring it to a boil over high heat. Add the broccoli rabe and blanch it for 2 to 3 minutes, until just tender. Drain the rabe in a large colander and then run cold water over it for about 30 seconds to stop the cooking.

Spread a clean kitchen towel on a countertop and lift the broccoli rabe onto it. Wrap it up and squeeze gently to absorb excess water. Set aside.

Heat a large sauté pan over medium-high heat. Add the olive oil, red pepper flakes, garlic, and anchovy paste and sauté for 30 seconds, stirring to help the anchovy paste melt into the rest of the ingredients. Add the tomatoes and sauté for 2 minutes, just until the skins start to wrinkle.

Put the broccoli rabe in the pan and sauté until heated through, about 3 minutes. Season to taste with salt and pepper. Serve immediately.

tip: Blanching broccoli rabe takes the edge off its natural deep bitterness. If you enjoy that punch, blanch the rabe for only a minute or skip that step altogether. Sauté the pieces of rabe in a tablespoon of olive oil for 2 to 3 minutes before adding the remainder of the ingredients as instructed.

alongside

LINGUINE WITH WHITE CLAM SAUCE ✦ STEAMED MUSSELS WITH WHITE WINE, BUTTER, AND SHALLOTS
SAUSAGE AND PEPPER ✦ SPAGHETTI AND MEATBALLS ✦ ROASTED PORK LOIN SANDWICHES ✦ GRILLED RIB-EYE STEAKS
SIMPLE RISOTTO **128** WITH ROASTED PEPPERS AND PARMIGIANO-REGGIANO FLAKES

coconut cilantro toasted israeli couscous serves 4

Unlike the tiny grainlike flecks of semolina couscous that fluffs and softens as it steams in aromatic water, Israeli couscous is similar in texture to pasta. Miniature pearls swell up in cooking liquid and turn velvety soft, similar to risotto, and the finished product spoons out thick and rich. Mild coconut milk lends its muted flavor and viscosity to this version, which is a perfect accompaniment to main courses featuring Asian, Latin, or tropical ingredients.

1 cup Israeli couscous

1¾ cups light coconut milk
(one 13.5-ounce can)

¼ cup water

½ teaspoon kosher salt

10 grinds fresh black pepper
(about ⅛ teaspoon)

⅛ teaspoon cayenne

½ cup fresh cilantro, chopped

Heat a medium deep sauté pan with a lid over medium-high heat.

Add the couscous and toast it for 3 to 4 minutes, until it turns golden and smells like baking bread.

Add the coconut milk, water, salt, pepper, and cayenne. Bring the liquid to a gentle boil, cover the pan, and decrease the heat to low. Simmer for 15 minutes, until the couscous is tender and creamy and the liquid has been mostly absorbed.

Stir in the cilantro, adjust the seasoning to taste, and serve immediately.

alongside

✦ ROASTED SALMON AND SESAME
   BRAISED BOK CHOY **97**
✦ PEPPER AND CUMIN CRUSTED
   SEARED SCALLOPS
✦ CRUSHED RED PEPPER AND GARLIC
   SAUTÉED SHRIMP
✦ LEMONGRASS CHICKEN STIR-FRY
✦ PINEAPPLE AND PORK KEBABS
✦ LAMB CURRY

sugar snap peas with grana padano crust

serves 4 to 6

Sweet and crunchy, as their name suggests, sugar snap peas don't need to be fussed over to make them presentable. Here a high-heat roast tenderizes the peas just a bit and then tucks them in under a browned, sizzling blanket of cheese, which adds salty texture. A natural string usually runs down the seam of each pea. Pull it from the top end and discard it if it's apparent.

1 pound sugar snap peas, stem ends trimmed and discarded

1 tablespoon extra virgin olive oil

¼ teaspoon kosher salt

⅛ teaspoon freshly ground black pepper (about 10 grinds)

½ cup freshly grated Grana Padano cheese (or a similar cheese, such as Parmesan)

Put a baking sheet in the oven and preheat the oven to 450°F.

In a large mixing bowl, toss the peas to coat with the olive oil, salt, and pepper.

Take the hot pan out of the oven and scrape the peas onto it in a single layer. Return to the oven and roast for 7 minutes.

Take the pan out, toss the peas with a spatula, and then push them together a bit, so most of them are touching at the edges. Sprinkle the cheese over the surface of the peas. Return the pan to the oven and roast for 7 to 10 minutes longer, until the peas are just tender and the cheese is a crisp crust on top.

Scoop the peas onto a small serving plate. Scrape any browned and crisp bits of cheese from the pan and add to the peas. Serve immediately.

alongside

PANFRIED SOFT-SHELL CRABS ✦ RAVIOLI WITH SIMPLE MARINARA ✦ GARLIC AND SHALLOT MARINATED LONDON BROIL
HERB AND LEMON CRUSTED ROAST CHICKEN BREAST ✦ PANKO AND PISTACHIO CRUSTED TROUT

lime rice serves 4 to 6

Simple white rice is a staple side for good reason. It's adaptable and accommodating, and it complements many main dishes and fellow accompaniments. But it deserves a makeover, and it doesn't take much to jazz it up. Follow this recipe's lead and create your own variations, subbing other citrus (lemon would be nice with roasted chicken), chopped herbs, or a drizzle of flavored oil or vinaigrette to match your meal.

. . . .

2½ cups water

1 teaspoon unsalted butter

½ teaspoon kosher salt, plus salt to taste

1½ cups long-grain white rice or white basmati rice

Finely grated zest and juice of 1 lime

¼ cup minced scallion (about 2 scallions)

Bring the water to a boil in a covered medium saucepan or a medium deep sauté pan over high heat. Uncover and stir in the butter, salt, and rice. Return the liquid to a boil, cover, and decrease the heat to low.

Slowly simmer the rice for 20 minutes. Remove from the heat and keep covered for 5 minutes more. Uncover and fluff the rice with a fork.

Add the lime zest, juice, and scallion to the rice and toss gently to combine. Serve immediately.

tip: To swap long-grain brown rice for the white rice, there are a few adjustments. Follow the directions, simmering 1½ cups of brown rice in 2⅔ cups of water for 40 minutes. Let the rice rest off the heat, covered, for 10 minutes before proceeding.

alongside

STEWED TURKEY THIGHS AND POBLANOS ✦ CHICKEN FAJITAS

GRILLED ORANGE CHILE PORK TENDERLOIN ✦ THAI BIRD STIR-FRIED BEEF

LEMONGRASS SHRIMP AND SCALLOP STIR-FRY ✦ BEAN AND CHEESE BURRITOS WITH AVOCADO SALSA

sesame braised bok choy serves 4 to 6

Bok choy's potential and versatility get lost in translation, leaving it underutilized. This mild cabbage is bright with steadfast crunchy stems in stir-fries and soft and yielding in a warm, steamy braise like this one. Baby bok choy, rather than large bok choy, works best in this recipe since the small halves remain intact as the vegetable melts into the liquid.

½ cup water

2 tablespoons low-sodium soy sauce

1 tablespoon dark brown sugar

1 teaspoon sesame oil (light or dark)

1 teaspoon mirin (rice cooking wine)

1 tablespoon safflower or vegetable oil

2 cloves garlic, thinly sliced

4 to 6 baby bok choy (about 1¼ pounds), halved lengthwise and tough base trimmed off

¼ cup chopped roasted salted peanuts (optional)

Combine the water, soy sauce, brown sugar, sesame oil, and mirin in a medium mixing bowl or spouted measuring cup.

Heat the safflower oil in a large deep sauté pan with a lid over medium-high heat. Add the garlic and sauté for about 20 seconds, until fragrant.

Place the bok choy in the pan cut side down. Pour the liquid over the bok choy, cover the pan, and decrease the heat to medium. Braise for 5 minutes, uncover the pan, and flip the bok choy cut side up using tongs. Cover the pan again and braise for 10 more minutes, until the white ends of the bok choy are very tender and the leafy tops are wilted.

Transfer the bok choy to a shallow serving bowl. Raise the heat to high and simmer the remaining liquid for 2 to 4 minutes to reduce it by about half. Drizzle it over the bok choy. Sprinkle with the peanuts and serve immediately.

alongside

SEARED FIVE-SPICE PORK TENDERLOIN ✦ GINGER GARLIC STIR-FRY WITH CHICKEN, BEEF, OR TOFU
VEGETABLE FRIED RICE ✦ UDON NOODLES WITH SPICY EGGPLANT, ZUCCHINI, AND CARROTS
SAUTÉED SHRIMP AND BAY SCALLOPS WITH SRIRACHA GLAZE
RED-COOKED BEEF TENDERLOIN AND BROWN RICE ✦ BROILED TERIYAKI STRIP STEAK

spiced rice pilaf serves 4 to 6

Baked pilaf infuses aromatic flavor and aroma into softening grains like the slow simmering of risotto. This one
is fragrant with the warmth of garam masala, an Indian blend that includes 10 to 15 different spices like cumin,
coriander, cinnamon, black pepper, cardamom, fennel, chiles, and others. Whole grain brown rice takes longer to cook
than white rice, so this recipe requires more time than a simple stovetop steam, but the results are worth the wait.

1 teaspoon cumin seeds

1 tablespoon coconut oil (see Tip) or
vegetable oil

½ small yellow onion, diced small
(about ¾ cup)

2 cloves garlic, minced

1½ cups brown basmati or long-grain
brown rice

2½ cups chicken stock or vegetable broth
(homemade or low-sodium store-bought)

½ teaspoon garam masala

½ teaspoon dried oregano

Kosher salt

Preheat the oven to 350°F.

Heat a medium deep sauté pan with an ovenproof lid over medium-
high heat. Add the cumin seeds and toast for 2 minutes, until fragrant.
Remove the seeds from the pan and set aside in a small bowl.

Return the pan to the heat and add the coconut oil to melt it. Add the
onion and sauté for 3 minutes, until soft and fragrant. Add the garlic and
cumin seeds and sauté for 30 seconds more.

Add the rice to the pan and stir to coat it with the oil. Cook the grains
for about 2 minutes, until they begin to turn translucent.

Add the stock, garam masala, and oregano. Bring the liquid to a rapid
boil, stir the rice once or twice, cover the pan with a lid or tightly with
foil, and transfer to the oven. Bake for 40 minutes. Remove from the
oven and let sit on the stovetop, covered, for 10 minutes more.

Fluff the finished rice with a fork, season to taste with salt, and serve
immediately.

tip: Coconut oil is solid at room temperature and comes in jars
stocked in the baking or oil aisle. It has a distinct coconut smell and
lends its very subtle flavor to recipes. If you don't like coconut or if
you can't find it, substitute equal amounts of butter or liquid oil like
safflower or olive oil.

alongside

CHILE-DUSTED BAKED COD ✦ CURRY SHRIMP OR TOFU ✦ CUMIN AND CORIANDER SPICED BRAISED CHICKEN
OR TURKEY THIGHS ✦ CILANTRO AND GARLIC MARINATED FLANK STEAK ✦ BUTTERNUT SQUASH AND LENTIL STEW
ROASTED LAMB SHOULDER

smoked gouda grits serves 4 to 6

Grits are like a good pair of jeans: Dress them up or down and they'll fit right in at any affair. These are simple enough for a Tuesday-night supper but easily indulgent enough to impress as part of a fancier meal. Skip instant grits altogether as their texture and flavor don't stand up to creamier, bolder, coarser, and less-processed stone-ground varieties.

- -

2 cups whole or low-fat milk, plus more as needed

2 cups water, plus more as needed

1 teaspoon kosher salt, plus more to taste

¼ teaspoon freshly ground black pepper (about 20 grinds), plus more to taste

½ teaspoon sweet paprika

1 cup medium-grind stone-ground grits (not quick-cooking)

1 tablespoon unsalted butter

¾ cup grated smoked Gouda (about 3 ounces)

Pour the milk and water into a large, wide pot over medium-high heat. Add the salt, pepper, and paprika and whisk to combine. Bring the liquid to a boil. Slowly add the grits, whisking constantly and briskly.

Cover the pot, decrease the heat to low, and simmer, stirring and scraping the bottom of the pot every 4 to 5 minutes, for 30 minutes, until the grits are thick, creamy, and soft. If they thicken too much into a stiff mass that becomes difficult to stir, add water or milk in ¼ cup increments and continue cooking. The cornmeal needs time to soften and cook completely in the liquid over the low heat.

Add the butter to the grits and stir it in as it melts. Fold the cheese into the grits, stirring to incorporate and melt it completely. Season the grits with more salt and pepper to taste. Serve immediately.

tip: Spread leftover grits into a square baking dish or loaf pan, cover tightly, and refrigerate. Cut slices and panfry in a large sauté pan with 1 tablespoon of vegetable oil over medium-high heat until heated through and just browned along the edges. Serve with a fried or poached egg for a fast, filling breakfast.

alongside

SPICY SAUTÉED OR GRILLED SHRIMP ✦ BUTTERMILK-MARINATED GRILLED CHICKEN
GARLIC AND HERB PAN-ROASTED BONE-IN PORK CHOPS ✦ BOURBON HONEY BABY BACK RIBS
PIMIENTO AND CHIVE QUICHE ✦ THREE-BEAN CHILI, WITH OR WITHOUT MEAT

ginger honey carrots   serves 4 to 6

Cooked carrots, like so many other throwback sides, too often suffer cooking abuse, jostling around in bland, boiling water until mushy soft. Scraped out into a seeping watery pile next to wrinkled green peas, an orange mound of homogenous carrot coins is a sad site. But this preparation does right by the sweet, earthy root, coaxing its sugars with a quick sauté and then cloaking the cuts in a sweet and spicy simmer sauce. Fresh ginger packs a punch that heat seekers will love.

1½ tablespoons honey

1¼ cups water

2 teaspoons rice vinegar

½ teaspoon kosher salt, plus salt to taste

1 tablespoon unsalted butter

1½ pounds carrots, sliced diagonally into 1-inch chunks

1 clove garlic, thinly sliced

1 (2-inch) chunk fresh ginger, peeled and grated on a Microplane or very finely minced

Freshly ground black pepper

Whisk the honey, water, vinegar, and salt together in a small mixing bowl and set aside.

Heat the butter in a medium deep sauté pan or a medium saucepan over medium-high heat. Add the carrots and sauté for 5 minutes, until they start to release some water and the outsides become just slightly tender. Add the garlic and ginger and sauté for 30 seconds.

Pour the liquid over the carrots and bring it to a boil. Cover the pan and decrease the heat to medium-low to simmer for 5 minutes, until the carrots are mostly tender when pierced with a knife. Remove the lid, return the heat to medium-high, and boil the liquid and carrots 10 to 12 minutes, stirring once or twice, until the liquid is nearly gone.

Season to taste with more salt and the pepper as needed. Serve immediately.

alongside

FIVE-SPICE-RUBBED ROASTED CHICKEN BREASTS ✦ ROASTED TURKEY LONDON BROIL STUFFED WITH HERBS AND APPLES ✦ TOFU FRIED RICE ✦ LAMB AND CHICKPEA CURRY ✦ ORANGE BEEF AND SNOW PEA STIR-FRY

summer squash sauté serves 4 to 6

In the summer months when zucchini and little pattypan squash are tumbling abundantly out of farmers' market crates at bargain prices, swap them for the yellow summer squash called for here or mix and match the varieties for a colorful dish that puts the fleeting bounty to great use. Trim tiny tough stem ends from all squash, especially pattypan, before cooking.

1 tablespoon unsalted butter

1½ pounds yellow squash, quartered lengthwise and sliced ¼ inch thick

5 large basil leaves, stacked, rolled tightly, and sliced into skinny ribbons crosswise

2 tablespoons finely chopped fresh chives

Finely grated zest of 1 large lemon plus juice of ¼ lemon (about 1 tablespoon juice)

½ teaspoon kosher salt

⅛ teaspoon freshly ground black pepper (about 10 grinds)

2 ounces ricotta salata cheese, cut into ¼-inch cubes (about ½ cup)

Melt the butter in a large sauté pan over medium-high heat. Add the squash and sauté for 5 to 7 minutes, until tender with a bit of a bite remaining.

Transfer to a serving bowl and add the basil, chives, lemon zest and juice, salt, and pepper. Toss to combine. Sprinkle with the cheese and serve immediately.

alongside

BARBECUE BAKED CHICKEN ✦ TURKEY FONTINA CHEESEBURGERS ✦ BEEF, PEPPER, AND ONION KEBABS
RAVIOLI PRIMAVERA ✦ LEMON AND WINE SWORDFISH STEAKS ✦ SPANISH RICE AND PINTO BEAN QUESADILLAS

chapter five

Warm-Weather Cookouts

A scene survey at any backyard barbecue reveals an important truth: The picnic table alongside the grill holds more weight at the party than the grill itself. This chapter features requisite old standbys packed with taste memories that entice even the most sophisticated palates. But it also fires up new ideas, flavors, and textures with original recipes guaranteed to win you points—in case you're losing them in the bocce match. Most of these can be made ahead, are easily transportable (for bring-a-dish gatherings), and will dutifully escort anything that comes off the grill.

red potatoes with cider mustard and candied bacon serves 6 to 8

If you're looking for an alternative to creamy potato salad (like Vintage Potato Salad, page 114) for a change of pace or to pacify mayo skeptics, look no further. This sweet and sour mélange is crowned with shards of salty, sugary candied bacon and can be served hot, warm, or at room temperature.

- 2½ pounds red potatoes (8 or 9 medium), quartered and cut into 1-inch chunks
- 2 tablespoons extra virgin olive oil
- ½ teaspoon kosher salt
- ¼ teaspoon freshly ground black pepper (about 20 grinds)
- 6 slices thick-cut bacon
- 2 tablespoons dark brown sugar
- 1 small yellow onion, thinly sliced (about 1 cup)
- 2 cloves garlic, minced
- ½ cup apple cider vinegar
- 3 tablespoons water
- 1 tablespoon pure maple syrup
- 1 teaspoon whole grain or stone-ground Dijon mustard

Preheat the oven to 400°F.

In a large mixing bowl, toss the potatoes with the olive oil, half of the salt, and half of the pepper. Spread them out on a baking sheet in a single layer. Reserve the bowl.

Cover another baking sheet with a piece of parchment paper cut to fit it. Set the bacon strips on the pan, evenly spaced. Distribute the brown sugar across the slices and rub the sugar into one side of each.

Put the baking sheets in the oven on separate racks. Cook the bacon for 15 to 20 minutes, or until crisp. Take care to not overcook because the sugar will burn. Take the bacon out of the oven and move the strips to a paper-towel-lined plate to cool completely. Carefully lift the parchment paper and pour the melted bacon grease that pools on it into a small bowl or empty jelly jar. Scoop out 2 tablespoons of the grease and add it to a large sauté pan. Store any remaining grease for another use.

Continue roasting the potatoes for 30 minutes longer, until tender and just starting to brown a little. Flip the potatoes over using a spatula once or twice. ➡

alongside

GRILLED PORTOBELLO AND ZUCCHINI SANDWICHES ✦ BURGERS: BEEF, PORK, TURKEY, OR BEAN
GARLIC BUTTERMILK MARINATED PORK CHOPS ✦ PULLED PORK SLIDERS ✦ BOURBON HONEY BABY BACK RIBS

While the potatoes cook, heat the bacon grease in the large sauté pan over medium heat. Add the onion and cook for 7 minutes, until softened and starting to turn blond. Add the garlic and cook for 2 minutes more. Pour in the vinegar, water, maple syrup, and mustard and whisk to combine. Heat the mixture for 1 minute and then turn off the heat, cover, and set aside.

When the potatoes are done, dump them back into the large mixing bowl and pour the warm vinegar mixture over the top. Add the remaining half of the salt and pepper and toss to combine. Let the warm potatoes soak up the vinegar for about 30 minutes.

Transfer the potatoes to a medium platter. Crumble the bacon across the top and serve.

If you plan to make ahead, let the potatoes and vinegar cool and then refrigerate in an airtight container. Bring to room temperature or warm in the microwave and sprinkle the bacon crumbles on top just before serving. The bacon crumbles can be refrigerated in a resealable plastic bag for up to 2 days.

zucchini spiral with toasted walnuts and goat cheese

serves 6 to 8

A kaleidoscope of marinated zucchini makes a surprisingly impressive simple salad. You can marinate and arrange the spiral ahead of time, but sprinkle on the nuts, cheese, and basil just before serving. If you are making the dish for a smaller crowd and anticipate leftovers, reserve some of the toasted walnuts to add to the leftovers later so they don't get soft in the moisture of the other ingredients.

¼ cup extra virgin olive oil

3 tablespoons white balsamic or white wine vinegar

1 clove garlic, minced and smashed to a paste (see Tip, page 60)

¼ teaspoon sugar

½ teaspoon kosher salt

⅛ teaspoon freshly ground black pepper (about 10 grinds)

1 large zucchini (about 1 pound), sliced into ⅛-inch rounds (see Tip)

½ cup walnut halves, toasted and coarsely chopped

4 ounces goat cheese, crumbled

5 large basil leaves, sliced into very thin ribbons

In a large mixing bowl, whisk together the olive oil, vinegar, garlic, sugar, salt, and pepper. Add the zucchini slices and toss several times to coat with the oil mixture. Cover the bowl and refrigerate to marinate for at least 30 minutes and up to 1 day.

Arrange the zucchini slices on a large round serving plate (12 inches or more in diameter) in a spiral, starting with the center of the plate and working outward in a counterclockwise pattern, overlapping the slices about ¼ inch or so. Drizzle any remaining marinade across the top of the zucchini.

Scatter the walnuts, goat cheese, and basil across the spiral and serve immediately.

tip: Thick rounds of zucchini won't work as nicely as ultra-thin slices, which absorb the marinade and make for silkier bites with hardly any crunch. A mandoline promises consistently thin cuts that hand-slicing doesn't guarantee.

alongside

LAMB BURGERS WITH SPICED YOGURT SAUCE ✦ GARLIC AND OREGANO CRUSTED RIB-EYE STEAKS
YOGURT SCALLION MARINATED CHICKEN ✦ TURKEY SHAWARMA ✦ FALAFEL WITH GRILLED VEGETABLES
SHRIMP AND SWORDFISH KEBABS ✦ LINGUINE WITH LEMON, FRESH HERBS, AND CHERRY TOMATOES

grilled veggie and asiago fusilli *serves 8 to 10*

If you're on the hunt for layers of flavor, this recipe is it. Smoky grill char on a mix of sweet summer vegetables; creamy, tart basil dressing; and sharp, salty Asiago cheese all mingle with the twisty twirls of fusilli for an out-of-the-ordinary pasta salad that could become your seasonal standard. Choose the firm aged variety of Asiago called stravecchio instead of the creamier semisoft varieties.

Vegetable oil for the grill

1 medium eggplant (about 1 pound), sliced crosswise or lengthwise ¼ inch thick

2 medium zucchini (about 1½ pounds), sliced lengthwise ¼ inch thick

3 bell peppers (about 1½ pounds), green, orange, and yellow, seeds and veins removed, quartered

1 medium red onion, cut into ¼-inch thick rounds

⅓ cup balsamic vinegar

⅔ cup extra virgin olive oil

½ cup loosely packed fresh basil leaves

1 small clove garlic

3 tablespoons mayonnaise

1 teaspoon coarse smoked salt or kosher salt

1 teaspoon sugar

¼ teaspoon freshly ground black pepper (about 20 grinds)

2 cups grape tomatoes, halved

1 pound fusilli or rotini pasta

1 cup grated Asiago cheese

alongside

+ GRILLED GARLIC BUTTERMILK MARINATED CHICKEN BREAST
+ SHRIMP CAESAR SALAD
+ BEEF, SALMON, OR VEGGIE BURGERS
+ SWEET AND SPICY ITALIAN SAUSAGES

Heat a grill to medium-high. Brush the grates with vegetable oil and repeat as needed. Depending on the size of your grill, cook the vegetables in batches. Lay the eggplant out in a single layer across the grates and grill 2½ to 3 minutes per side, until grill marks appear and the eggplant softens. Stack the cooked pieces in a pile on a platter. The retained heat in the pile will continue to soften the eggplant and keep it from drying out.

Grill the zucchini for 2 to 2½ minutes per side, until soft and floppy with grill marks, and add to the pile on the platter.

Grill the peppers for about 3 minutes per side, until the skin is charred in spots and the peppers just start to soften. Add to the platter

Grill the onion about 2 minutes per side, until charred and slightly wilted. Add to the platter.

Combine the vinegar, olive oil, basil, garlic, mayonnaise, salt, sugar, and pepper in a blender and blend until completely smooth.

Cut the grilled vegetables into bite-sized pieces (about 1 inch) and put them in a large serving bowl along with the tomatoes. Add ½ cup of the vinegar mixture and toss to coat the vegetables with it. Let the vegetables marinate in the dressing while you prepare the pasta.

Cook the pasta according to the package directions. Drain it and run cold water over it until it is completely cooled. Shake excess water from the pasta and add it to the serving bowl with the veggies. Pour the remaining vinegar mixture over the pasta, add the Asiago, and toss to combine and coat the pasta with the dressing.

Serve immediately or cover and refrigerate for up to 1 day. Let the pasta salad warm at room temperature for about 30 minutes before serving if refrigerated.

carrot radish relish *serves 6 to 8*

This is quick to fix with the help of a shredder disk on a food processor, and it will brighten an entire picnic table spread in color and freshness. Heap some alongside grilled grub as a cool side salad or offer it as a topper or condiment for burgers (especially good on ground pork burgers), grilled chicken, or fish tacos.

3 cups grated radish (about 8 ounces radishes)

4 cups grated carrot (about 1 pound carrots)

1 teaspoon kosher salt, plus more as needed

3 tablespoons minced seeded jalapeño pepper

1 tablespoon finely grated lime zest (about 2 limes)

2 tablespoons fresh lime juice (1 or 2 limes, depending on juiciness)

1 tablespoon safflower or vegetable oil

2 teaspoons honey

Pile the grated radish and carrot into a large strainer set in the sink or inside a large, wide bowl. Sprinkle the salt into the vegetables and toss several times. Set aside for 30 minutes, allowing some of the excess water to drain out of the vegetables.

Scrape the radishes and carrots into a large mixing bowl and add the jalapeño and zest. Toss several times to combine.

In a small bowl, whisk together the lime juice, oil, honey, and a pinch of salt. Pour the mixture over the vegetables and toss again to incorporate the juice. Season with additional salt to taste. Serve immediately or refrigerate in an airtight container for up to 2 days.

alongside

CAJUN BLACKENED FISH ✦ WOOD-PLANK-ROASTED SALMON ✦ GROUND PORK AND GINGER BURGERS
FRIED OR GRILLED FISH TACOS ✦ GRILLED LIME-MARINATED CHICKEN ✦ PULLED PORK SANDWICHES
BLACK BEAN AND BULGUR BURGERS

classic creamy coleslaw serves 8 to 10

Coleslaw is to a backyard barbecue what a good pair of perfectly fitting jeans is to a wardrobe. This simply shredded, well-dressed salad goes with practically everything and can be a focal point or an accessory as a condiment to sandwiches, burgers, and dogs. Dress it up or down with the rest of the menu. Its simplicity; its perfect balance of sweet, salty, tangy, and creamy; and its satisfying crunch that lasts for several days after being dressed make this coleslaw a mainstay.

6 cups shredded cabbage (a small head, about 1 pound; see Tip)

2 cups coarsely grated carrot (about 1 large carrot, about 3 ounces)

1 teaspoon kosher salt

⅔ cup mayonnaise

⅓ cup sour cream

1 teaspoon Dijon or stone-ground mustard

1 tablespoon plus 1 teaspoon white distilled vinegar

2 teaspoons sugar

2 tablespoons grated sweet onion (Vidalia, white, or spring onion bulb)

1 teaspoon celery seeds

Kosher salt and freshly ground black pepper

Toss the cabbage and carrot together in a large colander set in the sink or in a large bowl. Sprinkle with the salt and toss again. Let the cabbage and carrot wilt, releasing water, for 1 hour.

Meanwhile, make the dressing (preparing ahead allows the flavors to meld). In a medium mixing bowl, whisk together the mayonnaise, sour cream, mustard, vinegar, sugar, onion, and celery seeds until creamy and combined. Season to taste with the salt and pepper. Cover and refrigerate until the vegetables are ready.

Rinse the salted cabbage and carrots with cold water. Shake any excess water from the colander and then pat the vegetables dry with a clean kitchen towel or paper towels. Transfer to a large mixing bowl.

Fold the dressing into the vegetables, turning to coat several times with a rubber spatula.

Serve immediately or, for maximum flavor, cover and refrigerate for at least 30 minutes and up to 5 days. Toss several times before serving.

tip: To shred cabbage, cut the cored head into quarters or eighths and then slice the stack of leaves crosswise into ⅛-inch pieces. For the carrots, either shred on the large holes of a box grater or run through the food processor fitted with the shredder blade plate.

alongside

FISH TACOS ✦ BURGERS: BEEF, PORK, TURKEY, OR VEGGIE ✦ FRIED CLAM STRIPS
LOBSTER ROLLS ✦ SPICY BARBECUE GRILLED CHICKEN BREAST
SLOW-COOKER PULLED PORK SANDWICHES ✦ STICKY BROWN SUGAR MOLASSES RIBS

tomato and avocado bean salad serves 6 to 8

When peak tomato season rolls around, you don't have to do much to juicy slices of vine, beefsteak, or bulbous heirloom tomatoes to make them a perfect side dish. Here they are splayed out in all their red ripe (or yellow, orange, green, or striped) glory. You can make the salad with halved or quartered grape or cherry tomatoes and cubed avocados instead, tossing everything together in a jumble to be scooped from a bowl. But the composed version, with slices fanned around a mound of marinated beans, is much more striking.

¼ cup white balsamic or white wine vinegar

¼ cup extra virgin olive oil

1 teaspoon Dijon mustard

¼ teaspoon honey

¼ teaspoon kosher salt

⅛ teaspoon freshly ground black pepper (about 10 grinds)

¼ cup minced red onion or spring onion bulb

1½ cups cooked cannellini beans or 1 (15-ounce) can, drained and rinsed

1 cup shelled and cooked frozen edamame

1 pound ripe summer slicing tomatoes, any color or variety (such as vine, Roma, beefsteak), cored and sliced ¼ inch thick

2 ripe avocados, peeled, pitted, and sliced ¼ inch thick (see Tip)

In a large mixing bowl, whisk together the vinegar, olive oil, mustard, honey, salt, and pepper. Add the onion and whisk to incorporate. Set aside about a third of the dressing.

Dump the beans and edamame into the bowl with the other two-thirds of the dressing and stir to coat. Set aside.

Arrange the tomatoes along the perimeter of a large serving plate or platter, overlapping the slices just a bit. Situate the avocado pieces on top of the tomatoes but down a little bit closer to the center of the plate. Drizzle the reserved vinaigrette over the top of the tomatoes and avocados. (Brushing the vinaigrette on the surface of the avocados will help prevent browning.)

Scoop the bean mixture into the center of the plate so the pile is framed by the tomato and avocado. Season with additional salt and pepper if you like. Serve immediately or cover and refrigerate for up to 1 hour before serving.

tip: To slice an avocado, cut it in half and remove the pit to discard it. Hold one half, cut side up, in the palm of one hand. Use a sharp knife to cut the avocado fruit in strips lengthwise without cutting through the shell. Now run a large metal spoon between the shell and the fruit and lift the fruit away from the shell. Once you remove the strips, scrape up any of the avocado that's still stuck to the shell with the spoon. In this recipe, add the extra scraped bits to the beans.

alongside

BROILED OR GRILLED SWORDFISH WITH LEMON ✦ STRIP STEAKS WITH BLUE CHEESE BUTTER
SHRIMP AND SCALLOP RISOTTO ✦ GRILLED ZUCCHINI AND ONION TACOS
CHIPOTLE-RUBBED PORK TENDERLOIN ✦ SOY SAUCE AND SESAME MARINATED CHICKEN BREASTS

quick pickled red onion slaw   serves 6 to 8

A tall pile of this cooling slaw can sit in as a side salad or serve as a crunchy topping for burgers, sandwiches, or tacos. The cabbage and onions pickle during a good, long stay in the fridge with no more effort than it takes to prepare a garden salad. Add some lime juice and zest for extra flavor or minced jalapeño for some heat. Napa cabbage is best here because its milder, thinner, and more tender leaves give way to the vinegar, softening in a way that heartier cabbage varieties won't.

1 pound napa cabbage (about 1 small head or ½ medium head)

1 medium red onion, halved through the root and very thinly sliced (1 cup sliced)

2 tablespoons red wine vinegar

2 tablespoons white distilled vinegar

1 teaspoon sugar

¼ teaspoon kosher salt

Slice the cabbage ¼ inch thick horizontally. Discard the core end. Rinse and drain well and then spin or pat dry. Toss the cabbage and onion together in a 13 by 9-inch glass baking dish.

In a small mixing bowl, whisk together the vinegars, sugar, and salt. Pour the mixture over the cabbage and onions and toss several times to dress the vegetables with the vinegar. Cut a piece of plastic wrap the length and width of the dish. Press it down on the surface of the slaw. Cut another piece and cover the dish tightly with it. Refrigerate for at least 4 hours and up to 2 days.

Toss the slaw several times before serving to redistribute the vinegar mixture that pools at the bottom of the dish.

alongside

GRILLED SHRIMP OR FISH TACOS ✦ SWEET AND SPICY PULLED PORK ✦ TURKEY BURGERS
GARLIC GINGER SALMON ✦ LEMONGRASS VERMICELLI **176**

Vintage Recipe, Forever

In 1944, at age 19, Rosemary Foote was a newlywed in St. Louis, Missouri, without the foggiest idea of how to exist in her new vocation. She had grown up an only child in a great big house filled with Irish immigrant aunts, uncles, and working parents, including a mother who was a nightclub singer. Under the circumstances of her upbringing, she was doted on by the adults and ushered into a privileged girlhood of private school, elocution lessons, and horseback riding. She definitely never learned how to cook.

As a just-minted missus, she confessed to her husband that she had no idea what to do with her time while he worked and held up his duties in the U.S. submarine service. An engineer and the son of industrious parents, he created a weekly to-do list for her, and she set to task, doing laundry on Mondays, cleaning on Tuesdays, and so forth. To this day, Thursday is grocery day.

With her mother-in-law's help, Rosemary overcame her kitchen ineptitude and became the extended family's best source of excellent food and heirloom recipes.

Almost sixty years after Rosemary became Mrs. Foote, my friend Denise married Rosemary's grandson, Kevin. A food enthusiast and avid home cook, Denise found a kindred spirit in Grandma Foote and recognized her as the wellspring of meals around which the family would spend holidays and reunions. One of Grandma Foote's most treasured recipes is her potato salad, which she invariably made in enormous quantities to feed the crowd of resident guests who gathered annually for decades in the summer at Rehoboth Beach, Delaware. Rosemary cooked for a week

before the beach reunion and packed daily servings of the potato salad in jumbo mason jars, which would come out for lunchtime each day. It wasn't the beach without that potato salad.

After several years of heaping the creamy potatoes on her plate, Denise slipped into the kitchen of the beach house one afternoon with a pen and paper and asked Rosemary for the recipe. A formal one didn't exist, of course, as she made it just the way she made it, quantifying by her eye and without instructions. So Denise dug out measuring cups and spoons, transferring each of the ingredients and noting the amounts as Rosemary prepared it. In the end, Denise captured a close rendition of that potato salad and has been making it ever since.

For all the time we spend searching the Internet for recipes with five-fork ratings and reviews written by perfect strangers, we'll never find ones that taste as good as those gifted to us by the generations that paved the path to our own modern-day kitchens. When Rosemary Foote died in the summer of 2012, Denise requested two things of her estate: a refrigerator magnet that says "Rosemary's Kitchen" and her recipe collection, which is kept in a small plastic toolbox. "It's amazing how much food helps you remember people," she said.

No doubt those taste memories and that potato salad will live on for generations to come, starting with Denise's daughter, Grandma Foote's great granddaughter, Erin Rosemary. Denise shared the recipe for Vintage Potato Salad (page 114) with me for this book.

vintage potato salad serves 8 to 10

There are hundreds of potato salad recipes, ranging from the standard American version, which you can buy at a grocery deli, thick with sweet mayo coating over Idaho potatoes, to gussied-up gourmet, calling for fresh-plucked herbs, a French vinaigrette, and potatoes from Peru. Or try Red Potatoes with Cider Mustard and Candied Bacon, (page 105). This recipe falls squarely into the creamy classic camp and has stood the test of time (see page 113). A goodly amount of hard-boiled eggs adds a deviled dimension to the mayonnaise dressing. The keys to its flavors and sturdy demeanor are proper preparation and extra time (see Tip).

3 pounds unpeeled russet potatoes (about 8 medium)

6 large eggs

¾ cup mayonnaise

¼ cup sour cream

1 tablespoon yellow mustard

1 teaspoon kosher salt

¼ teaspoon freshly ground black pepper (about 20 grinds)

1 tablespoon fresh lemon juice (about ½ small lemon)

2 medium stalks celery, sliced ¼ inch thick (about 1 cup)

½ cup finely chopped green bell pepper (about ½ small pepper)

2 tablespoons pickle relish (sweet or dill)

Put the potatoes in a large Dutch oven or saucepan. Add enough cool water to cover them by about an inch. Cover the pot and set it over high heat to bring the water to a boil. When the water begins to boil, uncover the pot and cook the potatoes for 30 minutes, until tender all the way through when poked with a fork. Drain the potatoes and let them cool completely at room temperature.

Meanwhile, put the eggs in a medium saucepan or deep sauté pan and fill it with cold water to cover the eggs. Cover the pot and set it over high heat to bring the water to a boil. Once the water boils, turn off the heat and let the eggs sit in the hot water under the cover for 15 minutes. Drain the eggs and run cold water over them for about 30 seconds to cool them enough to handle. Peel the eggs and then refrigerate until cold.

In a large mixing bowl, whisk together the mayonnaise, sour cream, mustard, salt, black pepper, and lemon juice. Cover and refrigerate.

Once the potatoes have cooled completely, peel them using your fingers or a paring knife. Cut the potatoes into 1-inch chunks and add them to the bowl with the mayonnaise mixture.

alongside

HARD-SHELL STEAMED CRABS WITH OLD BAY ✦ GRILLED HALIBUT WITH HERBS AND LIME JUICE
HAM AND CHEESE ON BRIOCHE BUNS ✦ LEMON CAYENNE CRAB CAKES
BLUE CHEESE AND RED ONION BURGERS ✦ SWEET AND SPICY GRILLED CHICKEN

Halve the cooled peeled eggs and cut each half into 4 chunks. Add the eggs to the bowl. Don't worry about the yolks separating from the whites, which they will. Just scrape everything into the potatoes. Add the celery, bell pepper, and relish. Use a large rubber spatula to stir, coating all of the ingredients with the mayo mixture. Cover the salad and refrigerate for at least an hour and up to 5 days.

tip: You can't rush this or any potato salad, especially the cooling step. If you skip it, the residual heat from the potatoes will turn the pile of spuds and dressing into a soggy, sweaty mess. To avert disaster, plan ahead and make this in a few steps. At the very least, cook and cool the potatoes and eggs first. You can do this hours before you assemble the salad, or even a day ahead, refrigerating both until you are ready to proceed. While you're in the kitchen, whisk together the mayonnaise dressing mixture, cover, and refrigerate up to a day ahead. The celery and pepper can be chopped and stored, too, if you want to check another prep task off your list. Once all of these steps have been done, assembling the salad takes no time at all. But don't forget to factor in at least an hour for the flavors to mingle. The yellow mustard becomes part of the whole with some time, though it dominates the flavors when you first mix it in. The salad keeps remarkably well for several days, so, like Grandma Foote (see page 113), you can refrigerate it and serve it, in mason jars or not, for a number of picnics at the beach.

broccoli sesame crunch serves 6 to 8

Blanching and shocking the broccoli—boiling it briefly and then bathing it in cold water to halt the cooking—is the key to making it bright green and crunchy with the slightest tenderness in its bite. Alternatively, you can steam it briefly until just barely fork-tender. Make the salad with raw broccoli or steam it too long and you won't make it to the same happy place where it mingles with crunchy sesame seeds and cashews and perks up under the salty brightness of miso vinaigrette.

. . . .

2 pounds broccoli crowns, stem ends trimmed

Kosher salt

2 tablespoons miso paste (mild white or other variety)

1 tablespoon low-sodium soy sauce

1 teaspoon sesame oil (light or dark)

2 tablespoons rice vinegar

½ cup thinly sliced scallions (2 or 3 large scallions)

2 tablespoons toasted sesame seeds

1 cup roasted salted cashews

Cut the broccoli into bite-sized florets and slice the stems into ¼-inch pieces. Fill a large saucepan with water, salt it generously, and bring it to a boil over high heat. Add the broccoli and blanch it for 2 minutes (it will be overly soft and soggy in the salad if you blanch any longer). Drain and dunk it in a large bowl of ice water or run very cold water over it until it is completely cool. Shake the colander of any excess water and then leave the broccoli to drain for at least 15 minutes. (Skipping this step guarantees a watery pool of vinaigrette at the bottom of the salad bowl when you serve it!) The blanching, cooling, and draining step can be done up to a day ahead.

Whisk together the miso, soy sauce, sesame oil, and vinegar, breaking up any miso clumps. Once the broccoli is sufficiently drained, transfer it to a serving bowl, pour the miso mixture over it, and toss several times to dress it with the liquid. Add the scallions, sesame seeds, and cashews and toss again to combine. Serve immediately or refrigerate for up to 2 days. If you make the salad ahead, add the sesame seeds and cashews just before serving so they retain their crunch longer.

alongside

TERIYAKI SALMON ✦ SPICY CHICKEN OR TOFU STIR-FRY ✦ BEEF SATAY ✦ BANH MI (ANY VARIETY INCLUDING TOFU, SHRIMP, CHICKEN, BEEF) ✦ BOK CHOY AND CARROT UDON NOODLES ✦ GROUND PORK AND GARLIC GINGER BURGERS

sugar and spice baked beans serves 10 to 12

There are Boston baked beans and there are barbecue beans. The former are heady with deep, dark molasses and rich from thick slabs of salt pork, while the latter are usually spiked with flavors that give a nod to the grilled and smoked foods they often accompany. These beans fall somewhere in between. Either way, baked beans from scratch take a good long while but still far fewer hours than if they had to be cooked by the heat of the surrounding earth in a hole dug out of the ground, the way the Native Americans made them. Dump the dried beans in a pot and soak them overnight. Then set the oven to do its work in the morning and be glad you saved time skipping out on all that digging. You can make these up to 2 days in advance and warm on the stovetop before serving. Add a splash of water if the beans need thinning while they reheat.

2 ancho chiles (see Tip)

1 cup hot water

½ cup dark brown sugar

¼ cup molasses

¼ cup tomato paste

2 tablespoons spicy brown mustard

2 tablespoons plus 1 tablespoon cider vinegar

¼ teaspoon hot sauce, such as Tabasco

4 ounces bacon (about 4 thick slices), cut into ¼-inch pieces

1 medium yellow onion, finely diced (about 1 cup)

1 poblano pepper, seeds and veins removed, finely diced (about ⅔ cup)

1 jalapeño pepper, seeds and veins removed, finely diced (about ¼ cup)

4 large cloves garlic, roughly chopped

1 pound dried navy beans or Great Northern beans, soaked in cold water overnight

5 cups water

Kosher salt and freshly ground black pepper

alongside

SLOW-ROASTED OR GRILLED MARINATED BABY BACK RIBS ✦ HONEY BOURBON BEEF BRISKET
BARBECUE CHICKEN ✦ BALSAMIC PORTOBELLO BURGERS ✦ MAPLE MUSTARD PULLED PORK
SMOKED BRATWURST ✦ BEEF, TURKEY, OR PORK BURGERS

Preheat the oven to 325°F.

In a small bowl, soak the anchos in the 1 cup of water, hot enough to steep tea for at least 10 minutes.

Once the anchos have softened, take them out of the water, trim the stems off, cut them open, and scrape or rinse out the seeds. Set them aside and pour the soaking water into a large mixing bowl. Whisk in the brown sugar, molasses, tomato paste, brown mustard, the 2 tablespoons of vinegar, and the hot sauce.

Heat a 5½-quart Dutch oven or similar ovenproof large pot over medium heat. Add the bacon and cook until crisp, stirring occasionally, about 10 minutes. Add the onion, poblano, jalapeño, and garlic and cook for 5 minutes, until the onion and peppers soften.

Stir in the beans, anchos, sauce, and the 5 cups of water. Cover the pot (use tightly wrapped foil if you don't have a lid that fits the pot) and bring the liquid to a boil. Transfer the covered pot to the lower middle rack in the oven and bake for 2 hours, stirring once halfway through.

Uncover the beans, increase the oven temperature to 350°F and bake for 1 more hour, until the beans are tender and the sauce thickens and coats the beans.

Remove from the oven, cover, and cool for at least 15 minutes. The sauce will thicken even more as it cools. Stir the remaining tablespoon of vinegar into the beans and season them to taste with the salt and pepper.

tip: Ancho chiles are dried poblano peppers. You can find them packaged (usually in cellophane bags) in the produce section or in the ethnic foods aisle of a grocery store. They are mild with a sweet, raisiny aroma. If you're cooking for a mixed crowd and are worried about the heat tolerance of some palates, omit the jalapeño. Skipping out on both the jalapeño and the poblano will leave the beans devoid of spice, though still sweet and flavorful. Regardless of the variety, always wash your hands thoroughly after handling chiles and their seeds to avoid irritating or burning your skin and eyes.

timeless macaroni salad serves 8 to 12

Make four varieties of "gourmet" pasta salads and set them on a table that's also hosting classic American macaroni salad, and you're going home with a lot of the fancy stuff. It's practically a condition of our citizenship that most of us go weak in the knees for a nostalgic scoop of the salad that tops roll call at summer backyard barbecues and picnics from sea to shining sea. Here's my mother's recipe, which makes me want to change into shorts and sandals and look up in the sky for fireworks every time I taste it.

1 pound elbow macaroni

1 cup mayonnaise

¼ cup white distilled vinegar

¼ cup sugar

2 teaspoons yellow mustard

1 teaspoon kosher salt, plus more to taste

½ teaspoon freshly ground black pepper (about 35 grinds), plus more to taste

2 medium stalks celery, finely diced (about 1 cup)

½ medium green bell pepper, seeds and veins removed, finely diced (about ½ cup)

¼ cup minced yellow onion (about ½ small onion)

1 medium carrot, grated

Cook the pasta according to the package directions. Drain it and run cold water over it, stirring as you do to cool it completely and prevent it from cooking further. Shake out any excess water and let it drain and dry in the colander while you prepare the rest of the salad.

In a large mixing bowl (large enough to fit all of the macaroni too), whisk together the mayonnaise, vinegar, sugar, mustard, salt, and pepper. Stir in the celery, pepper, and onion. Dump in the macaroni and use a big spatula to fold it into the mayonnaise mixture. Scatter the grated carrot over the top and stir it into the macaroni.

Adjust the seasoning to taste with additional salt and pepper. Cover the bowl and refrigerate for at least 4 hours or overnight before serving. The salad will keep up to 5 days.

alongside

CHILE HONEY BABY BACK RIBS ✦ BUFFALO CHICKEN AND BLUE CHEESE BURGERS ✦ GRILLED SHRIMP PO' BOYS
GRILLED HAMBURGERS AND HOT DOGS ✦ BUTTERMILK-MARINATED GRILLED TURKEY TENDERLOIN WRAPS
MIXED VEGGIE KEBABS WITH SPICED HONEY BALSAMIC GLAZE

lemon couscous with olives and oven tomatoes

serves 6 to 8

Couscous is a good alternative to pasta, offering a change of pace but the same adaptable blank canvas that takes to countless diverse additions. Serve this version at room temperature, warm, or cold. Place the hot cooked food directly on top of the couscous, allowing the juices and residual marinades and seasonings to soak into the grains below.

oven tomatoes

2 pounds plum or Roma tomatoes (about 8 large), quartered lengthwise

5 large cloves garlic, peeled and smashed

½ teaspoon kosher salt

¼ teaspoon freshly ground black pepper (about 20 grinds)

2 tablespoons extra virgin olive oil

couscous

1½ cups water

1½ cups couscous or 1 (10-ounce) box

Finely grated zest and juice of 1 lemon (about 2 tablespoons zest and ¼ cup juice)

2 tablespoons extra virgin olive oil

½ teaspoon kosher salt

¼ teaspoon freshly ground black pepper (about 20 grinds)

1 cup pitted olives, roughly chopped (a single type or a variety of kalamata, picholine, cerignola, or your favorite) ➜

alongside

WHOLE ROASTED BRANZINO WITH WHITE WINE SAUCE ✦ PAN-SEARED SCALLOPS WITH SWEET PEA PESTO
SPIT-ROASTED LEG OF LAMB ✦ GARLIC-STUDDED ROAST PORK LOIN ✦ GRILLED EGGPLANT, ZUCCHINI, PEPPER, ONION,
AND FOCACCIA PLATTER ✦ ARUGULA AND RED PEPPER STUFFED CHICKEN

Preheat the oven to 325°F. Line a baking sheet with parchment paper. Arrange the tomato quarters across the baking sheet in a single layer. Scatter the garlic around the tomatoes. Sprinkle the salt and pepper across the tomatoes and then drizzle the olive oil all over. Gently toss the tomatoes a little by hand to coat them with the oil and resituate in a single layer. Roast the tomatoes for 1½ to 2 hours, until they shrivel just slightly and their pulp begins to dry.

To make the couscous, bring the water to a boil in a medium saucepan with a lid over high heat. Stir in the couscous, cover the pan, and turn off the heat. Let the couscous steam for 5 to 7 minutes, until all of the water is absorbed. Remove the lid and fluff the couscous with a fork.

In a large, wide serving bowl, whisk together the lemon zest, juice, olive oil, salt, and pepper. Stir in the olives. Scrape the couscous into the bowl and fold in with the olive mixture until well combined. Set aside or refrigerate until ready to serve. The couscous can be made a day ahead and refrigerated. Serve it cold or bring it to room temperature before adding the hot tomatoes and serving with a warm meal.

Add the tomatoes, the roasted garlic, and any oil and juices to the couscous. Toss gently to combine.

tip: While the oven is going, think ahead by roasting an extra batch of the tomatoes, refrigerating what isn't used for this recipe in an airtight container with a heavy-handed pour of olive oil for up to 2 weeks. You'll run out of them long before you run out of ideas for how to use them. A low and slow roast draws out the natural sugars of tomatoes as water evaporates, creating soft, satiny bites that have the pop of sun-dried tomatoes without the chew or sour notes. They'll elevate any salad, make a perfect bruschetta or pizza topping, and are a wonderful side dish on their own, adorned with nothing more than vibrant extra virgin olive oil and crunchy coarse sea salt. In this recipe, I like to leave the roasted tomato quarters whole for a more dramatic presentation, but you can chop them smaller to distribute them throughout the couscous for larger crowds.

burger platter serves 6 to 8

The usual suspects in the burger-topping category have earned their keep, but a little variation might just suggest a better burger. Substitute a plain slice of cheese with this smoky spread; swap the raw onion for sweet strands of sautéed Vidalia tangled up with mushrooms; and make the tomato slice even better with a quick marinade. Set each out in jars or small serving bowls where the ketchup, mustard, and relish usually sit.

guajillo cheddar spread (makes 1 cup)

2 guajillo chiles

8 ounces sharp Cheddar cheese, grated

1 tablespoon mayonnaise

1 teaspoon Dijon mustard

Heat a small sauté pan over medium-high heat. Add the chiles to the pan and toast each side for 1 to 2 minutes, until blackened sections appear on the chile skin. Add enough water to cover the chiles (about 1½ cups). Bring the water to a boil, cover the pan, and remove it from the heat. Let the chiles sit for 10 minutes to soften.

Discard the hot water and then cut the stems off the chiles. Slice them open and pluck out the seeds, discarding them. Cut the chiles into several big pieces.

Combine the cheese, mayonnaise, mustard, and softened chiles in a food processor and process until smooth, about 1 minute. Serve immediately or refrigerate in an airtight container for up to 2 weeks.

Bring the cheese spread to room temperature before serving.

alongside

CLASSIC GRILLED HAMBURGERS OR ANY VARIATION (PORK, CHICKEN, TURKEY) ✦ BLACKENED CHICKEN SANDWICHES
PULLED OR SLICED SLOW-ROASTED PORK SHOULDER ✦ ROASTED RIB-EYE SANDWICHES ✦ GRILLED VEGETABLE PANINI

sweet and savory onions and mushrooms (makes 1¼ cups)

2 tablespoons unsalted butter

1 large Vidalia onion, halved and sliced into
  very thin half-rings (2 cups)

8 ounces button or cremini mushrooms,
  thinly sliced (3 cups)

2 tablespoons malt vinegar

1 teaspoon dark brown sugar

¼ teaspoon kosher salt

⅛ teaspoon freshly ground black pepper
  (about 10 grinds)

Melt the butter in a large sauté pan over medium-high heat. Add the onion and cook for 15 minutes, stirring every 2 minutes, until it starts to brown. Add the mushrooms and cook for 5 minutes, scraping up the brown bits from the bottom of the pan as the mushrooms release their water.

Stir in the vinegar and brown sugar and cook for another minute, until the vinegar thickens a bit. Season with the salt and pepper to taste. Serve warm.

marinated tomatoes (about 16 slices)

2 tablespoons extra virgin olive oil

1 tablespoon red wine vinegar

½ teaspoon dried oregano

Pinch of sugar

¼ teaspoon kosher salt

⅛ teaspoon freshly ground black pepper
  (about 10 grinds)

1 pound beefsteak tomatoes, cored and
  thinly sliced

In a small mixing bowl or spouted measuring cup, whisk together the olive oil, vinegar, oregano, sugar, salt, and pepper to make the marinade.

Layer the tomatoes in a shallow bowl, drizzling each layer with some of the marinade. Cover and refrigerate for at least 30 minutes and up to 1 day before serving.

backyard pickle jar makes about 2 quarts

Plunk down a colorful mix of homemade pickles on your barbecue buffet table and call them a side salad, sandwich topper, or snack. You can fiddle with the ratios of vegetables or use all of a single type instead, but I like the variety inspired by the Italian pickled veggies called giardiniera, which frequent antipasto platters. These pickles are a great way to use up a summer bumper crop from the garden or a farm share.

2 cups distilled white vinegar

2 cups water

4 cloves garlic, quartered

3 tablespoons sugar

1 tablespoon kosher salt

¼ teaspoon hot red pepper flakes (more if you prefer your pickles spicy)

2 medium carrots (about 8 ounces), peeled and sliced ⅛ inch thick on a sharp diagonal (1½ cups)

2 medium salad turnips or baby turnips (about 5 ounces), peeled and sliced ⅛ inch thick (1 cup sliced)

1 small zucchini (about 6 ounces), sliced ¼ inch thick (1½ cups)

2 Kirby cucumbers (about 4 ounces), halved crosswise and then quartered, or 1 regular cucumber, peeled, quartered, and cut into 2-inch lengths

4 ounces green beans, halved crosswise (1 cup)

Combine the vinegar with the water in a large saucepan over medium-high heat. Add the garlic, sugar, salt, and red pepper flakes and bring the liquid to a rapid boil.

Add the carrots, turnips, zucchini, cucumbers, and green beans and let them sit in the hot liquid for 1 minute.

Turn off the heat and carefully transfer the veggies and liquid to a large glass bowl or baking dish to cool completely, about 1 hour. Once cooled, transfer the vegetables and liquid to airtight containers (preferably glass jars) and refrigerate until cold before enjoying. Store the pickles in the refrigerator for 2 to 3 weeks.

tip: Adapt this recipe to your taste. If you prefer sweet pickles, add another tablespoon or two of sugar. If you love your pickles with some heat, increase the amount of hot red pepper or add a sliced chile pepper that ranks higher on the Scoville scale (try jalapeño). A longer soak in the brining liquid on the stove produces softer pickles, so if you like yours more tender with less crunch, let the liquid come back to a boil after you add the veggies and before removing from the heat to cool.

alongside

HAMBURGERS ✦ GRILLED SAUSAGES AND KIELBASA
ROASTED PORK SANDWICHES ✦ GRILLED VEGETABLES AND PROVOLONE ON FOCACCIA BREAD
STEAMER CLAMS AND DRAWN BUTTER WITH BOILED CORN ✦ HONEY BARBECUE BRICK CHICKEN

chapter six

Intimate Gatherings

Dinner parties showcase personal food affinities or celebrate specific cuisines. They stir conversation and ignite debate. They are comfortable and inclusive. These intimate gatherings are a great time to put forth extra kitchen effort to create truly memorable meals. The recipes in this chapter are designed to impress or simply to welcome special friends with a dinner that shows you appreciate them. Sumptuous without being ostentatious, these dishes accessorize the main course at both formal dinners and casual get-togethers.

simple risotto *serves 4 to 6*

Among cooks unfamiliar with making risotto, there's a sense of unease and intimidation that mirrors the way Dorothy and her entourage felt about The Great and Powerful Oz upon arrival in the Emerald City. Of course, then they discovered the force to be reckoned with was really a simple man behind the curtain, working hard with what he had to make something downright impressive. Risotto is just the same. A few ingredients and the right touch make for a dish so luxurious that first-timers are sure they can't do it themselves. It's all in the technique, you know, like clicking your heels three times. Use this basic recipe as a dependable base for further flavoring with meats, vegetables, or herbs. Substitute fish or seafood stock, or vegetable or mushroom broth for a vegetarian dish. See page 130 for suggested add-ins and flavoring techniques.

2 tablespoons unsalted butter or extra virgin olive oil

1 cup finely diced yellow onion

3 cloves garlic, minced

1 cup Arborio or carnaroli rice

½ cup dry white wine (such as Chablis or pinot grigio)

4 cups warm chicken stock (homemade or low- or no-sodium store-bought)

½ cup freshly grated Parmesan cheese

1 teaspoon kosher salt

¼ teaspoon freshly ground black pepper (about 20 grinds)

Melt the butter in a Dutch oven or a large, wide, deep sauté pan over medium heat. Add the onion and sweat for 5 minutes, stirring with a wooden spoon every 30 seconds or so, until the onion softens and starts to become translucent. Add the garlic and cook for 30 seconds more.

Add the rice and stir to coat it with the onion, garlic, and butter. Sauté the rice for 2 minutes, until the grains start to give away some of their stark whiteness as they toast in the oil.

Pour in the wine and stir until it is almost completely absorbed into the rice, about 1 minute.

Add the warm stock ½ cup at a time (keep it in a small saucepan over low heat), stirring regularly but not constantly as the rice absorbs the liquid. Adjust the heat of the burner so that the liquid maintains a simmer, with steady, slow bubbles surfacing often. Add more liquid when the previous amount is almost completely absorbed, every 2 minutes or so. Run the wooden spoon through the middle of the rice. If enough liquid has been absorbed, you'll see the bottom of the pan at the separation line that forms from the spoon for a second before the thick rice and liquid fills it back in.

alongside

GRILLED RACK OF LAMB WITH HERB BUTTER ✦ VEAL OR CHICKEN SCALOPPINE ✦ FLOUNDER FRANCESE WITH ALMONDS AND CAPERS ✦ ROASTED OR GRILLED ZUCCHINI, EGGPLANT, AND RED PEPPERS WITH BASIL VINAIGRETTE BROILED BUTTERFLY JUMBO SHRIMP WITH HOT RED PEPPER FLAKE BREADCRUMBS

Continue this process until all of the liquid has been added and the rice is tender with only a bit of chew, but not at all mushy. As the rice cooks and releases its starches, the surrounding liquid will become thick and creamy and the rice will plump and soften. After adding the last of the broth, test for doneness by the rice grain. Do not cook until nearly dry. The end result should be dense with al dente rice but still semifluid (a little looser than rice pudding) so that a hot spoonful spreads slowly across a plate.

Remove the risotto from the heat and stir in the cheese, salt, and pepper. Adjust the seasoning to taste. Serve immediately.

Risotto Tips and Tricks

Risotto is surprisingly straightforward and uncomplicated, but overlooking a few important steps will result in something subpar.

1. Sweating the aromatics (usually onions and garlic) is the first step in layering flavor. It shouldn't be hurried along with a speedy sauté. Slowly sweating the ingredients brings out their sweetness and prevents scorching, the taste of which will last all the way through to your last forkful.
2. Toasting the rice before adding the liquid promotes a nutty flavor and coats the exterior starches with some of the cooking fat before the long simmer.
3. Adding a splash of dry white wine to get things started may be a personal preference (shared with most chefs), but risotto made without wine is flat and devoid of a flavor I consider to be part of risotto's signature charm.
4. Stirring in warm stock a little at a time creates the creamiest risotto. There's lots of chatter and controversy around this last point, and some cooks who are big on shaving off cook time swear that a sizable glug of cold stock and minimal stirring yields the same results. While I've concluded that risotto doesn't need to be manned and stirred constantly, I am a believer that it should be simmered slowly in increments of warm stock and stirred often.

Once you've mastered the technique of risotto making, you can customize it to your taste. Here are some thoughts to help you riff on the basics.

Aromatics
Yellow onions and garlic typically make up the aromatic base of risotto, but you can substitute sweet onions like cippoline or Vidalia, shallots, leeks, red onions, or any other bulb onion, and any variety of garlic including garlic scapes when they are seasonally available.

Rice
Arborio and carnaroli are the two rice varieties most commonly used for risotto. Both are short to medium grain with a pearly white exterior. Some cooks opt for the slightly longer and starchier grain of carnaroli, citing its creamy al dente results, but both produce reliably delicious risotto. Other rice varieties like long-grain white or brown rice are not suited to the risotto cooking technique. Whole grains, like farro and barley, can be cooked like risotto, with similar but chewier, less creamy results.

Vegetables
Consider the constitution of particular vegetables to determine the best point in the cooking process to add them. Hard vegetables like butternut squash should be cut into very small pieces and added early on, along with the onions, to give them plenty of time to cook. Extra liquid might also be necessary since the squash will absorb some of the stock, stealing a little from the rice kernels. On the other hand, tender, watery vegetables like zucchini should be added a little later lest they collapse into mush under the heat, moisture, and stirring. Cut zucchini into small cubes and stir them in after the first or second addition of stock. Unless you want tomatoes to melt into the risotto as it cooks, add quartered grape or cherry varieties or cubes of larger types and stir the pieces in just to warm them through when the risotto is nearly done. Mushrooms, however, should be added up front, cooked down with the aromatics, and simmered with the rice for the best taste and texture results.

Meat

Little bits of meat add excellent flavor to risotto. Try ham, sopressata, bacon, and pancetta. To contribute both the flavor and crispness of bacon and pancetta, cook small bits of either in the pot until crisp. Lift the bits out with a slotted spoon, leaving most of the rendered fat in the pot, and move them to a paper-towel-lined plate. Cook the onions and garlic in the fat, adding oil if necessary, and proceed with the recipe. Sprinkle the crispy pieces over the risotto just before serving. Ham and hard sausages can be added along with the rice and simmered with the rest of the ingredients, infusing flavor into the whole dish.

Seafood

Fish generally cooks quickly and should be added to risotto toward the very end of cooking to avoid tough bits of seafood throughout tender, creamy rice. Add shrimp with the last ladle of stock and stir it into the hot rice to cook it through. Other fish and shellfish can be cooked separately and added as a garnish on top just before serving.

Cheese

Parmigiano-Reggiano cheese is part of the standard recipe, but crumbles of blue cheese or grated sottocenere, a creamy Italian cheese speckled with truffle bits, add a new dimension and extra lusciousness to the final results.

Herbs

Add chopped fresh herbs just before serving, stirring them into the hot grains for a vibrant boost of flavor. Dried herbs can be sprinkled in early on with a ladleful of stock and given time to rehydrate and lend their taste to the pot.

za'atar chickpea mash serves 4 to 6

Rich with brown butter, these chickpeas are a nice alternative to whipped potatoes, with the same texture. Thick, creamy labneh, a Lebanese yogurt cheese, adds background tang to the mixture. The Middle Eastern spice mix za'atar, a combination of sumac, sesame seeds, and other herbs, adds extra depth to the finished dish. Reheat leftovers or spread on flatbread or crackers directly from the refrigerator, as you would hummus.

4 tablespoons (½ stick) plus 1 tablespoon unsalted butter

½ cup minced yellow onion

2 cloves garlic, chopped

4 cups cooked chickpeas (8 ounces dried chickpeas, cooked, or two and a half 15-ounce cans, drained and rinsed)

¾ cup chicken stock (homemade or low-sodium store-bought)

¼ cup labneh or plain Greek yogurt

½ teaspoon kosher salt

2 tablespoons za'atar, plus extra for garnish

alongside

✦ GRILLED OR ROASTED LAMB (CHOPS, LEG, OR SHOULDER)
✦ GRILLED HALLOUMI AND EGGPLANT WITH ALMOND MINT PESTO **135**
✦ HARISSA FLANK STEAK
✦ LAMB OR BEEF KOFTAS
✦ LEMON PEPPER ROASTED TURKEY BREAST
✦ BRAISED SUMMER VEGETABLES WITH CUMIN AND OREGANO

Melt 1 tablespoon of the butter in a large deep sauté pan over medium heat. Add the onion and cook, stirring occasionally, for 2 to 3 minutes, until starting to soften. Add the garlic and cook for 2 minutes more.

Turn off the heat and scrape the onion and garlic into a food processor along with the chickpeas, chicken stock, labneh, and salt. Process until smooth, about 30 seconds to a minute, stopping to scrape down the sides if necessary.

Wipe out the sauté pan and return it to the stove over medium heat. Add the remaining 4 tablespoons of butter and melt it, swirling it around as it becomes liquid. Keep a close eye on the butter as it starts to foam. If you look closely at the liquid butter as it cooks, you can see tiny specks of brown appear (which are the browning milk solids). Continue heating it until it starts to smell nutty and turns from off-white to golden to light brown. Immediately remove from the heat and stir in the za'atar.

Spoon the chickpea mixture into the brown butter and stir to combine. Warm through over medium heat for about 10 minutes. Season with additional salt to taste. Transfer to a serving bowl, sprinkle with an extra tablespoon or so of za'atar, and serve immediately.

tip: To use dried chickpeas, soak them overnight in a large Dutch oven or bowl with 8 cups of cold water. Alternatively, cover the beans with 8 cups cold water in a large Dutch oven or saucepan. Bring the water to a boil for 2 minutes, remove from heat, cover and soak for 1½ hours. Drain the beans and put them in a large Dutch oven or saucepan with 10 cups water. Partially cover the pot and bring the water to a boil over medium-high heat. Decrease the heat to medium and simmer for an hour or until they are tender with barely any bite left to them. Drain and use or refrigerate in an airtight container for up to 5 days or freeze for up to three months.

golden cauliflower with herbed breadcrumbs

serves 4 to 6

Cauliflower has an uphill battle to regain its reputation after repeated pummeling by boiling water baths. It's not its fault. Unwitting cooks have mishandled it. Don't be an unwitting cook. Roasting cauliflower caramelizes and deepens the flavors, maintains its substantial and sometimes downright meaty texture, and changes the stubborn minds of haters still scorned by the stink of a wet pile of blanched florets. Buttery, garlicky herbed breadcrumbs put the finishing touches on cauliflower done right.

1 medium head of cauliflower (about 2 pounds)

4 large cloves garlic, peeled and sliced in half lengthwise, plus 2 cloves garlic, minced

3 tablespoons extra virgin olive oil

1 teaspoon kosher salt

¼ teaspoon freshly ground black pepper (about 20 grinds)

1 cup panko breadcrumbs

2 tablespoons unsalted butter

Leaves from 2 sprigs fresh oregano, finely chopped

½ cup packed fresh parsley leaves, finely chopped

alongside

+ CURRIED LAMB STEW
+ FETTUCCINE WITH ROASTED GARLIC AND PARMESAN
+ ROASTED SALT-CRUSTED RIB-EYE
+ OSSO BUCO
+ EGGPLANT AND CHICKPEA CURRY
+ CHICKEN OR TURKEY POTPIE

Preheat the oven to 400°F.

Wash the cauliflower, discard the leaves, and slice in half lengthwise. Cut out and discard the tough stem core section and then split the cauliflower into medium-size florets.

Spread the florets and halved garlic cloves in a single layer across a large baking sheet. Drizzle with the olive oil and season with half of the salt and pepper. Fold the cauliflower and garlic with a rubber spatula to coat it with the oil and seasonings. Transfer to the oven and roast for about 45 minutes, until the cauliflower is tender and browning.

While the cauliflower roasts, toast the breadcrumbs in a dry sauté pan over medium-high heat, stirring often, just until golden brown, about 5 minutes. (Pay close attention to prevent burning.) Transfer them to a medium mixing bowl and set aside.

Melt the butter in the same sauté pan over medium heat. Stir in the minced garlic and sauté for about 1 minute, taking care not to burn it. Pour the melted butter and garlic over the toasted breadcrumbs and add the herbs. Stir well to combine everything. Season with the remaining ½ teaspoon of salt and ⅛ teaspoon of pepper.

Transfer the roasted cauliflower to a serving bowl or platter and sprinkle the breadcrumbs across the top. Serve immediately.

tip: Cauliflower colors and types vary from the most-recognized white to the uniquely spiky green Romanesco. Orange and purple varieties are said to be higher in vitamin content than their white cousins. Preparation methods are consistent regardless of the variety, so substitute colorful bunches you might stumble on in season at farmers' markets. And step away from the stovetop.

grilled halloumi and eggplant with almond mint pesto

Halloumi redefines grilled cheese. Creamy mild like mozzarella and salty like feta, this semifirm cheese with a high melting point can sit directly on hot grill grates without slipping right through them on contact. A quick rendezvous with the heat softens the slices just enough. The eggplant slices in this recipe are not seasoned before they hit the grill because the cheese and pesto are both salty, but add a sprinkle to taste once they come off the grill. Sandwich any leftovers between slices of grilled or toasted bread spread with the pesto.

½ cup sliced almonds, toasted (see Tip, page 181)

½ cup loosely packed fresh mint leaves

1 small clove garlic

¼ teaspoon kosher salt

⅛ teaspoon freshly ground black pepper (about 10 grinds)

¼ cup plus 2 tablespoons extra virgin olive oil

1 (8-ounce) block halloumi cheese

1½ pounds baby eggplant (about 4)

Heat a grill to medium-high.

Combine the almonds, mint, garlic, salt, pepper, and ¼ cup of the olive oil in a small food processor or blender and process into a coarse paste, about 30 seconds to a minute. Stop to scrape down the sides if necessary.

Cut the halloumi in half diagonally and then slice each half into ⅛-inch-thick triangles. Trim the eggplant stems and discard and then slice the eggplant ¼ inch thick lengthwise. Brush both sides of each slice of eggplant with the reserved olive oil.

Grill the eggplant for 3 to 4 minutes per side, until soft and dark. Season the slices to taste with salt and pepper and then stack on a platter. Grill the cheese for 1 to 2 minutes per side, until light grill marks appear and the cheese softens.

Arrange the hot eggplant and cheese on a serving dish. Spoon the pesto into a small condiment bowl and set on the dish. Serve immediately.

alongside

TAHINI BUTTERMILK MARINATED CHICKEN THIGHS WITH WARM PITA ✦ PAN-SEARED BABY LAMB CHOPS WITH ZA'ATAR CHICKPEA MASH **132** ✦ GRILLED OCTOPUS AND MUSSELS IN WHITE WINE GARLIC SAUCE WITH LINGUINE PORK MEDALLIONS IN WHITE WINE LEMON SAUCE ✦ RICE AND PINE NUT STUFFED GRAPE LEAVES WITH YOGURT SAUCE

lemon cream english peas serves 4 to 6

Plump, fresh English peas are vastly different from frozen green peas that wrinkle upon contact with hot water and mush with ease under the slightest press of a fork. Bright beads popped from their pod are vibrant in color and flavor and stay pleasantly firm if cooked properly and quickly. This recipe skips any contact with a boiling bath and heightens the sweetness of the peas with a hot stir with butter and shallots and a gentle simmer in rich cream.

1 tablespoon unsalted butter

¼ cup minced shallot (1 small to medium shallot)

3 cups shelled fresh English peas (3 pounds in the pod)

½ cup heavy cream

1 tablespoon finely grated lemon zest (1 large or 1½ medium lemons)

½ teaspoon kosher salt

⅛ teaspoon green peppercorns (about 20 grinds)

1 tablespoon minced fresh chives

Melt the butter in a large sauté pan over medium heat. Add the shallot and sweat it in the butter, stirring once or twice, for 1 minute. Stir in the peas and cook for 3 minutes, stirring every 30 seconds or so, until they start to become bright green from the heat.

Add the cream and lower the heat to medium-low. Simmer for 5 to 7 minutes, stirring often, until the peas are tender but not wrinkly and the cream has thickened to a coating on the peas.

Stir in the lemon zest, salt, pepper, and chives. Adjust the seasoning to taste and serve.

alongside

MOREL MUSHROOM AND RICOTTA RAVIOLI ✦ GARLIC AND HERB MARINATED LOLLIPOP LAMB CHOPS

PAN-ROASTED CHICKEN BREAST ✦ ASPARAGUS AND FENNEL RISOTTO ✦ BROILED BACON-WRAPPED SCALLOPS

dijon beluga lentils serves 4 to 6

Black lentils, also called Beluga lentils, are tiny, shiny, smooth, and round and keep their shape plus a bit of a bite when cooked (unlike other lentil varieties, which soften significantly and begin to fall apart). Their nutty, earthy flavor joins with other deeply savory ingredients here in a recipe that's a nice alternative to grain side dishes and would make a perfect substitution for bread-based stuffing. Enjoy leftovers cold with goat cheese, arugula, and a toasted baguette.

1 cup black lentils

2¼ cups of water

2 tablespoons unsalted butter

1 medium carrot, finely diced (½ cup)

1 large stalk celery, finely diced (½ cup)

½ cup minced shallot (about 1 large shallot)

8 ounces cremini mushrooms, sliced and coarsely chopped (about 2½ cups)

½ teaspoon chopped fresh thyme leaves (2 or 3 sprigs)

3 tablespoons Dijon mustard

2 tablespoons extra virgin olive oil

2 teaspoons white wine vinegar

1 teaspoon honey

½ cup loosely packed fresh parsley leaves, coarsely chopped

Kosher salt and freshly ground black pepper

Combine the lentils with the water in a medium saucepan over medium-high heat. Bring the water to a boil, lower the heat to medium-low, and partially cover the pan. Simmer for 20 minutes, until the lentils are tender with a slight bite.

While the lentils simmer, melt the butter in a large sauté pan over medium heat. Add the carrot, celery, and all but 1 tablespoon of the shallot and sweat them in the butter, stirring every minute or so, for 7 to 10 minutes, until the vegetables start to soften. Stir in the mushrooms and thyme and sweat for 10 minutes, stirring occasionally, until the mushrooms are about half their original volume and most of the water from the vegetables has cooked off.

In a small mixing bowl, whisk together the mustard, olive oil, vinegar, honey, and the reserved tablespoon of minced shallots.

Strain any remaining water from the cooked lentils and put them in a serving bowl along with the hot vegetables. Add the mustard mixture and the parsley to the bowl. Mix everything thoroughly, season to taste with the salt and pepper, and serve warm.

alongside

CHERRY ALMOND STUFFED ROASTED TURKEY BREAST ✦ PEPPER-CRUSTED PORK LOIN ✦ SEARED SCALLOPS WITH GREMOLATA ✦ FRESH HAM WITH ROSEMARY AND GARLIC ✦ PAN-ROASTED COD WITH OLIVE OIL HERBED BREADCRUMBS ✦ LAMB BURGERS ✦ SQUASH AND WILD RICE STUFFED PORTOBELLOS

poblano queso fundido serves 4

Melted cheese has the universal appeal of cute puppies and chocolate chip cookies, which is to say that most people are rendered defenseless in the face of it. Queso fundido is simply cheese melted with add-ins like mushrooms, peppers, or spicy chorizo sausage (but not to be confused with the Americanized processed cheese sauce sold in a jar and called "queso dip"). This version, intended as an accompaniment rather than an appetizer, skips the meat so it can adapt to more meals. Manchego cheese, a sheep's milk with creamy, salty characteristics, lays a foundation for a medley of peppers and caramelized onions. A scoop folded up into a warm tortilla is like a Mexican fondue and is a decadent contribution to a meal.

1 tablespoon extra virgin olive oil

1 small yellow onion, halved and sliced into thin strips

1 medium poblano pepper, seeds and veins removed, sliced into strips ⅛ inch thick

1 small red bell pepper, seeds and veins removed, sliced into strips ⅛ inch thick

1 small jalapeño pepper, seeds and veins removed, minced

1½ cups grated queso quesadilla or Monterey Jack cheese (4 ounces)

1½ cups grated manchego cheese (opt for a softer, younger variety aged less than 6 months, which melts better than more aged cheeses) (4 ounces)

2 cloves garlic, thinly sliced

6 warmed small flour or corn tortillas, halved

Preheat the oven to 375°F.

Heat the olive oil in a large sauté pan over medium-high heat. Add the onion and sauté for 10 minutes, until softened and starting to brown. Add the poblano, bell pepper, and jalapeño and sauté, stirring often, for 10 minutes more.

While the peppers cook, put an empty 9-inch pie plate in the oven for 5 minutes. Remove the plate and sprinkle the cheeses across the bottom. Return the plate to the oven for 5 more minutes.

Stir the garlic into the peppers and sauté for 30 seconds, then remove the pan from the heat.

Spoon the poblano mixture across the top of the melting cheese and return the plate to the oven for 10 more minutes, until the cheese is melted and starting to brown and bubble on top.

Stack the tortillas on top of each other and wrap them in a piece of aluminum foil. Add them to the bottom rack of the oven while the queso fundido bakes for the final 10 minutes. Alternatively, warm the stack (not wrapped in foil) for 1 minute in the microwave. Keep the warmed tortillas covered in a basket with a clean kitchen towel for serving.

Serve the fundido immediately with the warmed tortillas.

alongside

CHILE-RUBBED STEAK ✦ SPICY BRISKET CHILI ✦ PORK CARNITAS TACOS
GRILLED MARINATED CHICKEN BURRITOS ✦ SHRIMP FAJITAS WITH FRESH SALSA ✦ RICE AND BEAN STUFFED PEPPERS

warm kale cannellini serves 4 to 6

Beans are so often relegated to an auxiliary role, but here they are the focal point. Their own starches thicken the braising liquid into a creamy sauce tickled pink by tomato and made heartier by bits of kale, which surrenders their toughness and soften into the warmth of the mixture. Piquant cheese and fresh, grassy parsley brighten each spoonful of this simple braise.

2 tablespoons extra virgin olive oil

1 small yellow onion, halved lengthwise and thinly sliced

4 cloves garlic, minced

1 small bunch (8 to 12 ounces) kale (curly, dinosaur, or Tuscan), tough stems removed and discarded, leaves torn or chopped into 1-inch pieces

¼ cup tomato paste

3 cups chicken stock (homemade or low-sodium store-bought)

2 tablespoons balsamic vinegar

4½ cups cooked cannellini beans or 3 (15-ounce) cans, drained and rinsed

Kosher salt and freshly ground black pepper

½ cup freshly grated Grana Padano, Parmesan, Pecorino Romano, or Locatelli cheese

¼ cup packed fresh flat-leaf parsley, very finely chopped

In a large deep sauté pan or a Dutch oven, heat the olive oil over medium heat. Add the onion and sauté for 5 minutes, until it softens and starts to brown. Add the garlic and cook for 30 seconds.

Turn the heat up to medium-high, add the kale, and cook, stirring occasionally, for 3 minutes, just until it starts to wilt. The volume of the leaves will seem unruly at first but will shrink down quickly. Add the tomato paste and spread it around with the kale, garlic, and onion to help it melt. Pour in about ½ cup of the chicken stock and scrape up any bits stuck to the bottom of the pan. Add the rest of the stock and the vinegar and stir occasionally for 5 minutes to incorporate the tomato paste while the kale wrinkles and reduces to less than half of its original volume.

Decrease the heat to medium again, stir in the beans, and partially cover the pot. Braise the mixture for 20 minutes, stirring every few minutes, until the liquid thickens with the bean starches. The resulting consistency should be stewlike, not soupy, and similar to the thickness of baked beans in their sauce. If it's still quite loose after 20 minutes, uncover the pot and continue to simmer for an additional 5 minutes, until the liquid has thickened.

Season to taste with the salt and pepper. Scrape the cannellini beans and kale into a wide serving bowl and top with the cheese and parsley. Serve immediately.

alongside

SLOW-COOKED PORK LOIN WITH VIDALIA ONIONS AND WHITE WINE
ROAST COD WITH OREGANO AND ROSEMARY ✦ SALT AND LEMON ZEST SEARED SCALLOPS
CHICKEN SCALOPPINE ✦ VEAL SALTIMBOCCA ✦ STUFFED SHELLS WITH FIRE-ROASTED TOMATOES

roasted fingerlings with warm rosemary vinaigrette serves 4 to 6

Small, long fingerling potatoes look a little like fat fingers, though they might actually have been named for their resemblance to tiny fingerling fish. Regardless, potato lovers favor them for their buttery flavor and smooth, waxy texture. This double cooking method coaxes their inner tenderness with a parboil and achieves crunchy crispness during an oven roasting. Dress the fingerlings with the warm vinaigrette or serve it alongside in a tiny pitcher for guests to apply as they prefer.

2 pounds fingerling potatoes

3 tablespoons plus 1 tablespoon extra virgin olive oil

1 small clove garlic, minced

1 small shallot, minced (about 1 tablespoon)

½ teaspoon minced fresh rosemary

2 tablespoons sherry vinegar

½ teaspoon Dijon mustard

½ teaspoon kosher salt

⅛ teaspoon freshly ground black pepper (about 10 grinds)

alongside

+ CHICKEN WITH BRAISED GREENS, PANCETTA, AND PROVOLONE
+ BEEF WELLINGTON
+ CHICKEN-FRIED STEAK WITH PEPPER GRAVY
+ PORK CHOPS WITH APPLE CIDER CREAM SAUCE
+ SLICED LAMB SHANKS WITH ANCHOVY ROSEMARY SPREAD
+ MUSTARD MAPLE GLAZED PLANKED SALMON
+ MUSSELS WITH SOPRESSATA AND GARLIC BROTH

Place a baking sheet on the middle rack of the oven and preheat the oven to 425°F.

Put the potatoes in a large saucepan and cover them by about an inch with cold water. Cover the pot and set it over high heat to bring the water to a boil. Once the water boils, uncover the pot and continue boiling the potatoes for 10 minutes. Drain the potatoes and set them aside for 5 minutes, until cool enough to handle.

Slice them on a sharp diagonal and put them back in the saucepan or add them to a large mixing bowl. Drizzle the peanut oil over the potatoes and toss to coat them well. Take the hot baking sheet pan out of the oven and spill the potatoes out onto it. Spread the fingerlings into a single layer and then return the pan to the oven. Roast the potatoes for 40 minutes, tossing once halfway through to help more surface area get crispy.

While the potatoes roast, make the vinaigrette. Pour the 1 tablespoon of olive oil into a large sauté pan over medium heat. When the oil is hot, add the garlic, shallot, and rosemary and cook them for about 3 minutes, stirring often, until the shallot softens slightly. Remove the pan from the heat and whisk in the vinegar, mustard, and remaining 3 tablespoons of olive oil.

When the potatoes are golden brown, crisp, and tender throughout, take them out of the oven and scrape them onto a serving platter. Season with the salt and pepper, drizzle the warm vinaigrette over them, and serve immediately.

roasted acorn squash with orange oil serves 4 to 6

Sweet and simple, this dish, as with most roasted squash recipes, requires very little fuss. A short roast results in tender rustic slices brightened by orange olive oil. Add an extra squeeze of fresh juice if you like. There's no need to struggle with peeling the skin off the scalloped grooves of the squash, because it softens into an edible outer edge in the heat of the oven.

Finely grated zest and juice of 1 small orange (about 1 tablespoon zest and ⅓ cup juice)

1 tablespoon plus 1 tablespoon extra virgin olive oil

1 large acorn squash (about 1½ pounds)

¼ teaspoon kosher salt

⅛ teaspoon freshly ground black pepper (about 10 grinds)

Leaves from 2 small sprigs fresh thyme

Preheat the oven to 375°F.

In a small mixing bowl, mix the zest and 1 tablespoon of the olive oil. Set aside.

Cut the squash in half through its equator. Scrape out the seeds with a spoon and discard. Set each half cut side down and cut again into ½-inch-thick half-moons. Add them to a large mixing bowl with the orange juice, the remaining tablespoon of olive oil, the salt, pepper, and thyme. Toss to coat the squash with all of the ingredients.

Arrange the squash in 2 or 3 layers inside a 9- or 10-inch pie plate. Scrape any of the juice and oil that remains in the bottom of the bowl on top of the squash. Cover the dish with aluminum foil and bake for 30 minutes, until the squash is tender.

Drizzle or brush the hot squash with the reserved zest and oil mixture. Adjust the seasoning to taste with additional salt and pepper before serving.

alongside

APPLE AND SAUSAGE STUFFED TURKEY BREAST ROULADE ✦ PAN-SEARED CRISPY THYME CHICKEN
ORANGE-SOY MARINATED PORK RIBS ✦ HARISSA-RUBBED LAMB CHOPS
TORTELLINI WITH ALMOND ARUGULA PESTO ✦ ROASTED CUMIN SALMON ✦ WILD MUSHROOM RISOTTO

red quinoa with cherries and smoked almonds serves 4 to 6

This warm grain salad comes together as quickly as a pot of rice but offers a lot more to mull over with each bite. I love the tangy chew of dried cherries, but if you prefer them softer, stir them in to simmer and steam with the quinoa. They lend their sweet perfume and relax into silkier bits in the heat. Smoked almonds are spectacular in this mix, but if you can't find them or if you don't care for their flavor, roasted and salted almonds work perfectly well too.

1½ cups chicken or vegetable stock (homemade or low-sodium store-bought) or water

1 cup red quinoa

½ cup dried cherries, coarsely chopped

½ cup smoked almonds or roasted salted almonds, coarsely chopped

¼ cup minced fresh chives

1 tablespoon extra virgin olive oil

1 teaspoon sherry vinegar

Kosher salt and freshly ground black pepper

Boil the chicken stock in a medium saucepan over medium-high heat. Stir in the quinoa, cover the pot, decrease the heat to low, and simmer for 15 minutes. Remove the pot from the heat and let the quinoa sit, covered, for 10 minutes more. Uncover and fluff the quinoa with a fork.

Add the cherries, almonds, chives, olive oil, and vinegar and toss briskly with a fork to combine everything. Season to taste with the salt and pepper and serve immediately.

alongside

PEPPER AND THYME PAN-SEARED PORK TENDERLOIN ✦ SWEET AND SPICY SLOW-ROASTED BABY BACK RIBS
DUCK CONFIT WITH MIXED GREENS ✦ PAN-ROASTED CHICKEN WITH MUSHROOM CREAM SAUCE
HERB, CHARD, AND EGGPLANT STUFFED PORTOBELLO CAPS

bulgur with apricots, golden raisins, and pistachios serves 4 to 6

Rice pilaf lovers will appreciate this alternative, which borrows some of the same cooking technique and features a combination of sweet and savory stir-ins. These particular ingredients are typical in Middle Eastern cuisine, but once you master the approach, you can tinker with substitutions that match other meals. Try almost any combination of dried fruits, nuts, and herbs against the same backdrop of tender, chewy bulgur.

2 tablespoons unsalted butter

¼ cup minced shallot (about 1 small shallot)

1¾ cups chicken stock (homemade or low-sodium store-bought) or water

½ cup chopped dried apricots (about 14 whole apricots)

½ cup golden raisins

1 cup medium bulgur

½ cup fresh parsley leaves, finely chopped

Kosher salt and freshly ground black pepper

½ cup roasted salted pistachios, chopped

Melt the butter in a medium deep sauté pan or a medium saucepan over medium heat. Add the shallot and sweat it for 3 minutes, stirring every 30 seconds or so. Add the stock and bring the liquid to a boil over medium-high heat. Stir in the apricots, raisins, and bulgur. Bring the liquid back to a boil, cover the pan, decrease the heat to low, and simmer and steam the fruit and bulgur for 12 to 15 minutes, until the liquid is absorbed and the bulgur is tender but still a little bit chewy.

Fluff the bulgur with a fork. Scatter the parsley and mix it in with the fork. Season to taste with the salt and pepper. Scoop into a serving bowl and sprinkle the pistachios across the top. Serve immediately.

alongside

ZA'ATAR-CRUSTED ROASTED PORK LOIN ✦ ROASTED CHICKEN WITH YOGURT HERB SAUCE
PAN-SEARED DUCK BREAST WITH POMEGRANATE PEPPER SAUCE ✦ SPICY SCALLOPS WITH WATERCRESS SAUCE
BROILED FLOUNDER WITH HERBED BREADCRUMBS ✦ BRAISED LAMB SHANKS

roasted beets with shaved fennel and marcona almonds   serves 4 to 6

Choose any beet variety you like for this recipe: candy striped, orange, or the most prevalent red beet, whose color is so intense it's almost intimidating. Once roasted, the skins of the beets slip off to reveal the shiny, sweet, tender bulb shaped like a Christmas tree ornament. The fennel will turn deep pink when mixed with the beet slivers, completing a tone-on-tone backdrop for bright emerald speckles of chives, tanned marcona almonds, and bright white crumbles of cheese. Pick smaller beets over larger ones, as they'll cook in less time, or add 10 to 15 extra minutes for bigger beets.

1½ pounds fresh beets, trimmed of greens and root end, washed, and patted dry

3 tablespoons plus 2 tablespoons extra virgin olive oil

1 teaspoon kosher salt

¼ teaspoon freshly ground black pepper (about 20 grinds)

3 tablespoons sherry vinegar

1 small fennel bulb, cored and shaved or very thinly sliced (1 cup)

3 tablespoons plus 1 tablespoon minced fresh chives

½ cup Marcona almonds, coarsely chopped

¼ cup (2 ounces) crumbled goat or feta cheese (optional)

Preheat the oven to 375°F.

Cut a large sheet of aluminum foil, set the beets in the center of it, and drizzle them with 2 tablespoons of the olive oil. Sprinkle half of the salt and pepper over the beets and then use your hands to toss gently and coat them with the oil and seasonings. Wrap the beets, folding the ends of the foil in and up to the center to create a package. Set the package on a baking sheet pan. Roast for 45 to 50 minutes, until the beets are tender when pierced with a paring knife.

While the beets cook, whisk the remaining 3 tablespoons of olive oil and remaining ½ teaspoon salt and ⅛ teaspoon pepper with the vinegar in a medium mixing bowl.

Remove the beets from the oven, open the foil packaging, and let them cool for about 10 minutes. When they are cool enough to handle, peel the beets either by rubbing gently with a paper towel or by using a paring knife to scrape away the skin. Quarter the beets and cut each quarter into bite-sized wedges, piling them in to the bowl with the oil mixture. Add the fennel and 3 tablespoons of the chives and toss to combine. Spoon the mixture into a serving bowl or platter, sprinkle with the reserved chives, the almonds, and the cheese, and serve.

To prepare ahead, wait until just before serving to add the reserved chives, almonds, and cheese. Serve cold or at room temperature.

alongside

SHEPHERD'S PIE ✦ LAMB SHOULDER CHOPS WITH PORT SAUCE ✦ PENNE WITH BITTER GREENS AND GARLIC SAUCE
BRAISED PORK SHOULDER WITH WHITE BEANS AND ORANGES ✦ PAN-SEARED TURKEY TENDERLOINS WITH PORCINI SAUCE

bacon cheddar spoonbread *serves 4 to 6*

Now that you're here, I'll tell you the truth. Spoonbread and soufflé are nearly the same. I knew if I listed this as soufflé, you might chicken out under the false pretense that soufflés are too hard, and your intimate dinner party would be subpar. If you're terrified of trying your hand at soufflé, starting with spoonbread is smart because it's a little huskier than its dainty cousin, making for more structurally sound results. Spoonbread looks fancy but tastes country and is an excellent alternative to usual starch sides like rice and potatoes.

1 cup stone-ground white or yellow cornmeal, plus cornmeal for the baking dish

4 slices thick-cut bacon (4 or 5 ounces), cut crosswise into ½-inch pieces

½ cup minced yellow onion (about 1 small onion)

3 cloves garlic, minced

2½ cups whole milk

1 cup grated sharp Cheddar cheese

Kosher salt and freshly ground black pepper

4 large eggs, separated

Preheat the oven to 375°F. Generously butter the inside of a 1½-quart soufflé dish or round straight-sided ovenproof baking dish. Sprinkle a couple teaspoons of cornmeal around the dish as if you're flouring a cake pan.

Set a large heavy Dutch oven or saucepan over medium heat. When the pot is hot, add the bacon and cook, stirring occasionally, until crisp, about 10 minutes. Lift the crisp pieces out with a slotted spoon and set them on a paper-towel-lined plate to cool.

Add the onion to the bacon grease in the pot and cook for 5 minutes, until it starts to soften, stirring every 30 seconds or so. Stir in the garlic and sauté for 2 minutes. Pour in the milk and bring it to a boil. Slowly add the cornmeal, whisking quickly to prevent lumps as the mixture thickens. Cook for about 2 minutes, whisking regularly, and then turn off the heat. Add the Cheddar and stir until it melts into the cornmeal. Stir in all but 2 tablespoons of the bacon. Season with the salt and pepper and taste the mixture before moving on to adjust the seasoning to your preference. This is the base of the spoonbread and the source of most of the flavor, so season it well. Turn off the heat.

alongside

BRAISED BROWN SUGAR AND CIDER PORK SHOULDER ✦ OVEN-FRIED CHICKEN
GRILLED OR BAKED SMOKED SAUSAGES AND STEWED GREENS ✦ BEAN AND TURKEY CHILI
TOMATO JALAPEÑO SPARERIBS ✦ SLOW COOKER WHOLE CHICKEN WITH CARROTS AND ONION

Put the egg yolks in a large mixing bowl and beat them together. Add a heaping tablespoon of the hot cornmeal to the yolks and quickly stir it together. Repeat this twice more to raise the temperature of the egg yolks enough that they won't cook when the rest of the hot cornmeal is added. Use a large rubber spatula to scoop the rest of the cornmeal into the mixing bowl and fold to combine.

Put the egg whites in a clean, dry bowl and whip them to medium peaks, using a handheld electric beater or a whisk, so they flop over just slightly when you lift the beaters or whisk upright. Fold the whites into the cornmeal mixture with the rubber spatula in 3 additions. Pour the mixture into the soufflé dish. Sprinkle the reserved 2 tablespoons of bacon across the top.

Set the soufflé dish on a baking sheet and transfer to the oven to bake for 45 minutes, until it is set (not jiggly when you shake the side of the pan), has puffed up about an inch above the dish, and is golden brown across the surface. Note that the spoonbread will rise high well before it's cooked through, so trust the timing and avoid checking early and often, which will cause the puffiness to sag in the changing temperature of the oven. Serve immediately to show off the impressive billow straight from the oven, which will deflate soon after.

potato stracciatella   serves 6 to 8

Potato gratin is one of the most beloved accompaniments, fitting into menus of all genres and audiences. This version starts with rich velouté, one of the five mother sauces of classic French cuisine. The silky liquid becomes the famously homey Italian egg drop soup named stracciatella for the tiny strands that form when beaten eggs hit hot stock. Here the stracciatella is fortified with fresh herbs, spinach, and grated piquant Parmesan. It is the liquor that coaxes starches from thinly sliced potatoes as it bubbles around them, turning them tender under a crust of brûléed cheese.

. . . .

2 pounds russet potatoes (about 4 medium-large), sliced into ¼-inch rounds

3 cups chicken stock (homemade or low-sodium store-bought)

2 tablespoons unsalted butter

1 small shallot, minced (about 2 tablespoons)

2 cloves garlic, minced

2 tablespoons unbleached all-purpose flour

2 large eggs

1 cup fresh parsley leaves, roughly chopped

2 cups fresh baby spinach, roughly chopped

1 teaspoon kosher salt

½ teaspoon freshly ground pepper

½ cup plus ½ cup finely grated Parmesan cheese

Heat the oven to 400°F. Butter a 9-inch springform pan and wrap aluminum foil to cover the bottom and seams to prevent leaking.

Combine the potatoes and stock in a medium saucepan and cover. Bring to a boil and then decrease the heat to medium-low and simmer for 5 minutes, until the potatoes are barely tender. Lift the potatoes out of the stock with a large slotted spoon or spatula and set them aside in a bowl. Don't fret if some of the potatoes break apart. Reserve the liquid in the pot.

Melt the butter in a separate medium saucepan over medium-high heat. Add the shallot and garlic and sauté until fragrant, about 1 minute. Sprinkle the flour into the pan, whisking briskly to break up lumps. Cook the mixture for 2 minutes, until the flour becomes light golden and smells like toasting bread.

Add the reserved stock very slowly, a little at a time, whisking constantly and vigorously to form a smooth paste and then a lumpless liquid. Bring the liquid to a boil. Stir occasionally for about 5 minutes, until the liquid thickens and coats the back of a spoon. Decrease the heat to medium-low.

Beat the eggs in a small mixing bowl. Slowly pour them into the stock, whisking constantly. The stock will thicken as thin strands of eggs form throughout the liquid.

alongside

PAN-SEARED ROSEMARY RACK OF LAMB ✦ GRILLED T-BONE STEAKS WITH GREMOLATA
SLOW-ROASTED BEEF BRISKET ✦ SIMPLE LEMON HERB ROAST CHICKEN OR TURKEY BREAST
ROASTED PORK LOIN WITH GARLIC SHALLOT GRAVY

Add the parsley, spinach, salt, pepper and ½ cup of the cheese and stir to combine. Turn off the heat.

Arrange a third of the potato slices in a slightly overlapping layer at the bottom of the springform pan. Ladle on about 1 cup of the sauce. Continue layering the potatoes and ladling sauce until all of the potatoes and liquid have been used. Sprinkle the remaining ½ cup of cheese on the top layer of potatoes and sauce.

Place the springform pan on a baking sheet and transfer to the oven to bake for 1 hour, until the top is browned and the potatoes are very tender. Remove from the oven and let sit for 15 minutes before loosening the ring of the springform pan to slice into wedges and serve.

tip: If you don't trust your knife skills to cut even slices of potatoes, use a mandoline set at ¼ inch on the dial. It's important in this and all gratin recipes for the potatoes to be thin and uniform to prevent a mix of perfectly done and either over- or underdone spuds. A simple, inexpensive mandoline will come in handy here and in other recipes that call on a steady hand for consistent cuts, like Zucchini Spiral with Toasted Walnuts and Goat Cheese, page 107.

parmigiano polenta two ways *serves 4 to 6*

Polenta, originally considered a peasant food, is a staple side dish that's become a regular at casual suppers and sophisticated dinners alike. The cornmeal is traditionally simply cooked in water or sometimes stock, but milk lends a creamy richness, which elevates its rustic plainness into something more indulgent. This recipe gives you the option of scooping out big, soft spoonfuls like you would mashed potatoes or baking the polenta and cutting it into hot slices crusted with melted cheese.

6 cups whole milk

1 small yellow onion, peeled and halved through the root

3 cloves garlic, halved

2 teaspoons kosher salt, plus more for seasoning

1½ cups stone-ground polenta (also called stone-ground corn grits)

1 cup freshly grated Parmigiano-Reggiano cheese

2 tablespoons unsalted butter

Pour the milk into a large heavy saucepan over medium heat. Add the onion, garlic, and salt and slowly bring the milk to a boil, giving the onion and garlic time to infuse their flavors into the milk.

Once the milk boils, decrease the heat to medium-low. Fish out the onion and garlic with a slotted spoon and discard both. Pour the polenta into the milk in a steady stream, whisking constantly to prevent lumping. After about 5 minutes, when the polenta is too thick to whisk, switch to a wooden spoon.

Big, dramatic bubbles will surface slowly and regularly, popping audibly and releasing puffs of steam each time they do. If the heat is too high, the polenta will bubble rapidly and become too thick and dry before the corn has time to swell and soften. Cook this way at a bare simmer, stirring often but not constantly, for 45 minutes. It will seem that the polenta is soft and thick after 20 or 30 minutes, but a taste will confirm that the grains are not cooked through yet. If your polenta starts to appear too dry and gloppy, add more milk, about ¼ cup at a time, to soften it and spare it from becoming too stiff.

While the polenta cooks, preheat the oven to 400°F and butter a 9-inch pie plate if you want to bake it. ➜

alongside

BAKED SAUSAGES WITH PEPPERS AND ONIONS ✦ EGGPLANT PARMESAN ✦ POACHED EGGS IN TOMATO SAUCE WITH SMOKED MOZZARELLA ✦ ROASTED PORK RIBS WITH CHERRY SAGE SAUCE ✦ PORTOBELLO MUSHROOMS STUFFED WITH SHIITAKE AND HERB RICOTTA ✦ CHICKEN CACCIATORE ✦ PANCETTA AND BEEF STEW

After 45 minutes, when a spoonful of polenta is smooth and soft without much chew left to the tiny grains, stir in half of the Parmigiano-Reggiano and the butter. You can serve the polenta at this stage, doling out spoonfuls directly to waiting plates. If you do, add all of the cheese and season with additional salt to taste.

Alternatively, season the polenta to taste and then pour it into the prepared pie plate, sprinkle the remaining ½ cup of cheese across the top, and bake for 10 to 15 minutes, until the cheese has melted into a crust on the surface. Remove from the oven and let it rest for 5 minutes before cutting the polenta into wedges to serve.

chapter seven

Potlucks and Parties

Potlucks are practically a variety show of side dishes, prized for expansive displays of flavors and ideas. Contributing to one is like participating in a recital, demonstrating a little bit of individual craft and flair. Most potluck recipes are hearty enough to stand alone but abundant enough for everyone in a crowd to enjoy a spoonful. This chapter's variety of recipes offers options for matching or fitting into themes set by party hosts. The lineup includes both familiar flavors and range enough to elevate the basics to potluck surprise. All of the recipes yield enough to serve a group of about ten adults.

jambalaya-stuffed peppers makes 16

Smoky and textured, warm and saucy, jambalaya is one of those one-pot wonders that suits a crowd. Here poblano peppers package the rice studded with sausage, chicken, and shrimp into individual vessels that fill up ample space on a potluck plate.

. . . .

8 small to medium poblano peppers

¼ cup water

6 ounces smoked kielbasa or andouille sausage, cut into ¼-inch cubes (about 1 cup)

2 boneless, skinless chicken thighs (6 to 8 ounces), cut into ½-inch pieces

1 small yellow onion, finely diced (about 1 cup)

1 small red bell pepper, seeds and veins removed, cut into ¼-inch dice (about 1 cup)

3 cloves garlic, chopped

½ cup white basmati rice

1½ cups chicken stock (homemade or low-sodium store-bought)

½ teaspoon kosher salt

¼ teaspoon freshly ground black pepper (about 20 grinds)

12 ounces raw, unpeeled 16/20 shrimp (see Tip for peeling and deveining, page 15) or 8 ounces peeled and deveined shrimp, finely diced (about 2 cups)

alongside

+ BROILED FLANK STEAK WITH CHIMICHURRI SAUCE
+ LEMON CHICKEN SCALOPPINE
+ CUMIN AND CHILI RUBBED SLICED PORK LOIN
+ HERBED BREADCRUMB BUTTERMILK CHICKEN CUTLETS
+ GRILLED SMOKED SALT STRIP STEAKS

Preheat the oven to 450°F.

Cut the top off of the poblano peppers. Discard the stems and chop the pepper tops into ¼-inch pieces (about ½ cup); set aside. Cut each pepper in half lengthwise and cut the seeds and ribs out with a paring knife.

Pour the water into the bottom of a 13 by 9-inch baking dish. Arrange the poblano halves, cut side up, inside the dish so they all fit snuggly. Cover with foil and roast for 15 to 20 minutes, until the peppers begin to soften from the steam but are still sturdy and holding their shape. Remove from the oven and set aside, covered with the foil. Leave any remaining water in the pan. Lower the oven temperature to 375°F.

In a large deep sauté pan over medium-high heat, sauté the sausage for 2 minutes, stirring often, until some of the fat is released into the pan. Add the chicken and cook for 2 minutes, stirring regularly. Stir in the onion, bell pepper, reserved poblano pieces, and garlic and cook for 7 minutes more, until the vegetables are tender with a bit of crunch.

Stir in the rice, coating it with the fat and juices from the pan. Add the stock, bring the liquid to a boil, and cover the pan. Decrease the heat to low and simmer for 20 minutes, until the rice is tender.

Turn off the heat, uncover the pan, and stir in the salt, pepper, and shrimp, fluffing the rice and vegetables as you stir. The shrimp will start to cook in the heat of the rice mixture and finish cooking in the oven.

Scoop 2 or 3 heaping tablespoonfuls of the rice mixture into each poblano half. Return to the oven, uncovered, and bake for 20 minutes. Serve immediately.

tip: To make ahead, roast the peppers, cook the rice, and refrigerate both, covered. Before assembling the poblanos, warm the rice through with ¼ cup water in a large, deep sauté pan over medium heat. Stir in the shrimp and proceed with the recipe.

roasted red pepper orzo salad serves 8 to 10

You can make this cold pasta salad just before it's served or ahead of time, refrigerating it for up to two days. If assembled moments before dishing it out to eat, the orzo and veggies slip and slide against one another in the dressing. After a day in the fridge, the pasta soaks up the dressing and flavors, plumps a bit, and sticks to the other ingredients. Either way it's delicious.

2 pounds red bell peppers (about 5 medium)
  or 1 pound store-bought roasted
  red peppers

1 pound orzo

3 packed cups fresh baby spinach, coarsely
  chopped

½ cup minced red onion (about ½ medium
  onion)

½ cup toasted pine nuts (optional)

½ cup extra virgin olive oil

3 tablespoons fresh lemon juice
  (about 1 medium lemon)

3 tablespoons red wine vinegar

¼ teaspoon sugar

2 tablespoons fresh oregano leaves
  (2 sprigs)

⅔ cup crumbled feta (about 4 ounces)

Kosher salt and freshly ground black pepper

Preheat the oven to 450°F. Line a large baking sheet with aluminum foil and arrange the peppers in a single layer. Roast them for 30 to 40 minutes, turning with tongs every 10 to 15 minutes, until the skins are blistered and blackened in spots across the surface. Transfer the peppers to a large bowl and cover it with foil or plastic wrap. Let the peppers rest for about 20 minutes, until wilted and cool enough to handle.

Meanwhile, cook the orzo in salted water according to the package directions. Drain it and run cold water over it until all of the orzo is completely cooled. Shake out any excess water and pour the orzo into a large, wide mixing bowl.

Pluck the stems off the peppers and discard them. Peel the blackened skins from each pepper and then pull the seeds out of the insides, disposing of both. Drizzle any juices that remain in the bowl over the cool pasta (pour through a fine-mesh strainer if lots of seeds are floating in the juice). Mince the peppers and add them to the bowl with the orzo along with the spinach, onion, and pine nuts.

Combine the olive oil, lemon juice, vinegar, sugar, oregano, and cheese in a blender and blend until smooth, about 30 seconds. Pour the dressing over the pasta and toss to coat the ingredients with it. Season to taste with the salt and pepper.

alongside

GRILLED OLIVE OIL AND LEMON MARINATED MAHIMAHI ✦ BLACKENED CHICKEN AND GRILLED ROMAINE
BROILED SWORDFISH ✦ BASIL AND GARLIC SHRIMP ✦ ROMAINE WITH LEMON GARLIC CROUTONS AND
PARMIGIANO-REGGIANO **69** WITH CREAMY GARLIC DRESSING **78**

hearty chickpea tabbouleh serves 6 to 8

Tabblouleh is about the parsley, with sparse flecks of bulgur simply serving as a textural accompaniment. This salad celebrates the freshness of authentic tabbouleh and bulks it up with more grains, veggies, and chickpeas for a hungry crowd. Traditional recipes frown on chopping the herbs in a food processor, but it sure makes quick work of it. Serve it just as it is or with pita and thick, creamy labneh.

. . . .

1 cup fine or medium bulgur (see Tip)

¼ cup fresh lemon juice

¼ cup water

1½ cups ¼-inch diced fresh tomato (plum or beefsteak, about 8 ounces)

1½ cups ¼-inch diced English cucumber (about ½ large English cucumber) or peeled and seeded regular cucumber

1½ cups cooked chickpeas or 1 (15-ounce) can, drained and rinsed

4 packed cups fresh parsley leaves, finely chopped (1 cup)

1 packed cup fresh mint leaves, finely chopped (⅓ cup)

2 tablespoons extra virgin olive oil

2 teaspoons kosher salt, plus more to taste

Mix the bulgur with the lemon juice and water in a small bowl. Set aside to soak for 30 minutes while you prepare the other ingredients.

Put the tomato, cucumber, chickpeas, parsley, and mint into a large glass mixing bowl. Toss to combine. Scrape the bulgur into the bowl along with the olive oil and salt and mix again to combine thoroughly. The bulgur will still be a little bit firm but will continue to soften as the tabbouleh sits. Cover the bowl and refrigerate for at least 2 hours or overnight.

Stir again and adjust the seasoning to taste before serving.

tip: Bulgur is available in fine, medium, or coarse grinds. If you're using the coarser grind, add an extra ¼ cup of water or lemon juice to the soaking liquid and soak for a little longer before mixing with the other ingredients. The cucumbers and tomatoes add a good amount of water too, which will be absorbed by the grains as it rests in the refrigerator.

alongside

CORIANDER LAMB KEBABS ✦ WHOLE ROASTED BRANZINO WITH THYME AND GARLIC
ROASTED EGGPLANT STUFFED WITH FETA, ZUCCHINI, AND TOMATOES ✦ FALAFEL PITA PLATTER
GROUND BEEF AND LAMB KIBBEH WITH YOGURT OLIVE OIL SAUCE

layered esquites corn salad serves 6 to 8

In Mexico, esquites is a street food snack of corn sprinkled with chile powder, salt, the herb epazote, lime, and cheese and served in a cup. This recipe is based on the same concept and demands to be served with grilled steaks and margaritas. Sure, it takes more effort than steaming a pot of cobs does, but if someone else is manning the grill and you've got a salt-rimmed glass of refreshment, what do you care? You can make the salad up to one day ahead, cover tightly, and refrigerate until ready to serve.

1 tablespoon unsalted butter

6 cups fresh or thawed frozen corn kernels (6 medium ears)

1 bunch scallions (4 or 5), white and green parts thinly sliced separately

3 cloves garlic, minced (about 1½ tablespoons)

¼ teaspoon chipotle powder

1 teaspoon kosher salt

½ cup loosely packed fresh cilantro leaves, finely chopped

¼ cup minced jalapeño (1 large or 2 small)

⅓ cup sour cream

2 tablespoons mayonnaise

2 teaspoons finely grated lime zest (1 or 2 limes)

2 tablespoons fresh lime juice (1 or 2 limes)

¾ cup crumbled feta cheese or cotija cheese (about 3 ounces)

Melt the butter in a large sauté pan over medium-high heat. Add the corn and cook for 10 minutes, stirring every minute or so, until the kernels are hot and their starchy rawness has turned into sweet crunchiness.

Add the white parts of the scallions and the garlic and cook for another 2 minutes. Stir in the chipotle powder and salt. Remove from the heat and set aside to cool completely. (To cool quickly, spread the corn out across a baking sheet pan or a large platter.) Once the corn is cool, mix in the green parts of the scallions, the cilantro, and the jalapeño. Add more chipotle powder if you like a little more heat.

In a small bowl, combine the sour cream, mayonnaise, lime zest, and lime juice.

Layer the ingredients in a 9-inch pie plate, starting with one-third of the corn. Top with one-half of the sour cream mixture. Sprinkle with one-third of the feta. Repeat the layering, ending with a layer of corn sprinkled with feta. Serve immediately or cover and refrigerate for up to 1 day.

alongside

SMOKED-SALT-CRUSTED STRIP STEAKS ✦ FLANK STEAK, CHICKEN, OR VEGGIE FAJITAS
SHRIMP AND SCALLOPS SAUTÉED WITH CHILE LIME BUTTER ✦ GRILLED MAHIMAHI AND PINEAPPLE
FIRE-ROASTED POBLANOS STUFFED WITH BLACK BEANS, RICE, AND CHEESE

eggplant feta rollatini serves 6 to 8

These little parcels of tender roasted eggplant filled with flavored ricotta are blanketed lightly with a simple sauce. Eggplant slices for rollatini are usually breaded and fried parmigiana style, but this version skips that step, yielding lighter results that are perfect for a side dish. If you prefer, you can substitute a teaspoon of chopped mint for the tablespoon of parsley in the cheese filling.

. . . .

1 large eggplant (about 1¼ pounds)

Kosher salt and freshly ground black pepper

1 cup ricotta cheese

4 ounces crumbled feta cheese (⅔ cup)

½ cup grated Parmesan cheese

1 teaspoon finely grated lemon zest (1 medium lemon)

1 tablespoon plus 2 tablespoons minced fresh parsley

½ cup canned crushed tomatoes

1 teaspoon minced fresh oregano

1 small clove garlic, coarsely chopped

¼ cup extra virgin olive oil for brushing

Trim the eggplant of its stem and then peel off ½-inch strips of the eggplant skin lengthwise, leaving strips of skin remaining to make stripes (trimming some of the skin cuts back on its toughness in the finished dish). Cut the eggplant into ¼-inch rounds. Sprinkle the slices with several pinches of salt and pile them into a large colander for 30 minutes.

Meanwhile, mix the ricotta, feta, half of the Parmesan, the lemon zest, and 1 tablespoon of the parsley in a medium bowl. Season to taste with the salt and pepper. Cover and refrigerate.

Preheat the oven to 450°F.

In a small mixing bowl, combine the remaining 2 tablespoons of parsley with the tomatoes, oregano, and garlic. Set aside.

Rinse the eggplant slices with cold water and spread them across a clean kitchen towel. You'll want about 24 medium to large rounds to stuff with the cheese. Roast the smaller rounds and snack on them if you like. Pat the other slices dry and arrange them in single layers across 2 baking sheets. Brush both sides of each piece of eggplant with olive oil. Transfer to the oven and bake for 8 minutes, until softened. Flip each slice and bake for 3 minutes longer. Remove and let the slices cool just enough to handle.

alongside

GRILLED LEMON CHICKEN ✦ FENNEL AND MINT MUSSELS ✦ GREEK SALAD WITH WARM PITA ✦ CRUSHED RED PEPPER AND WHITE WINE SHRIMP AND LINGUINE ✦ BASIL AND MINT RISOTTO ✦ FRITTATA DI PASTA

Lower the oven temperature to 350°F. Spread a thin layer of the crushed tomato mixture across the bottom of a 9 by 13-inch baking dish. Spoon about 1 tablespoon of the cheese mixture onto the center of each eggplant slice. Roll the eggplant onto itself over the cheese and place each one seam side down in the baking dish. Pack the rollatini into the dish in snug rows.

Spoon the remaining tomato sauce over the eggplant and sprinkle the remaining ¼ cup of Parmesan on top. Bake for about 25 minutes, until the eggplant is tender, the filling and sauce is bubbling, and the cheese is browned on top. Cool just slightly before serving.

If you make this in advance and refrigerate (up to 2 days ahead), reheat in a 350°F oven for about 15 minutes or until the filling is hot.

frittata di pasta serves 8 to 10

My neighbor, Anna, packs a wedge of this frittata in her kindergartener's school lunch box because her own Italian mother did the same for her when she was young. Peanut butter and jelly wasn't part of the repertoire during her first-generation Italian-American childhood. Spaghetti pie is a classic Neapolitan repurposing of leftovers and is as adaptable as spaghetti itself. It can be served warm, at room temperature, or cold, in thick triangles or skinny slices. Here is the basic recipe to which you can add whatever you like. Try tiny cubes of crisp pancetta, chopped oven tomatoes, tuna, olives, pepperoni, cooked crumbled sausage, or a variety of cheese. Beware, however, that the addition of wet ingredients, like ricotta or juicy fresh tomatoes, may compromise the structural integrity of the frittata.

- 1 pound spaghetti
- 2 tablespoons extra virgin olive oil
- 1 medium yellow onion, halved and very thinly sliced (about 1½ cups)
- 1 small zucchini or yellow squash, finely diced (about 1 cup)
- 4 cloves garlic, minced
- 1 cup canned crushed tomatoes
- 2 teaspoons minced fresh oregano leaves (2 sprigs)
- 1 cup grated Pecorino Romano cheese
- ½ teaspoon kosher salt, plus more for seasoning
- ¼ teaspoon freshly ground black pepper (about 20 grinds)
- 6 large eggs
- 10 large fresh basil leaves, very thinly sliced
- ¼ cup plus ¼ cup peanut or vegetable oil

Cook the spaghetti according to the package directions. Reserve ¼ cup of the cooking water and then drain and rinse the spaghetti with cold water until of it has cooled. Leave it to drain in the colander.

Heat the olive oil in a large deep sauté pan over medium heat. Add the onion slices and sweat them for 8 to 10 minutes, stirring every minute or so, until softened and just starting to brown. Add the zucchini and cook for 2 minutes, stirring occasionally. Stir in the garlic and sauté for 30 seconds.

Add the tomatoes and oregano and simmer for about 10 minutes. Stir in the reserved pasta water to thin the sauce a bit and turn off the heat. If your pan can accommodate it, add the spaghetti and cheese to the sauce and toss it with tongs several times to coat the strands. Otherwise transfer to a large mixing bowl. Season with the salt and pepper to taste, using a little more than you usually would since the eggs have to share some of that seasoning and will mute it a little once cooked. If the pasta tastes just a bit too salty and peppery, you've got it right.

Whisk together the eggs and basil and pour the mixture over the pasta. Use tongs again to coat the spaghetti with the eggs. →

alongside

EGGPLANT PARMESAN ✦ BOUILLABAISSE ✦ BAKED ITALIAN SAUSAGE AND PEPPERS
GRILLED CHICKEN CAESAR SALAD ✦ BASIL BREADCRUMB AND CHARD STUFFED PORTOBELLO MUSHROOMS

Heat ¼ cup of the oil in a 12-inch cast-iron skillet or deep sauté pan over medium heat (use a pan that is 12 or more inches in diameter or divide the pasta into 2 smaller pans. Smaller pans won't accommodate an entire pound of the pasta at once.) When the oil is hot (you can see it starting to ripple under the heat or it sizzles vehemently when flicked with a few drops of water), gently pour in the pasta. Level it as well as you can into an even thickness. Fry for 15 minutes, rotating the pan a quarter turn every 2 to 3 minutes so the pasta browns evenly. Resist the urge to constantly poke at the pasta or check the bottom. If you sense that the pasta is starting to burn at all, decrease the heat to medium-low.

After 15 minutes, turn off the heat. Situate a baking sheet, bottom side down, over the pan (the handle of the skillet should be parallel to you and the long sides of the baking sheet should be perpendicular to you). Very carefully flip the pan over, holding the baking sheet tightly on top of it. Set it down. Lift the pan to turn out the frittata and sprinkle some salt on the browned top. Return the skillet to medium heat on the stovetop. Pour in the remaining ¼ cup of the oil and let it spread out across the bottom.

Nudge the frittata, browned side up, back into the skillet and repeat the frying and rotating process for another 15 minutes.

Turn off the heat and use the baking sheet to flip the frittata out again. Sprinkle a few more pinches of salt on the newly browned side. Let the frittata cool for 10 minutes or so before slicing into wedges or skinny pieces (or cool to room temperature before slicing, depending on how you plan to serve it).

spicy peanut noodle twirl serves 8 to 10

Here's a bowl of chin-spattering, cheek-mussing twirls of cool, thin noodle strands dressed in a spicy, velvety sauce that begs to be freed from the pasta salads category. Audibly crunchy strips of pepper and carrot pal around perfectly with familiar Asian flavors they know well from other dishes. And bright emerald and white scallions partner with salty bits of roasted peanuts to serve as the accessories that finish the whole ensemble like Harry Winston jewels on the Red Carpet. While you can cook the noodles ahead of time and make the sauce the day before, the salad is best dressed just before serving, since the noodles soak up the sauce and get sticky when refrigerated.

1 pound spaghetti

¼ cup all-natural creamy peanut butter

¼ cup soy sauce

¼ cup rice wine vinegar

2 tablespoons brown sugar

2 teaspoons sesame oil (light or dark)

1 tablespoon sriracha

1 clove garlic

2 medium carrots, julienned (use a mandoline set at ⅛-inch julienne or cut by hand)

2 medium red bell peppers, seeds and veins removed, sliced into very thin strips

4 scallions, white and green parts, sliced diagonally into ⅛-inch disks (about ¾ cup)

½ cup roasted salted peanuts, chopped

Cook the spaghetti according to the package directions. Drain it in a colander and rinse it with cold water until the noodles are no longer warm to stop the cooking.

Combine the peanut butter, soy sauce, vinegar, brown sugar, sesame oil, sriracha, and garlic in a blender. Blend until completely smooth, stopping to scrape down the sides of the blender with a rubber spatula once or twice, about 30 seconds.

Transfer the spaghetti to a large, wide serving bowl. Pour the peanut butter sauce over the pasta and toss to completely coat the noodles with the sauce. Add the carrots, peppers, and scallions to the bowl and toss again to incorporate them. Sprinkle the peanuts over the top of the noodles just before serving.

tip: Oversized veggies are clunky against skinny spaghetti, so if you don't trust your knife skills to pull off thin julienne strips of carrots and peppers, grate the carrots coarsely and finely dice the peppers.

alongside

CHARRED SATAY-STYLE CHICKEN OR BEEF SKEWERS ✦ GARLIC AND CHILI MARINATED GRILLED, SAUTÉED, OR ROASTED TOFU CUBES OR FILLETS ✦ COCONUT-MARINATED SHRIMP OR CHICKEN KEBABS ✦ THINLY SLICED GARLIC-STUDDED ROASTED PORK TENDERLOIN ✦ GINGER GROUND PORK OR TURKEY BURGERS

shells with fontina, sweet onions, and chard

serves 6 to 8

It's no secret that petite cippoline onions are high-maintenance. Peeling them requires patience and the foresight that their sweet, silky results are worth every minute that passes while you pull off their outer skins. Here they melt into balsamic vinegar and honey and then infuse a creamy, cheesy blend tangled with softened chard. At potlucks this recipe is a sophisticated alternative to macaroni and cheese. At the dinner table it pairs perfectly with low-maintenance roasted meats that you can ignore while you prepare the pasta. Choose the slightly sharper and more pungent Italian Fontina Val d'Aosta over milder varieties from Denmark or the U.S.

1 tablespoon plus 2 tablespoons
　　unsalted butter

1 tablespoon extra virgin olive oil

1 pound cippoline onions, halved and peeled

2 tablespoons balsamic vinegar

1 tablespoon honey

1 medium bunch Swiss chard (about
　　12 ounces), sliced crosswise ¼ inch thick

1 pound medium pasta shells

2 tablespoons unbleached all-purpose flour

2 cups chicken stock (homemade or
　　low-sodium store-bought)

1 cup plus ½ cup grated Fontina Val d'Aosta
　　cheese (about 6 ounces)

1 teaspoon kosher salt

⅛ teaspoon freshly ground black pepper
　　(about 10 grinds)

Melt 1 tablespoon of the butter along with the olive oil in a large sauté pan over medium heat. Add the onions and sweat them for 5 minutes, stirring often as they soften and start to brown slightly. As they cook, push the onions with the back of a wooden spoon, squishing the layers and separating them.

Add the vinegar and honey and stir well to distribute both throughout the onions. Cover the pan and continue to cook the onions for 5 minutes, stirring once or twice, until they are very soft and the vinegar and honey become thick and syrupy.

Add the chard to the pan and stir to combine, scraping up any brown bits from the bottom of the pan as the chard releases some of its water. Cover the pan again to cook for 5 minutes, stirring twice while the chard wilts into the onions. Uncover and continue cooking for 5 minutes, until soft and less than half of its original volume.

Cook the pasta shells according to the package directions while you continue with the rest of the recipe. Preheat the oven to 375°F. Butter a 2-quart casserole dish (or an 8-inch square glass baking dish).

alongside

CHICKEN MARSALA ✦ ROASTED GARLIC AND ROSEMARY PORK LOIN ✦ VEAL SCALOPPINE ✦ ROASTED CHICKEN WITH
CARROTS, LEMONS, AND SCALLIONS ✦ ZUCCHINI AND EGGPLANT ROLLATINI

Scrape the onions and chard into a bowl and set aside. Return the pan to medium-high heat and add the remaining 2 tablespoons of butter to melt it. Whisk in the flour to form a paste and let it cook for 2 to 3 minutes, stirring regularly until it turns a light golden color and starts to smell nutty. Slowly add the chicken stock, whisking constantly to prevent lumps. Bring the liquid to a boil and stir regularly for 3 to 5 minutes, until it thickens slightly.

Drain the hot cooked pasta and add it to the chicken stock sauce along with the onions and chard. Stir to coat all of the ingredients with the sauce. Sprinkle in 1 cup of the Fontina and stir to combine. Season with the salt and pepper to taste.

Transfer the pasta to the buttered dish, sprinkle with the remaining ½ cup of Fontina, and bake for about 15 minutes, until the cheese is melted across the top. Serve immediately.

tip: Suggested peeling techniques for cippoline onions include dropping them into boiling water to loosen the skins before sliding them off, as you would with pearl onions, but I find this makes them water logged and mushy. The simplest method is plucking and peeling the skins like any other onion, but with a little more determination.

oven-dried tomato tart gratin serves 6 to 8

This recipe puts tomatoes on a buttery herb crust pedestal. It's perfect for a summer boon of red ripeness, and the oven drying will also do wonders for off-season tomatoes that are a little bland. You can fiddle with the cheese to suit your tastes, but if you bump up the amount of provolone, consider opting for a mild variety. The sharp saltiness of firm, imported varieties needs the balance it gets from mellower mozzarella, lest it overpower the flaky oregano crust and the sweetness of the tomatoes.

1⅓ cups unbleached all-purpose flour, plus more for the work surface

1 teaspoon plus ½ teaspoon dried oregano

¼ teaspoon plus ¼ teaspoon kosher salt

8 tablespoons (1 stick) cold unsalted butter, cut into ½-inch cubes

1 large egg, separated

3 tablespoons ice water

1½ pounds slicing tomatoes, such as vine-ripe, beefsteak, Roma, or plum

¼ teaspoon freshly ground black pepper (about 20 grinds)

½ cup grated sharp provolone cheese

1 cup grated whole-milk or part-skim mozzarella cheese (fresh and buffalo mozzarella are too moist here)

Put the flour, 1 teaspoon of the oregano, and ¼ teaspoon of the salt in a food processor and pulse about 10 times to combine. Add the butter cubes and pulse about 30 times, until the butter becomes tiny bits coated with flour. Add the egg yolk and the ice water and pulse another 10 to 20 times, until a sandy, shaggy dough barely starts to clump together in the processor.

Dump the dough and crumbs out onto a very lightly floured surface and squeeze it all together into a ball. Flatten the ball into a 1-inch-thick disk, wrap tightly in plastic wrap, and refrigerate for at least 30 minutes and up to 24 hours.

Preheat the oven to 375°F. Take the dough out of the refrigerator and set it on a lightly floured surface. Smack it 5 or 6 times with a rolling pin to flatten slightly. Roll out into a rough circle about ¼ inch thick and 12 inches in diameter. Roll half of the dough up onto the rolling pin so it drapes over and then carefully set the dough into a 9-inch tart pan. Press it to fit snuggly across the bottom and up into the fluted sides. Press the rolling pin against the top edge of the tart pan to neatly trim off excess dough (discard scraps or reserve and bake free-form for another purpose). Refrigerate the dough for 20 minutes in the tart pan.

While the dough chills, core the tomatoes and slice them about ¼ inch thick. Arrange them side by side in a single layer on a baking sheet lined with parchment paper.

alongside

SALT-CRUSTED RIB-EYE STEAKS ✦ GRILLED SUMMER VEGETABLES AND PASTA
GRILLED MAHIMAHI WITH PESTO SAUCE ✦ CRISPY CHICKEN CUTLET AND BACON SALAD
PORK TENDERLOIN WITH HOT GARLIC GREENS ✦ LEMON AND WHITE WINE PANFRIED FLOUNDER

When the dough is cold, poke it several times with a fork across the bottom and up the sides. Cut a piece of parchment paper into a round to fit the diameter of the pan, plus an inch up the sides. Pour baking weights or about 2 cups of dried beans on top of the parchment to hold it down. Set the tart pan on a baking sheet and put it on the top rack of the oven. Put the tomatoes on the bottom rack and bake both for 20 minutes to dry out the tomatoes and blind bake the crust.

Take the tart shell and tomatoes out of the oven and set the tomatoes aside to cool slightly. They will have dried and wrinkled a bit. Carefully lift the parchment with the weights or beans out of the tart pan and set them aside to cool (store and reuse for another pie or tart). Brush the crust with the reserved egg white (discard whatever you don't use) and return the crust to the oven for 10 minutes more, until the edges start to turn a very pale golden color.

Assemble the tart. Mix the cheeses together in a small bowl and reserve about ½ cup for the top. Scatter half of the cheese across the bottom of the crust. Arrange half of the tomatoes in a single layer on top of the cheese. Sprinkle with pinches of the remaining oregano, salt, and pepper. Repeat this layering again and top the last layer of tomatoes with the remaining cheese.

Return the tart to the oven and bake for 20 minutes, until the cheese is melted and browned and the sides of the crust are golden. Let the tart rest for about 10 minutes before slicing to serve.

quintessential macaroni and cheese

serves 10 to 12

Despite its irrevocable popularity, my problem with macaroni and cheese has always been that for all its seducing richness and comfort, it can be terribly one-dimensional in flavor: just heavy with cheese and plain old macaroni. For me to continue to invest the time and money to make it, it needed to prove its worth in taste. So before I add milk to make the cheese sauce, I infuse it with onions and garlic. Next, I pack a punch of flavor into the sauce with dry mustard and miso paste, king of umami, that savory fifth taste sensation with the elusive definition that is rarely called on outside of Asian cuisine. (See Tip for suggested uses of the tub of miso in your fridge after you use it in this recipe.) Finally, I use a mix of cheeses, heavy on extra-sharp Cheddar, but balanced with melting cheeses to ensure smoothness not attainable with Cheddar alone (it tends to separate and seize when melted).

. . . .

3 cups whole milk

1 small yellow onion, peeled and halved

3 cloves garlic, halved

Pinch of cayenne

1 pound (4 cups) elbow macaroni

3 tablespoons unsalted butter

3 tablespoons unbleached all-purpose flour

1½ tablespoons red miso paste

1 teaspoon dry mustard

2 cups grated extra-sharp Cheddar cheese (8 ounces)

1 cup grated Gouda cheese (4 ounces)

1 cup grated Colby Jack cheese (4 ounces)

¼ teaspoon freshly ground black pepper (about 20 grinds)

Kosher salt

Preheat the oven to 375°F.

Combine the milk, onion, garlic, and cayenne in a medium saucepan over medium-high heat. Bring the milk to a rapid simmer so that bubbles pop up all along the sides of the pot and steam starts to rise and then immediately decrease the heat to low. Give the milk a stir and cover the pot. Steep the onions and garlic in the milk for 20 minutes.

Meanwhile, cook the macaroni. Bring a large Dutch oven or pot of water to a boil and add the pasta. Cook for 4 or 5 minutes, so that the macaroni is still slightly underdone. Drain and rinse it with cold water to prevent it from cooking any further. Set aside and reserve the pot for making the cheese sauce.

After 20 minutes, strain the milk of the onion and garlic or simply fish the solids out with a slotted spoon and discard them. Set the milk aside, off the heat but covered.

alongside

GRILLED OR SLOW-ROASTED BABY BACK RIBS ✦ BOILED CRAB, SHRIMP, OR LOBSTER
SPICY BARBECUE BAKED CHICKEN ✦ GRILLED VEGETABLE PLATTER ✦ HONEY BOURBON BEEF BRISKET OR PULLED PORK

Return the macaroni pot to medium heat and melt the butter in it. Scatter the flour across the surface of the butter, whisking briskly to prevent it from lumping while a smooth paste forms. Cook the paste (also called a roux) for 3 to 4 minutes, until it turns from blond to very light golden in hue and starts to smell like baking bread.

Whisk in the miso paste and mustard. Stir well to help the miso melt into the paste. Add the milk ¼ cup at a time at first, whisking constantly to work it into the paste. It will seize up a little with the first few additions of milk, but a thick, smooth paste and then a thinner sauce will form as the rest of the milk is whisked in. Once all the milk is added, raise the heat to medium-high to simmer the sauce, stirring often and scraping the bottom of the pot to prevent buildup of the paste. Let the sauce simmer until thickened, about 3 minutes. Dip a spoon into it and then run your finger down the back of the spoon to draw a line in the sauce that remains on the spoon. If the line holds, the liquid is thick enough.

Combine the grated cheeses in a large mixing bowl. Reserve 1 cup and stir the rest into the thick milk sauce until it is completely melted. Add the pepper and then dump the cooked macaroni into the sauce and stir to coat it thoroughly. Season with salt to taste. (Do not add salt before this, since the miso and cheese both add significant amounts of salt.)

Butter a 13 by 9-inch casserole or baking dish. Scrape the macaroni into the dish and sprinkle the remaining 1 cup of cheese over the macaroni. Bake for 20 to 30 minutes, until the cheese on top is melted and just starting to brown. Let the macaroni and cheese cool for about 10 minutes before serving.

tip: Miso, or Japanese bean paste, is a powerhouse of flavor. It is salty and savory, with vague notes of fermentation, which you can smell. Outside of Japanese recipes, try working it into ground meat for burgers, meatballs, or meat loaf; stirring a few tablespoons into soup and stew; blending a bit into dips or dressings (as in Broccoli Sesame Crunch, page 116); adding some to barbecue sauce or marinades.

orange and black bean quinoa *serves 8 to 10*

The mix of these ingredients looks like confetti in a bowl. Tiny flecks of fluffed quinoa, shiny black beans, glimmering orange bits, and speckles of bright green scallions make for an eye-catching grain salad. Be sure to let the quinoa cool and dry a bit before tossing with the rest of the ingredients so it doesn't get heavy and soggy with too much moisture. Segmenting or supreming an orange yields little bits of the vibrantly colored fruit without any of the chewy skin or membranes.

. . . .

2½ cups water

1½ cups quinoa

2 large oranges (navel or your favorite variety), finely zested and segmented (see Tip, page 185), and cut into ¼-inch pieces

1½ cups cooked black beans or 1 (15-ounce) can, drained and rinsed

½ cup thinly sliced scallion, green and white parts (about 4 scallions)

2 tablespoons extra virgin olive oil

½ cup crumbled queso fresco or feta cheese

½ teaspoon kosher salt, plus more to taste

Bring the water to a boil in a medium saucepan. Stir in the quinoa, cover, and turn the heat down to low. Let the quinoa simmer and steam for 15 minutes, until all the liquid is absorbed. Scrape the cooked quinoa into a wide serving bowl and let it dry slightly while it cools completely.

Meanwhile, put the zest and orange segments in a large mixing bowl with the beans, scallions, olive oil, and queso fresco. Toss everything together.

Scoop the orange and bean mixture on top of the cooled quinoa and fold all of the ingredients together to combine. Season with the salt and adjust to taste. Serve immediately or refrigerate in an airtight container for up to a day.

alongside

CHICKEN AND POBLANO FAJITAS ✦ CUMIN AND LIME MARINATED SKIRT STEAK
CHILE-DUSTED SAUTÉED SHRIMP ✦ MUSHROOM AND TOFU ENCHILADAS ✦ GRILLED PORK CHOPS AND PINEAPPLE

baked ditalini with fennel sausage and smoked mozzarella serves 10 to 12

Big, oozing trays of baked pastas, like lasagne and ziti, are potluck standards. They feed crowds, appeal to the masses, and stuff plenty of food onto one heaping, steaming serving spoonful. This dish pays homage to its predecessors but does a better job at sharing the stage with other party contributions. It's lighter in density and ingredients but full of rich flavor. A tumbling scoop of it covers the requisite cheesy pasta slot while leaving room for plenty more grazing.

2 tablespoons plus 1 tablespoon extra virgin olive oil

2 links (about 8 ounces) sweet Italian sausage

4 cloves garlic, minced

¼ cup plus ½ cup water

1 (28-ounce) can or 3 cups whole peeled tomatoes, squeezed by hand (see Tip)

1 pound ditalini

¼ cup thinly sliced fresh basil (about 20 leaves)

¼ cup fresh parsley, finely chopped

Leaves from 2 sprigs fresh oregano, chopped

½ cup freshly grated Parmesan cheese

8 ounces smoked mozzarella cheese, cut into ¼-inch cubes (1 cup plus ½ cup)

Kosher salt and freshly ground black pepper

Heat 1 tablespoon of the olive oil in a large deep sauté pan over medium-high heat. Squeeze the sausage out of its casings, break it into small bits, and drop it into the hot pan. Cook the meat for 5 to 7 minutes, breaking it up further with a wooden spoon, until a brown crust forms on the pieces and on the bottom of the pan.

Add the garlic and sauté with the sausage for 30 seconds. Pour in ¼ cup of the water and scrape the bits from the bottom of the pan as the water sizzles and evaporates. Add the tomatoes and another ½ cup of water and stir to combine. Decrease the heat to low, cover the pan, and simmer for 30 minutes, stirring occasionally.

While the sauce simmers, cook the pasta according to the package directions and preheat the oven to 375°F. If there is any lag between the time you cook the pasta and the time you assemble the dish, run cold water over the drained pasta to stop the cooking.

alongside

EGGPLANT OR CHICKEN PARMIGIANA ✦ CAESAR SALAD WITH GARLIC CROUTONS AND GRILLED CHICKEN OR SHRIMP
PORK MILANESE OR SALTIMBOCCA ✦ MARINATED VEGETABLES WITH CHARCUTERIE AND CHEESE

Once the sauce has simmered, stir in the remaining 2 tablespoons of olive oil, the basil, parsley, and oregano. Scrape the pasta into a 13 by 9-inch glass or enamel baking dish and pour the sauce on top. Add the Parmesan cheese and 1 cup of the mozzarella. Stir to coat the pasta with the sauce and incorporate the cheese. Season to taste with the salt and black pepper. Sprinkle the remaining ½ cup of mozzarella across the top of the pasta. Cover the dish with foil and transfer to the oven to bake for 15 minutes. Remove the foil and bake for 5 to 10 minutes more, until the mozzarella starts to bubble and brown. Serve immediately.

tip: To crush whole, peeled tomatoes, dump them and their juices (if using canned) into a large mixing bowl. Plunge your hands into the bowl and squeeze individual tomatoes in your palms, creating shaggy pieces of varying sizes.

tip: If needed, cook the pasta and the sausage sauce a day ahead and assemble just before baking. After draining the hot pasta, run cold water over it until it is no longer warm, to stop the cooking and prevent it from moseying beyond al dente. Shake out any excess water and then scrape the ditalini into a large bowl or storage container. Stir in a tablespoon of olive oil to prevent too much sticking, cover, and refrigerate until ready to use. Make the sauce as directed, simmer time included, and cool, cover, and refrigerate.

panzanella trifle   *serves 6 to 8*

The sole purpose of this salad's invention in Italy during the days of yore was to use up stale bread. Big chunks of hard, crusty day-old loaves were mixed with ingredients like onions, oil, water, herbs, and, later, juicy summer tomatoes. The hard bread became soft as it soaked in the flavorful liquid, and the bulked-up salad served as a meal. Here summer's bounty dresses oven-toasted croutons in a colorful salad studded with creamy bites of fresh mozzarella. The trifle dish you keep meaning to dig out of storage is the perfect vessel for displaying all the color of the vegetables, but if you don't have one, any large glass bowl or long baking dish will do. If you prepare the elements of the salad ahead, save the assembly for just before serving so as to reserve some of the crunch in the bread before it soaks up all the delicious juices.

. . . .

3 tablespoons plus 2 tablespoons extra virgin olive oil

½ teaspoon plus ½ teaspoon kosher salt

½ teaspoon garlic powder

6 cups ½-inch bread cubes (use ciabatta or baguette)

1½ pounds heirloom or salad tomatoes, cut into ½-inch chunks (about 4 cups)

2 small zucchini or summer squash (about 12 ounces), cut into ½-inch cubes (about 3 cups)

1 medium cucumber (about 12 ounces), peeled and cut into ½-inch cubes (about 2 cups)

1 roasted red pepper (page 155 or store-bought), quartered and cut into thin strips (about 1 cup)

3 tablespoons white balsamic or white wine vinegar

1 teaspoon honey

8 ounces small fresh mozzarella balls (bocconcini), quartered (about 1 cup)

6 large fresh basil leaves, torn into small pieces

alongside

PENNE WITH SAUTÉED SUMMER CORN AND PANCETTA ✦ RISOTTO-STUFFED ROASTED PORTOBELLOS
ROSEMARY AND THYME CRUSTED GRILLED PORK CHOPS ✦ CRAB AND LOBSTER BAKE ✦ GRILLED RIB-EYE WITH PARSLEY
GARLIC BUTTER ✦ BROILED SCALLOPS WITH LEMON BUTTER ✦ GRILLED OREGANO AND GARLIC CHICKEN BREAST

Preheat the oven to 425°F. Whisk 2 tablespoons of the olive oil with ½ teaspoon of the salt and the garlic powder. Drizzle the oil mixture over the bread cubes in a large bowl and toss several times to coat the bread. Spread the cubes out in a single layer on a baking sheet and bake for 15 minutes, until dark golden and very crunchy. Remove the cubes from the oven and let them cool completely.

In a large mixing bowl, combine the tomatoes, zucchini, cucumber, and red pepper and toss together. Whisk the remaining 3 tablespoons of olive oil with the vinegar, honey, and remaining ½ teaspoon of salt. Drizzle the vinaigrette over the vegetables and mix. Let the vegetables marinate at room temperature for 30 minutes.

Layer the salad in a 14-cup trifle dish. Using a slotted spoon, scoop 2 cups of the vegetables into the bottom of the dish. Dot this first layer with ¼ cup of the mozzarella followed by 1½ cups of bread cubes. Sprinkle some of the torn basil across the layer. Repeat the process. Pour any marinade and juices remaining in the mixing bowl over the top layer of vegetables before topping with the last of the bread cubes. Serve immediately.

lemongrass vermicelli serves 6 to 8

Rice noodles are a staple of Asian cuisine and are available in all sorts of shapes and sizes. Vermicelli is long, skinny strands that cook very quickly and is available dried or fresh in the ethnic sections of groceries or Asian supermarkets. This recipe calls for dried vermicelli. If you have trouble finding it, you can substitute angel hair pasta, though the texture won't be quite the same. These noodles are intended to be served at room temperature, but leftovers make an excellent lunch straight from the fridge.

¼ cup rice vinegar

3 tablespoons vegetable oil

3 tablespoons low-sodium soy sauce

2 tablespoons fish sauce

1 teaspoon sriracha

½ teaspoon sugar

2 tablespoons (about 1 stalk) minced lemongrass (see Tip)

1 cup grated English cucumber or peeled, seeded grated regular cucumber

½ cup lightly packed fresh cilantro leaves, coarsely chopped

¼ cup lightly packed fresh Thai basil leaves, coarsely chopped

¼ cup lightly packed fresh mint leaves, coarsely chopped

¼ cup minced scallion (about 2 scallions)

1 (14-ounce) package dried rice vermicelli

½ cup roasted salted peanuts, chopped

In a large mixing bowl, whisk together the vinegar, oil, soy sauce, fish sauce, sriracha, sugar, and lemongrass. Add the cucumber, cilantro, Thai basil, mint, and scallions, stir to combine, and set aside.

Bring a large pot of water to a rapid boil. Drop the vermicelli in and cook until tender, about 3 minutes, stirring regularly to prevent the strands from clumping and sticking. Drain the vermicelli in a large colander and run cold water over and through it to rinse off some of the starch and cool it completely. Shake the colander vigorously to rid the noodles of excess water. Add them to the large mixing bowl with the other ingredients.

Using tongs, toss the noodles repeatedly to coat them with the vinegar mixture, lemongrass, and herbs. Sprinkle with the peanuts and serve immediately.

tip: While sizable chunks of lemongrass stalks flavor broths or teas nicely, they are usually too tough to eat. Mincing the softer inner layers of the stalk breaks them down into chewable bits. To mince lemongrass, cut off the tough, woody top and bottom ends of the stalk. Then peel off the harder outer layer and discard. Cut the remaining core of the stalk into sections about 3 inches in length. Slice each piece in half lengthwise and set them cut side down. Cut the lemongrass into very thin half-moons and then run your knife through the pile several times to mince it into tiny bits. Tubes of lemongrass paste are available in grocery stores and can be substituted for equal measures of lemongrass in this recipe, but I tend to avoid them because of added oils and preservatives.

alongside

SPICY BASIL BEEF ✦ CRISPY PORK SPRING ROLLS ✦ STIR-FRIED VEGETABLES AND TOFU
CASHEW CHICKEN AND SHRIMP ✦ MUSSELS AND SQUID IN GARLIC CHILE BROTH

baked stuffed mushrooms makes 24 mushrooms

Mushrooms are meaty little things that add a springy chew and melt into earthy richness. They are contortionists that can work their way into dishes of all sorts. Here they're stuffed silly with themselves and laced with cheese, breadcrumbs, and a subtle kick of heat from chipotle chile powder. These are two-bite treats that complement a range of recipes, making them an ideal contribution to a community potluck table.

24 large stuffing mushrooms, white button or cremini

2 tablespoons extra virgin olive oil

½ small red onion, minced (about ⅔ cup)

2 large cloves garlic, minced

1 cup loosely packed fresh parsley leaves, minced (about ½ cup)

⅔ cup panko breadcrumbs

½ cup freshly grated Parmesan cheese

¼ teaspoon chipotle chile powder

Kosher salt and freshly ground black pepper

2 tablespoons unsalted butter, cut into ⅛-inch cubes

¼ cup dry white wine (such as pinot grigio or Chablis)

½ cup water

alongside

+ ROAST BEEF AU JUS
+ SPINACH MANICOTTI WITH PARMESAN CREAM
+ SHRIMP SCAMPI
+ BAKED COD WITH LEMON
+ MIXED GREENS WITH ALMONDS AND ROTISSERIE CHICKEN
+ ROASTED TURKEY AND GRAVY

Preheat the oven to 425°F.

Pluck the stems from each of the mushrooms or gently carve them out with a paring knife, taking care not to dig too deeply or gouge the mushroom cap. Set the stems aside on a cutting board and line up the mushrooms stem side up in a 13 by 9-inch baking dish. Chop the mushroom stems very finely.

Heat the olive oil in a large sauté pan over medium heat. Add the onion and garlic and sweat them for 3 to 5 minutes, stirring every minute or so and cooking until they are soft and the deep purple of the onion turns a much lighter shade of pink. Add the chopped mushroom stems to the pan and sweat them with the onion and garlic for another 5 minutes, until much of the water released from the mushrooms has cooked away and the stems shrink to about a third of their original volume. Remove the pan from the heat and let everything cool to about room temperature.

Add the parsley, breadcrumbs, cheese, and chipotle powder to the onions and mushrooms. Season to taste with the salt and pepper.

Carefully stuff heaping teaspoons of the cooked mixture into the mushrooms. Taking a second to tuck each spoonful in deep will help prevent the stuffing from toppling over out into the dish. Dot each mound of stuffing with 2 or 3 of the tiny butter cubes.

Mix the wine with the water and pour it into the baking dish through a space between the mushrooms (not over top of them, which will make the stuffing soggy) so they are sitting in the liquid. Bake for 25 minutes or until the mushrooms are tender and the stuffing just starts to brown and crisp and most of the liquid has evaporated. Serve immediately.

tip: The mixture of wine and water is a fragrant bath in which the mushrooms steam, but you can substitute chicken, mushroom, or vegetable broth, or simply use water instead.

chapter eight

Holiday Feasts

The holidays are notorious for plenty of things, not the least of which is food. These feasts are the birthplaces of tradition and recipe lore. Holiday tables are also the ultimate stage for side dishes and perhaps the place where accompaniments can most influence the entire meal. The recipes in this chapter jump off from the classics and dare to dabble in originality. The bulk of the chapter offers recipes that call on ingredients associated with the major fall and winter holidays. Several recipes take a little extra time and energy on account of being contributions to special occasions, but they are well worth it.

green beans amandine with frizzled shallots
browned brussels with maple butter
roasted roots and fruits with cider butter
blood orange wild rice
turnip and rutabaga gratin
coconut curry braised butternut
sweet tart cranberry relish
hazelnut and roasted mushroom brioche pudding
farro with figs, kumquats, and walnuts

black-eyed peas and smoky greens
garlic chive corn pudding
caramelized onion and roasted garlic herb stuffing
legacy cornbread dressing
light and fluffy yukon gold potatoes
smoked cheddar mashed potatoes
sugar-glazed sweet potatoes
roasted butternut and spuds

green beans amandine with frizzled shallots

serves 6 to 8

Green beans amandine were a staple for a number of years on my mother's holiday menu. They were the green amidst all of the luxurious, decadent, earth-tone starches, and they always hit the table last, just like my mom, who'd slump down in her chair, finally, after a full morning of nonstop kitchen shuffling. The beans were always blanched and shocked ahead of time in a quick-get-them-out-of-the-way hustle. And then later, just as the masses were hunkering in around the long stretch of table laden with gustatory delights, my mother would find the beans when the carved bird moved to its center place and revealed them waiting patiently for their finishing touches. The glory of this side dish is that it can be prepped entirely ahead—the beans cooked, the nuts toasted, and the shallots fried—and then warmed and composed in the time it takes everyone to figure out their seats at the table.

Kosher salt

4 cups water

1½ pounds green beans, trimmed

¾ cup vegetable oil

1 large shallot, halved and sliced into thin rings

¼ cup unbleached all-purpose flour

⅛ teaspoon freshly ground black pepper (about 10 grinds)

2 tablespoons unsalted butter

⅓ cup slivered almonds, toasted (see Tip)

Sprinkle a heaping teaspoon of salt into the water and bring it to a boil in a large, wide sauté pan over medium-high heat. Add the green beans and return the water to a boil. Cook the beans for 8 to 10 minutes, until fork-tender but not overly soft. Drain the beans in a colander and then run cold water over them to prevent them from cooking further. Set aside.

Heat the oil in a medium saucepan over medium-high heat to 375°F on a deep-fry thermometer. Alternatively, check the readiness of the oil by putting the handle side of a wooden spoon down into the hot oil. If bubbles rush up around the handle, the oil is ready. (Stay tuned to the oil temperature. The shallots will burn quickly if the oil is too hot, but they'll be soggy if the temperature drops too low.)

alongside

SALT AND CIDER BRINED TURKEY ✦ WILD RICE STUFFED CHICKEN BREASTS ✦ PORK TENDERLOIN WITH GRAINY MUSTARD CREAM SAUCE ✦ LAMB CHOPS WITH MINT PESTO ✦ EGGPLANT AND MASCARPONE MANICOTTI

In a small mixing bowl, toss the shallot rings in the flour and then lift them out, shaking off excess flour (use a slotted spoon or scoop the shallots into a fine-mesh strainer and shake the flour back into the bowl). Gently drop one or two rings into the hot oil to test its readiness. They should sizzle in a frame of bubbles as they cook. If they don't, raise the heat a touch and test again after about 1 minute. When the oil is ready, add the rings and fry for about 2 minutes, until golden and crisp. Lift the shallots from the hot oil with a metal or wooden slotted spoon and transfer them to a plate lined with paper towels to drain off excess oil. Sprinkle immediately with salt and pepper.

Melt the butter in the large, wide sauté pan over medium-high heat. Add the cooked beans and toss to coat them with butter and to heat all the way through, 2 to 3 minutes. Sprinkle the nuts over the beans and toss to combine. Scrape the beans and almonds into a serving dish, season to taste with additional salt and pepper, and scatter the shallots on top just before serving.

tip: Nuts can go from perfectly toasted to flat-out burned very quickly, so if you set to the task of toasting, keep your eyes on the prize for the few minutes required, lest you end up scattering scorched nutty remains into the trash. To toast, try one of these methods:

STOVETOP: Add nuts to a large, dry sauté pan over medium heat. Toss the nuts every 30 seconds or so, either by scooping and flipping with a spoon or spatula or tossing the nuts in the pan, flicking the pan by its handle with your wrist slightly. Toast for about 5 minutes total, until the nuts are lightly browned and fragrant, like baking bread.

OVEN: Spread the nuts across the center of a baking sheet and put them in a preheated oven (350° to 400°F) for about 5 minutes, until lightly browned and fragrant. Toss the nuts halfway through for uniform toasting. Keep a close eye on them: If they burn, you'll know it by scent first!

browned brussels with maple butter serves 4 to 6

Some people are evangelical about their favorite foods, determined to sway skeptics to their way of thinking and tasting. I'm this way about Brussels sprouts. If any preparation of these cruciferous bulbs is going to spur converts, it's this one. The maple butter is reminiscent of caramel, creating a sweet cloak over savory sprouts that become deeply browned and crisp wherever their surfaces meet the hot pan. The maple butter can be made a day ahead, cooled completely, and refrigerated. Bring to room temperature while the sprouts roast and then scrape it into the hot sprouts to melt it.

1 tablespoon plus 1 tablespoon extra virgin olive oil

2 pounds Brussels sprouts, stem ends trimmed, outer leaves peeled, and halved (quartered if large)

½ teaspoon kosher salt

¼ teaspoon freshly ground black pepper

3 tablespoons unsalted butter

2 tablespoons pure maple syrup

Preheat the oven to 425°F. Brush 1 tablespoon of the olive oil on a baking sheet and transfer it to the hot oven for 5 minutes.

Meanwhile, in a large mixing bowl, toss the sprouts with the remaining tablespoon of olive oil and the salt and pepper. Pour the sprouts out onto the hot baking sheet and spread into a single layer. (Take the time to place each sprout cut side down for especially crisped and browned sprouts.)

Roast the Brussels sprouts for 15 to 20 minutes, until fork-tender and a dark brown crust forms on the sides exposed to the baking sheet.

While the sprouts roast, melt the butter in a small saucepan over medium-high heat, swirling it around as it becomes liquid. Keep a close eye on the butter as it starts to foam. If you look closely at the liquid butter as it cooks, you can see tiny specks of brown appear (which are the browning milk solids). Continue heating it until it starts to smell nutty and turns from off-white to golden to light brown. Immediately remove from the heat and stir in the maple syrup. Stir briskly as the mixture sizzles and spurts. Set aside in the saucepan until the Brussels finish roasting.

Remove the Brussels from the oven and transfer to a serving bowl. Drizzle the maple butter all over, tossing to coat evenly. Serve immediately.

alongside

BACON-CRUSTED ROAST TURKEY ✦ APPLE, PEAR, AND SAGE STUFFED PORK LOIN ROULADE
SLOW-COOKED CHICKEN AND CIPPOLINE ✦ HERB-STUFFED LEG OF LAMB ✦ BUTTERNUT RICOTTA LASAGNE

roasted roots and fruits with cider butter

serves 6 to 8

As soon as these vegetables and fruits hit the piping-hot pan you can smell their sugars caramelizing—well before their interiors soften and their colors deepen in the heat. This simple jumble coated in a nutty, sweet, buttery sauce brings complex and contrasting flavors to the table. The girth of carrots and parsnips varies greatly, so aim to cut the pieces to promote even roasting. If the stem end of a carrot is 1 inch in diameter but the tip is much thinner, cut the thicker piece in half, keep the skinnier end whole, and chop the whole lot into equal lengths.

2 pounds carrots, cut into 2-inch pieces

2 pounds parsnips, cut into 2-inch pieces

2 medium firm, crisp apples (about 1 pound, Golden Delicious, Fuji, Honeycrisp), cored, quartered, and cut into 1-inch chunks

1 pound pears (2 Bosc, Anjou, or Bartlett or 4 Seckel), cored, quartered (Seckels halved), and cut into 1-inch chunks

3 tablespoons extra virgin olive oil

½ teaspoon kosher salt

¼ teaspoon freshly ground black pepper (about 20 grinds)

4 tablespoons (½ stick) unsalted butter

Leaves from 2 sprigs fresh thyme

2 tablespoons apple cider

2 teaspoons pure maple syrup

1 teaspoon apple cider vinegar

Put 2 baking sheet pans on separate racks and preheat the oven to 425°F.

In a large mixing bowl, combine the carrots, parsnips, apples, and pears. Add the olive oil, salt, and pepper and toss several times with a large rubber spatula or clean hands to coat the roots and fruits with the oil and seasonings.

Distribute the veggies and fruit evenly between the hot baking sheet pans and arrange in a single layer. Roast for 15 minutes. Remove both pans, toss everything with a heatproof spatula, and return the pans to the oven, switching racks, for another 15 minutes, until the roots and fruits are tender when poked with a fork.

Meanwhile, melt the butter in a small sauté or saucepan over medium heat. Add the thyme leaves and let them float in the butter for about 5 minutes. Keep a close eye on the butter as the milk solids (the tiny white speckles) separate from the golden butter and slowly begin to brown. As soon as the solids turn to a toasty brown color, turn off the heat and whisk in the cider, syrup, and vinegar.

When the roots and fruits have finished roasting, spoon them into a serving bowl and drizzle the cider butter over them, tossing gently to coat. Adjust the seasoning to taste and serve immediately or cover and keep warm until ready to serve.

alongside

WHOLE ROASTED DUCK WITH ONIONS AND HERBS ✦ CORNISH HENS WITH PORT WINE SAUCE ✦ ROAST PORK WITH SAUSAGE POMEGRANATE STUFFING ✦ SPICY MUSTARD TURKEY BREAST ✦ CRANBERRY MARMALADE GLAZED HAM

blood orange wild rice *serves 6 to 8*

Here's a nice alternative to the usual famed starchy sides of the holidays. The dark brown or blackish long grains of wild rice cook into chewy, nutty-tasting forkfuls. Seasonal blood oranges and ruby studs of cranberry brighten the mix, and toasted pecans add crunch. Serve as a substitute for, or in addition to, traditional stuffing or potato accompaniments.

1½ cups wild rice

3¼ cups water

2 blood oranges (substitute Cara Cara or navel), segmented (see Tip) and cut into ¼-inch pieces

½ cup dried cranberries

½ cup toasted pecans (see Tip, page 181), chopped

½ cup loosely packed fresh curly parsley, chopped

3 tablespoons almond oil or mild oil like safflower or vegetable

2 tablespoons cider vinegar

1 tablespoon pomegranate molasses (see Pomegranate Molasses Vinaigrette, page 177) or honey

½ teaspoon kosher salt, plus more to taste

⅛ teaspoon freshly ground black pepper (about 10 grinds), plus more to taste

Combine the rice and water in a medium saucepan over high heat. Bring the water to a boil and then lower the heat to medium. Simmer the rice, uncovered, for 45 to 55 minutes, until most of the grains start to split and are tender with plenty of chew. If any water remains, drain the rice in a fine-mesh strainer.

Transfer the cooked rice to a serving bowl and add the orange segments and any juice, the cranberries, pecans, and parsley. Toss to combine.

In a small bowl, whisk together the oil, vinegar, and pomegranate molasses. Drizzle over the rice and add the salt and pepper. Stir to coat the rice with the vinaigrette. Adjust the seasoning to taste. Serve warm or at room temperature.

tip: Using a sharp paring knife, cut the peel from the top and bottom of the oranges and stand the oranges up on one end. Working from top to bottom all the way around, cut the pith away, exposing the fruit beneath. Now pick up the orange in your palm and hold it over a bowl to collect juice as you cut the orange segments free from the membranes (the thin white skin that separates the orange pieces). Squeeze the remaining membrane for more juice before discarding it.

alongside

MULTIGRAIN SOURDOUGH AND GOAT CHEESE STUFFED PORTOBELLOS ✦ CINNAMON PEPPER PORK TENDERLOIN
TURKEY ROULADE WITH CORNBREAD STUFFING ✦ COQ AU VIN ✦ VEAL MEDALLIONS IN WHITE WINE SAUCE

Turnips for One

Motherhood is a gift and a thief. It dumps forth perpetual joy and demands silent selfless surrender at every turn. This dawned on me over a bowl of mashed turnips.

For most of my life, my parents have hosted the majority of holiday feasts for our extended family at their house. My mother juggles the hostess pressures as she hustles around the kitchen for hours, managing a dizzying turnstile of dishes in and out of the fridge and the oven, from stovetop to tabletop. She updates a mental checklist, of which no one has a copy, making sure the meal accounts for guest contributions, everyone else's favorites, weird quirks of company, persnickety palates of kids, and unwavering traditions. It's an exhausting endeavor.

One holiday, decades ago, I was circling the kitchen like a vulture, surveying the spread as it simmered, sautéed, baked, and browned. There was a small saucepan on the back burner in the shadows of everything else. The smell of its contents made me wrinkle my nose.

"What's this?" I prodded my mother, who had her head stuffed in the belly of the fridge, searching for something. She looked over for a split second and resumed her position.

"Turnips," she responded plainly.

"For what?" I retorted, probably with a petulant tone of disgust. I certainly didn't want those, and I couldn't imagine who would.

"For me," she said, "because I like them."

The turnips, mashed with butter, salt, and pepper, made it to the table in a little bowl that passed on through the hands of no takers until they landed near my mother. My brother and I snorted exaggerated revulsion at those stinky smashed roots over heaping plates of all the things we liked. She took a scoop of the soft, sweet, and pungent pulp, content not to share with anyone else. Those turnips made it to the table year after year. I didn't get why she bothered with them if no one else wanted any.

The realization finally seeped into me from the perspective of an adult. My mother's inclusion of that singular, simple recipe was her minimalist reward for offering an enormous meal for everyone else to enjoy. Probably beyond that, it was an inconspicuous override of all the days prior when she kowtowed to us age-appropriately ungrateful kids and gave up her own preferences in the name of temporary sanity. I can grasp it now even more when my own daughter pushes away an untouched plate of food that I arranged for her, or whines disapproval, or forgets her please and thank you.

Every mother deserves her bowl of turnips.

turnip and rutabaga gratin serves 6 to 8

These bulbs are no more homely in appearance than an average potato, but their orbed shapes and peculiar names continuously face turned-up noses. Root vegetable lovers are missing out on the duality of their sweetness and intensity in writing them off without a fair trial. Here the richness of the cream and cheese mellow the pungent edge of the turnips and rutabagas as everything bakes into a sturdy, sliceable round that is particularly perfect with roasts.

2 pounds small to medium turnips and rutabagas combined

1½ cups half-and-half

1 tablespoon prepared horseradish

1 clove garlic, minced

2 teaspoons minced fresh sage (4 or 5 leaves)

¼ teaspoon fresh thyme leaves (about 1 sprig)

1 teaspoon kosher salt

½ teaspoon freshly ground black pepper (about 35 grinds)

1½ cups plus ½ cup grated Gruyère cheese (about 6 ounces)

Preheat the oven to 375°F. Butter a 9-inch pie plate with 2-inch-high sides.

Peel the turnips and rutabaga and then slice both ⅛ inch thick. This is the perfect job for a mandoline if you don't trust your own hand and knife skills.

Measure the half-and-half in a spouted measuring cup and then whisk in the horseradish, garlic, sage, thyme, salt, and pepper.

Build the gratin. Arrange a spiral of alternating slices of turnip and rutabaga in the pie plate in one layer. Whisk the half-and-half to distribute the herbs, spices, and seasonings and then pour or spoon about ¼ cup over the layer. Sprinkle on about ⅓ cup of the 1½ cups cheese.

Repeat the layering process until you've used all of the turnip and rutabaga. Be sure to whisk the half-and-half each time or the flavoring ingredients will settle to the bottom.

Pour the last of the half-and-half over the assembled gratin and sprinkle the remaining ½ cup cheese across the top. Cover tightly with aluminum foil and set the pie plate on a baking sheet. Bake for 30 minutes. Remove the foil and bake for 45 minutes more, until the cheese becomes a light brown crust over the top and the turnips and rutabaga are tender when poked with a fork. Let the gratin rest for at least 20 minutes before slicing.

alongside

GARLIC PRIME RIB WITH BÉARNAISE SAUCE ✦ FILET MIGNON WITH RED WINE REDUCTION
SAUTÉED VEAL MEDALLIONS WITH APPLES AND ONIONS ✦ SLOW-ROASTED LAMB SHOULDER
CRANBERRY MUSHROOM STUFFED TURKEY BREAST ROULADE

coconut curry braised butternut serves 6 to 8

Big chunks of sweet butternut squash soften in a simmer and sauna of aromatic, mildly spicy coconut milk. Bright green pearls of peas stud the mixture with texture and color, and onions sweated in coconut oil thread savory notes through steaming spoonfuls of the thick stewlike combo. This is an excellent accompaniment to hefty meats, and it can also bulk up and round out meatless meals.

1 tablespoon coconut oil or vegetable oil

1 large yellow onion, halved and sliced into ½-inch-thick half-moons

3 cloves garlic, thinly sliced

1 cup fresh or frozen peas

1¾ cups (one 13.5-ounce can) coconut milk (light or regular)

2 teaspoons red curry powder or your favorite blend

½ teaspoon ground cumin

¼ teaspoon cayenne (optional if using hot curry powder)

1 large butternut squash (about 3 pounds), peeled, seeded, and cut into 1½-inch cubes (about 7 cups or 2¼ pounds precut store-bought)

Kosher salt and freshly black ground pepper

Preheat the oven to 400°F.

Heat the oil in a 5½-quart Dutch oven or large, wide ovenproof saucepan over medium-high heat. Add the onion and cook, stirring frequently, for 10 minutes, until softened and just beginning to turn blond and brown around the edges. Stir in the garlic and sauté for 30 seconds.

Add the peas and sauté for 2 minutes (or until thawed if using frozen peas). Pour in the coconut milk, sprinkle in the curry powder, cumin, and cayenne, and stir to combine.

Bring the liquid to a boil and add the squash. Stir to coat the squash with the seasoned coconut milk and combine with the onion and peas. Return the liquid to a boil, cover the pot, and transfer to the oven to bake for 30 to 40 minutes, until the squash is fork-tender but holds it shape when stirred gently. Season to taste with the salt and pepper. Serve immediately.

alongside

CORIANDER-CRUSTED ROASTED LEG OF LAMB ✦ SPICED ORANGE BRAISED DUCK LEG
CILANTRO CHICKPEAS AND BASMATI RICE ✦ BRAISED TURKEY LEG OR THIGHS WITH FRESH SCALLIONS
LENTILS WITH CARROTS AND YOGURT

sweet tart cranberry relish

In a crowd of earth-toned starches and proteins that dominate a holiday table, this brightly colored and intensely flavored blend of fruit will balance dinner plates with one heaping spoonful. Serve it chilled as a refreshing palate cleanser or at room temperature to complement warm turkey slices. It makes an excellent spread for requisite leftovers sandwiches.

. . . .

2 cups (8 ounces) fresh cranberries

2 small blood oranges or 1 medium navel orange, quartered and seeded

2 tablespoons pomegranate molasses (see Pomegranate Molasses Vinaigrette, page 77)

¼ cup sugar

1 Granny Smith apple, cored and grated (1 cup)

Combine the cranberries, oranges, pomegranate molasses, and sugar in a food processor and process until the fruit is finely chopped, about 30 seconds. Scrape the mixture into a medium mixing bowl and stir in the grated apple.

Serve immediately or refrigerate for up to 1 week.

alongside

ROASTED SAGE AND THYME TURKEY WITH GIBLET GRAVY ✦ CORNBREAD DRESSING STUFFED PORK LOIN
WILD MUSHROOM AND BRIE TART ✦ CHICKEN POTPIE WITH BISCUIT TOPPING
MAPLE BAKED HAM ✦ SEARED SALT AND PEPPER DUCK BREAST

hazelnut and roasted mushroom brioche pudding serves 8 to 10

Prepared and baked like a bread pudding, this rich, luxurious alternative to typical holiday stuffing gets sliced and served rather than scooped. It's wonderful straight out of the oven, but, like many bread puddings, it doesn't suffer from being made ahead and reheated. See the Tip for time-conscious make-ahead suggestions.

. . . .

2 pounds mixed mushrooms (portobello, cremini, white button, shiitake, oyster)

2 medium leeks, white and very light green parts only, sliced in half lengthwise and then into ¼-inch-thick half-moons (about 3 cups)

⅓ cup safflower or vegetable oil

1 teaspoon kosher salt

¼ teaspoon freshly ground black pepper (about 20 grinds)

8 cups 1½-inch cubes brioche bread (about 12 ounces bread)

1 cup hazelnuts

4 large eggs

3 cups half-and-half or a combination of cream and milk

½ teaspoon minced fresh rosemary

½ teaspoon minced fresh thyme leaves

Preheat the oven to 425°F and place 2 baking sheets on separate racks while it warms. Butter the inside of a 9½ by 5½-inch loaf pan and set aside.

Trim the mushrooms (plucking stems and scraping the gills from portobellos). Quarter the portobellos and cut them into ½-inch pieces. Quarter or halve the cremini, white button, and shiitake and chop the oyster mushrooms into bite-sized pieces.

Combine all of the mushrooms and the leeks in a large mixing bowl. Drizzle with the oil and sprinkle with half of the salt and pepper. Toss several times to coat the mushrooms with oil.

Take the hot baking sheets out of the oven and spill the mushrooms and leeks out evenly between them in single layers. Roast for 8 minutes. Toss them with a spatula, rotate the pans, moving the one on the top rack to the bottom and vice versa, and then continue to roast for 8 minutes, until the mushrooms are soft and tender and the leeks are starting to brown. Scrape everything into a large mixing bowl and set aside. Wipe the baking sheets clean with a dry paper towel after they cool a little.

Lower the oven temperature to 375°F. Spread the bread cubes across one of the baking sheet pans and put the hazelnuts in the center of the other. Bake both for 15 minutes, keeping a close eye on the hazelnuts so they don't burn. The bread should be assertively crunchy and golden brown. Take both out of the oven. Let the bread cubes cool completely.

alongside

ROASTED TURKEY WITH FENNEL, APPLE, AND POMEGRANATE GLAZE ✦ SLICED ROAST BEEF AU JUS
MAPLE MOLASSES CROWN ROAST OF PORK ✦ ROSEMARY AND GARLIC LEG OF LAMB

Dump the hazelnuts onto a clean kitchen towel. Fold up the sides and rub the hazelnuts until the skins come off. Pick out the skinless nuts and continue rubbing until the rest are bare. Discard the skins. Chop the roasted nuts coarsely. Reserve ¼ cup for topping and add the rest to the bowl with the roasted mushrooms and leeks. Add the cooled bread cubes and fold everything together.

Beat the eggs together with the half-and-half in a large spouted measuring cup or a medium bowl. Stir in the rosemary, thyme, and the remaining ½ teaspoon of salt and ⅛ teaspoon of pepper. Spoon about a quarter of the mushroom mixture into the loaf pan and drizzle a quarter of the egg mixture on top. Continue building these layers, making sure to reserve enough liquid to pour over the last layer. Press down on the assembled pudding with the rubber spatula to help the liquid soak into the bread. Sprinkle the ¼ cup reserved hazelnuts over the top. Let the mixture sit for 15 minutes.

Put the loaf pan on a baking sheet and transfer to the oven. Bake for 50 to 60 minutes, until the top is crisp and browned, the center of the pudding doesn't wobble much when you nudge it, and there are no traces of liquid bubbling up around the sides. Take it out of the oven and let it rest for at least 15 minutes.

Cut the pudding into thick slices in the pan or carefully invert the pudding onto a serving plate, repositioning it top side up again, and slice at the table.

The pudding can be made a day or two ahead. Bake as instructed and carefully invert the pudding onto a cooling rack to cool completely. Wrap tightly in aluminum foil and refrigerate. Reheat, wrapped in the foil in a 350°F oven for 20 minutes, until warm through the center of the loaf.

tip: You can make parts of the recipe ahead and assemble and bake just before serving. Roast the mushrooms and leeks and toast the bread and nuts a day ahead. Refrigerate the mushrooms and leeks in an airtight container and bring to room temperature before proceeding with the recipe. Store the bread cubes and nuts separately at room temperature in resealable plastic bags. Continue with the rest of the recipe the next day.

tip: Leeks collect dirt in their tight layers, so wash them well before using. After cutting into half-moons as instructed, float the leeks in a large bowl of cold water. Agitate the water and separate the layers to free dirt from the folds. The sediment will settle at the bottom of the bowl, so skim the surface to lift out the cleaned leeks rather than draining them.

farro with figs, kumquats, and walnuts serves 4 to 6

Tart, tangy kumquat; sweet, chewy figs; and crunchy, rich walnuts are ornaments of texture and flavor in this dish of grains. The farro soaks up the bright flavors of the kumquat puree and offers a lighter note to a table full of heavier holiday favorites.

4 ounces whole dried Mission figs, stems trimmed (about 15 figs)

½ cup very hot water, plus 1½ cups cooler water

1 cup farro (semipearled or presoaked if unhulled)

1 cup plus 1 cup kumquats

3 tablespoons walnut or extra virgin olive oil

2 tablespoons white balsamic or white wine vinegar

1 tablespoon honey

1 scallion, green and white parts thinly sliced separately

½ teaspoon kosher salt

¼ teaspoon freshly ground black pepper (about 20 grinds)

1 cup toasted walnut halves (see Tip, page 181), chopped

alongside

✦ ORANGE AND FENNEL STUFFED ROAST TURKEY
✦ CROWN ROAST OF PORK WITH FIG SAUCE
✦ LEG OF LAMB WITH POMEGRANATE
✦ BLOOD ORANGE BRAISED WHOLE CHICKEN
✦ PEPPERCORN BEEF TENDERLOIN

Place the figs in a medium bowl and cover with the ½ cup of very hot water. Soak the figs for 5 minutes.

Pour the 1½ cups cooler water into a medium saucepan. Lift the figs out of the soaking water with a slotted spoon and set them aside on a cutting board. Pour the fig water into the saucepan with the rest of the water and stir in the farro. Bring the water and farro to a boil over medium-high heat, then decrease the heat to medium-low and simmer, partially covered, for 20 minutes, until the farro is tender with some chew.

While the farro cooks, quarter the figs and add them to a medium mixing bowl or serving dish. Slice 1 cup of the kumquats into ¼-inch rounds, discarding seeds as you discover them. Add the slices to the figs.

Cut the remaining 1 cup of kumquats in half lengthwise, plucking out and discarding the seeds. Add the kumquats to a blender with the olive oil, vinegar, honey, scallion, salt, and pepper. Puree until smooth, stopping to scrape down the sides of the blender once or twice.

When the farro is done, drain any remaining water from the grains using a mesh strainer or small-holed colander. Add the hot farro to the bowl with the figs and kumquats. Pour the kumquat puree in the blender over the farro and toss to coat everything very well. Sprinkle the walnuts into the bowl and toss again to combine. Serve immediately.

tip: Farro is available as a whole grain or semipearled, which means it is refined in such a way that makes its cooking time quicker at the expense of some of the nutrients that disappear with part of the tough bran. Semipearled farro is tender and ready to eat after simmering for 20 to 25 minutes. If you opt to honor its whole grain lineage, be sure to soak unrefined grains overnight and plan for much longer cooking times, typically 30 to 45 minutes, in recipes.

black-eyed peas and smoky greens   serves 8 to 10

Wide, oversized, and sturdy, collard leaves could double as some sort of tropical handheld fan but are much more scrumptious when braised low and slow into a rich, dark, and silky soft "mess o' greens." Here they melt into a soft tangle with smoky, warm chorizo and buttery black-eyed peas, which are thought to bring luck to life if eaten on the eve of a new year. Serve with a hot, crisp slice of Heritage Cornbread (page 45).

1 tablespoon vegetable oil

8 ounces firm smoked chorizo (not the softer fresh variety), halved and cut into ½-inch slices

1 medium yellow onion, quartered and thinly sliced

1½ pounds collard greens

3 cloves garlic, thinly sliced

¼ cup plus 1¾ cup chicken stock (homemade or low-sodium store-bought), plus more as needed

3 cups cooked black-eyed peas or 2 (15-ounce) cans, drained and rinsed

1 tablespoon malt vinegar

½ teaspoon kosher salt

¼ teaspoon freshly ground black pepper (about 20 grinds)

½ teaspoon smoked paprika

Heat the oil in a large deep sauté pan over medium heat. Add the chorizo and cook for 5 minutes, stirring every minute or so while the sausage releases some of its fat and browns a little. Add the onion and cook with the chorizo for 10 minutes, until soft.

Meanwhile, cut the tough stems from the collard greens and wash the leaves thoroughly in several changes of cold water. Tear the clean leaves into pieces about 2 inches wide.

Add the garlic to the chorizo and onion and sauté for 30 seconds. Pour in ¼ cup of the stock and scrape the brown bits from the bottom of the pan as the liquid sizzles and cooks off. Add the collards in small batches, giving each pile of leaves a minute or two to wilt a bit. Once all of the leaves have shrunk down enough to make way for more ingredients (about 5 minutes' worth of slow additions of the leaves), add the remaining 1¾ cups of stock, the black-eyed peas, vinegar, salt, pepper, and paprika and stir well to combine.

Bring the liquid to a boil and then lower the heat to medium-low. Simmer until the liquid is nearly gone and the collard greens are very tender, about 45 minutes. If the starch from the beans thickens things too much, add ¼ to ½ cup more stock or water to loosen to desired consistency. Transfer to a large bowl and serve immediately.

alongside

BRINED AND BAKED FRESH HAM ✦ DEEP-FRIED TURKEY ✦ GARLIC BUTTERMILK BREADED PORK CHOPS
SLOW-ROASTED BARBECUE SPARERIBS ✦ SUGAR AND SPICE RUBBED BEEF BRISKET

garlic chive corn pudding serves 8 to 10

Soft, slightly sweet, and mostly savory, this warm pudding fits perfectly on a holiday buffet table. If you managed to freeze fresh summer corn kernels, use them here. Otherwise thawed frozen corn works well. The brightness of chives and sharp flavor of garlic add depth to the dish, but experiment with flavors you favor too. A variety of herbs (sage and thyme or fresh summer basil when the season permits), a sprinkle of crunchy bacon, or shreds of salty ham are excellent options. Add a tablespoon or two of sugar if you like your corn pudding especially sweet.

. . . .

1 teaspoon unsalted butter for the baking dish

3½ cups plus 1½ cups fresh or thawed frozen corn kernels (about 5 medium ears or 26 ounces frozen)

4 large eggs

1½ cups half-and-half

¼ cup sugar

2 cloves garlic

2 tablespoons unbleached all-purpose flour

1½ teaspoons baking powder

1 teaspoon kosher salt

¼ teaspoon freshly ground black pepper (about 20 grinds)

¼ cup chopped fresh chives or scallion

Preheat the oven to 375°F. Butter an 8-inch square baking dish with 1 teaspoon of butter.

Reserve 1½ cups of the corn and put the rest in a blender along with the eggs, half and half, sugar, garlic, flour, baking powder, salt, and pepper. Blend until smooth, about 30 seconds. Add the reserved 3½ cups corn and the chives and stir them into the blended mixture.

Pour the mixture into the baking dish and set the dish on top of a baking sheet. Bake for 1 hour and 15 minutes, until the top is golden brown and the center is set and barely jiggles when tapped with your fingertips. Let the pudding sit for about 15 minutes and then scoop out servings with a large spoon.

alongside

APPLE, ONION, AND THYME STUFFED ROAST TURKEY ✦ CIDER-BASTED CROWN ROAST OF PORK
SAUSAGE AND PEAR PORK ROULADE ✦ SPIRAL-SLICED BAKED HAM
BROILED LEMON HERB HADDOCK ✦ CRISP BUTTER ROAST CHICKEN AND GRAVY

caramelized onion and roasted garlic herb stuffing serves 6 to 8

Here is the taste most Americans imagine when they daydream about a hot scoop of classic Thanksgiving stuffing. This from-scratch version layers complex flavors of individual ingredients—sweet roasted garlic and caramelized onions, fresh herbs, and rich butter—and bakes them into sturdy sourdough bread cubes that soften but keep their shape after soaking in savory stock. Roasting the garlic and caramelizing the onions can't be rushed, so plan ahead to tackle this recipe with enough time to make it to Grandma's and consider employing the make-ahead tips below to streamline your cooking.

Butter or oil for the baking dish

2 heads of garlic

1 tablespoon extra virgin olive oil

1 tablespoon water

6 tablespoons plus 2 tablespoons (1 stick) unsalted butter

2 large onions (about 1½ pounds), yellow, Vidalia, or white, halved and thinly sliced

10 cups ½-inch cubed sourdough bread (about a 14-ounce bakery loaf, not sliced, packaged sandwich bread)

2 large stalks celery, finely chopped (about 1 cup)

1 tablespoon minced fresh sage (about 6 large leaves)

1½ teaspoons minced fresh rosemary (about 1 sprig)

1 teaspoon minced fresh thyme leaves (2 large sprigs)

2 cups turkey or chicken stock or vegetable broth (homemade or low-sodium store-bought)

Preheat the oven to 450°F. Butter or oil a 2½-quart casserole dish or a 9-inch baking dish.

Slice the heads of garlic in half through the equator. Cut a large piece of aluminum foil and set the 4 halves in the center of it. Drizzle the olive oil and water over the garlic. Pull the sides of the foil up toward the center and fold the ends inward to make a pouch around the garlic. Put the pouch on a baking sheet and into the oven to roast for 45 minutes.

Melt 2 tablespoons of the butter in a large deep sauté pan over medium heat. Add the onions and stir to coat them in the butter. Cook them for 45 minutes, stirring every 3 or 4 minutes, until they are a deep golden brown.

Meanwhile, spread the bread cubes out on a baking sheet pan and toast them on another rack in the oven for 10 minutes, until they are crunchy and just starting to brown. Remove them and let them cool completely.

Remove the garlic from the oven and very carefully open the pouch (hot steam will come up out of the pouch). Stick a paring knife into one of the cloves to be sure it is completely soft. Set aside to cool. Turn the oven down to 350°F.

alongside

BUTTER AND OLIVE OIL BASTED TURKEY (WHOLE OR BONE-IN BREAST)
GARLIC STUDDED ROAST PORK LOIN ✦ CLASSIC ROAST CHICKEN WITH CARROTS, ONIONS, AND CELERY
BAKED HERB-CRUSTED COD ✦ SLICED CROCK POT PORK SHOULDER WITH CIDER SAUCE

Once the onions are caramelized, add the remaining 6 tablespoons of butter to the pan and melt it. Stir in the celery and sweat the pieces for 5 to 7 minutes, until the celery just starts to soften. Add the sage, rosemary, and thyme and stir to combine everything well. Turn off the heat. Pop the garlic cloves out of their skins, or use a paring knife to scoop them out, and add them to the pan.

Dump the toasted, cooled bread cubes into the pan (if your pan isn't big enough to contain everything, transfer to a large mixing bowl). Fold the bread in with the rest of the ingredients. Drizzle the stock over the bread cubes 1 cup at a time, folding to moisten all the bread. Scrape everything into the buttered casserole dish and bake for 45 minutes, until the top is crisp and the stuffing is hot all the way through. Serve immediately.

tip: To make part of this recipe ahead, prepare everything up to adding the bread to the onion mixture. Store the toasted bread in a resealable plastic bag or airtight container and refrigerate the onion mixture (including the butter, celery, herbs, and roasted garlic). When you are ready to assemble the stuffing, warm the onion mixture in the same large deep sauté pan over medium heat and proceed with the recipe.

legacy cornbread dressing serves 8 to 10

My husband's grandfather Riley Fell knew his way around the kitchen and ran it according to his plans and preferences. For years he insisted on oyster dressing for holiday suppers, until finally Milly, his wife and the mother of their ten children, burst forth with the news that she hated that oyster dressing and wouldn't eat it anymore. In a rare moment of surrender, Riley changed course and made cornbread dressing, with Milly's cornbread ever after. Before he died, Riley dictated his intensely savory recipe to their daughter Grace so a trademark bit of them both joins the family at the Thanksgiving and Christmas table every year. Make Milly's cornbread a day ahead, cool completely, cut it, and leave it out to dry and stale for several hours or overnight.

½ pound pork breakfast sausage (about 4 links)

1 cup ¼-inch pieces onion (½ medium Vidalia onion or large yellow onion)

1 cup ¼-inch pieces celery (about 2 large stalks)

4 cloves garlic, minced (about 2 tablespoons)

1 teaspoon chopped fresh sage leaves (5 leaves)

1 teaspoon chopped fresh marjoram (about 10 leaves)

1 teaspoon chopped fresh thyme leaves (about 5 sprigs)

¼ teaspoon kosher salt

¼ teaspoon cayenne

1 loaf Heritage Cornbread (page 45), cut into 1-inch cubes and staled overnight

2 cups chicken stock (homemade or low-sodium store-bought) or homemade giblet stock

2 cups ¼-inch cubed unpeeled Rome apple (2 medium apples)

1 teaspoon bacon grease, butter, or oil for the baking dish ➡

alongside

APPLE AND HERB STUFFED ROAST TURKEY ✦ BAKED HONEY HAM ✦ OVEN-FRIED BUTTERMILK HERB CHICKEN
SAGE AND THYME RUBBED PORK LOIN ✦ FRIED CATFISH FILETS

Preheat the oven to 350°F.

Heat a large deep sauté pan or cast-iron skillet over medium heat. Push the sausage out of the casings and discard the casings. Break the sausage into bits with your fingertips and add them to the hot pan. Cook for 5 minutes, stirring with a wooden spoon and breaking the sausage into smaller bits as it cooks and just starts to brown.

Add the onion and celery to the sausage in the pan. Stir to coat them in the fat rendered from the sausage. Scrape up any browned bits from the bottom of the pan as the onion and celery release their water. Cook for 5 minutes as they soften. Add the garlic and decrease the heat to medium-low. Sweat the vegetables and garlic in the pan until softened and very fragrant, about 5 minutes more.

Turn off the heat. Add the herbs, salt, and cayenne and stir to incorporate them into the rest of the ingredients. If your pan is big enough to accommodate the broken cornbread bits and crumbs, add them now. Otherwise, put them in a large mixing bowl and scrape the sausage mixture into it. Gently fold it all together using a big spatula or wooden spoon. Drizzle the chicken stock over everything, stirring halfway through to be sure of even distribution. The cornbread should be moistened, not drenched. Add the apple chunks and fold them in.

Paint a 2½-quart oval casserole dish with the grease, butter, or oil. Scrape the cornbread mixture into it and even it out with a spatula or your hands. Cover the dish with aluminum foil and bake until hot all the way through, about 30 to 40 minutes.

tip: If you're making this for a holiday meal and have to consider cooking times and oven space, you can bake the dressing at whatever temperature your oven is set to for roasting meat (i.e., the turkey). Adjust the total time up or down accordingly. If you cook your turkey low and slow, at 325°F or less, then add 20 to 30 minutes to the total baking time for the cornbread. If your oven is set above 350°F for other dishes, bake the dressing for fewer minutes, checking to be sure it doesn't dry out in the higher temps. You can also work through the first few steps a day ahead, refrigerating until ready to proceed. Add the cornbread, stock, and apples just before baking.

light and fluffy yukon gold potatoes serves 6 to 8

Pale-yellow-skinned Yukon Golds are inherently buttery, making them a famed favorite in the spuds category. Passing cooked chunks through a basic, inexpensive handheld ricer maximizes their texture, which is less starchy than their russet brethren, and makes a soft, dry pile that simply stirs into creamy, smooth mounds. If your kitchen lacks a ricer, you can mash the potatoes by hand or whip with a handheld mixer, though the results won't be quite as fluffy.

- 3 pounds Yukon Gold potatoes, peeled and cut into relatively uniform chunks, about 1 inch thick
- 1 teaspoon plus ½ teaspoon kosher salt, plus more to taste
- ½ cup whole milk, half-and-half, or heavy cream
- 4 tablespoons (½ stick) unsalted butter
- ¼ teaspoon freshly ground black pepper (about 20 grinds), plus more to taste

alongside

- ✦ SLOW-ROASTED TURKEY WITH GRAVY
- ✦ LEMON THYME BAKED CHICKEN
- ✦ ROSEMARY-CRUSTED RACK OF LAMB
- ✦ BEEF BOURGUIGNONNE
- ✦ FILET MIGNON WITH BORDELAISE SAUCE

Put the potatoes in a large saucepan (at least 3 quarts) and fill to cover by an inch with cold water. Salt the water as you would if you were cooking pasta (about 1 teaspoon). Cover the pot and bring the water to a boil over high heat. When the water boils, turn the heat down to medium, uncover the pot, and simmer the potatoes for 15 minutes, until they are tender and start to break apart when poked with a knife or fork.

Drain the potatoes in a large colander and shake out the excess water.

Return the pot to the stovetop over low heat and add the milk and butter. Pile about ½ cup of potato chunks (more if you're using a larger ricer) into the ricer. Squeeze the potatoes through the ricer and into the pot with the milk and butter. Continue in batches until all of the potatoes have been riced. Stir the potatoes into the milk and butter until smooth and fluffy. Season with the remaining ½ teaspoon salt and the pepper, plus more to taste. Transfer to a serving bowl and serve immediately.

Mashed Potatoes: Standards and Variations

Mashed potatoes have everyone duped. They look so benign there in the bowl, pale and homely, wearing an understated gloss of melted butter. If you described them to people who'd never heard of them before, they'd wonder why anyone would bother with something that sounds so unremarkable: boiled, pulverized potatoes made soft by some milk or cream. Big deal.

But I've seen people nearly come to blows over mashed potatoes. In college, a couple of friends almost ended their relationship over a disagreement about how to season, when to add butter, and which way to mash (granted, this may have been a sign that each was destined to marry someone else, which they both did). I've read reviews of restaurants in which the critic hung the kitchen out to dry on account of lousy mashed potatoes. And most years at Thanksgiving, my sister-in-law and I start circling the pot of them, still on the stove, dueling forks in hand before anyone else has a go at them. I try to exercise some restraint when serving myself at the table, but I've always got one eye on the last serving . . . and so does she.

One of the ultimate comfort foods, mashed potatoes fuel contention because they are so tied to emotion, memories, and maybe a little bit of idealism. Despite their being a blank canvas for creative riffing, an informal poll of mashed potato lovers revealed that most folks converge as traditionalists when it comes to this classic. Potatoes, milk or cream, plenty of butter, salt and pepper make up the limited list of ingredients. But there are still countless variables that will set each version of the same basic recipe apart. Maybe you love yours thick and heavy, hand-mashed with some bumps and lumps left to remind you of the spuds' beginnings. I like mine light and fluffy after they get sent through a ricer and then whipped into hot milk. The guy next to me might prefer his strewn with heavy cream and butter and whirred into a creamy mass by the beaters of an electric hand mixer.

Personal preference makes the final decision. Here are some key factors that have a big impact on a seemingly simple but rather complex recipe.

Cooking Method

Boiling is the most common first step for making mashed potatoes. You can boil peeled or unpeeled potatoes, in water, stock or broth (chicken or vegetable) for extra flavor, or milk. Whatever the liquid of choice, nailing the cooking time makes all the difference. Boil the potatoes too long and your mash will be waterlogged and gluey. Undercook them and they will be unpleasantly lumpy with starchy bumps of vaguely raw potato. The times suggested in the recipes that follow consistently yield tender potatoes just right for mashing.

Baking whole, unpeeled potatoes is a good way to get a fluffy mash because the cooked flesh is dry and harder to make a wet mess of. But it's important that the potatoes bake tender all the way through and that they are peeled and mashed while still warm. This approach can be time consuming and slightly more arduous but yields a mash with great flavor and texture.

Mashing Method

Most of our grandmothers wouldn't make much of this category. They'd hand us their well-worn metal zigzag masher with its wooden handle and tell us to go to work until the lumps are gone and the potatoes are smooth and soft. All of us would be foolish to argue with any of them since it's true that hand-mashing yields good old-fashioned mashed potatoes that are thick and sturdy but still downy and scoopable. Of course, if you like a few chunks of potatoes in your mash, you can stop short of mashing until uniformly smooth and give them more of the "smashed" treatment, which yields a mix of textures.

If you're a fan of exceptionally light and fluffy spuds, though, a ricer or a food mill can't be beat. Chunks of cooked potatoes pass through tiny holes and pile high in skinny threads that turn velvety with a simple stir.

Electric beaters or a combination of the paddle and whisk attachments on a stand mixer will spin spuds soft, too. But the blades of a food processor or blender will only turn potatoes gluey as they overwork the starches in an instant. Strike those from your potato-mashing repertoire.

Regardless of which tool you use, make sure the liquid (milk, cream, or stock), butter, and creaming ingredients like sour cream or crème fraîche are either warm, melted, or at room temperature. Cold add-ins prompt seizing and gluey potato starches.

Potato Variety

Russet potatoes tend to dominate the top spot as the pick for mashed potatoes. Their dry flesh takes to the cooking methods and the repeated pummeling that turns them soft and smooth. Plus their distinct earthy flavor has staked its claim in taste memories that make us long for more of what we've always known.

Second to Russets are Yukon Golds, which boast an entirely different taste profile. Their waxier flesh is sweeter and slightly more buttery. They respond especially well to ricing, transforming into airy pale yellow spoonfuls of mashed potatoes.

Other varieties, like all-purpose white potatoes, small new potatoes, red potatoes, and sweet potatoes work too. Those with thin skins are the best for smashing into more textured, less smooth piles of skin-on potatoes.

Flavoring Agents

You can infuse flavor into mashed potatoes at various points in the cooking process. Add sprigs of fresh herbs, chunks of onions, or whole cloves of garlic to the cooking liquid and then fish out those solids to discard before mashing the potatoes. Or simmer milk with any of those aromatics and strain them out before mashing the milk in with the cooked potatoes.

Suggested Flavoring Ingredients

Milk, cream, butter (higher fat content makes for richer potatoes)	Truffle
	Chives
	Scallions
	Lemon zest
Chicken stock, vegetable or mushroom broth (in lieu of dairy)	Bacon
	Cream cheese
	Crème fraîche
Rosemary	Parmesan
Thyme	Ricotta
Sage	Mascarpone
Garlic	Cheddar
Ginger	Smoked Gouda
Lemongrass	Shallots
Cinnamon (for sweet potatoes)	Buttermilk
	Brown butter
Dill	Flavored oil (see chart on page 89 for ideas)
Horseradish	

Reheating

Mashed potatoes are loveliest when they go directly from the pot to the table. But in the hustle of holiday feast prep, follow these steps to make ahead and reheat. Make the potatoes as directed. When they are still warm, scoop them into a buttered casserole or soufflé dish, from which you will ultimately serve them. Let them cool to room temperature, then cover and refrigerate them. Take them out of the refrigerator 30 to 60 minutes before reheating. Cover the dish with foil in a 350°F warm oven for 30 minutes, or until hot through the center.

smoked cheddar mashed potatoes serves 6 to 8

These potatoes are sturdy from a good old-fashioned hand-mashing and smoldering with smoky flavor behind the natural creamy earthiness of russets. A pile of them, smoothed by the simple cheese sauce, stands up to chunks of meat and thick, rich sauces and gravies. Substitute your favorite cheese if you prefer.

3 pounds russet potatoes, peeled and cut into relatively uniform chunks, about 1 inch thick

½ teaspoon plus ½ teaspoon kosher salt, plus more to taste

¾ cup whole milk

2 tablespoons unsalted butter

½ cup plus ½ cup grated smoked Cheddar cheese (about 4 ounces)

3 tablespoons crème fraîche or sour cream

¼ teaspoon freshly ground black pepper (about 20 grinds), plus more to taste

Put the potatoes in a large saucepan (at least 3 quarts) and fill to cover by an inch with cold water. Add ½ teaspoon of the salt. Cover the pot and bring the water to a boil over high heat. When the water boils, turn the heat down to medium, uncover the pot, and simmer the potatoes for 15 to 20 minutes, until they are tender and break apart when poked with a knife or fork.

While the potatoes cook, combine the milk and butter in a small saucepan over medium heat. When the butter melts and the milk is scalding (just below a simmer, as tiny bubbles pop up in the milk around the edges of the pot and steam starts to rise), stir in ½ cup of the cheese until it is completely melted. Keep the milk mixture warm over low heat or off the heat, covered.

Drain the potatoes in a large colander and shake out the excess water. Dump the potatoes back into the pot over low heat. Pour the milk and cheese mixture over the potatoes (reheat gently first if the cheese starts to seize a little while it sits) and add the remaining ½ cup of cheese and the crème fraîche. Now mash the potatoes with a handheld masher, stirring after every 10 mashes or so. Keep working until the potatoes are smooth and thick. If the consistency is a little bit stiffer than you prefer, stir in a few tablespoons of milk until you reach the desired texture.

Season with the remaining ½ teaspoon of salt and the pepper, or more to taste. Transfer to a bowl and serve immediately.

alongside

BEEF TENDERLOIN WITH BACON CARAMELIZED ONIONS ✦ COFFEE-BRAISED SHORT RIBS
CIDER-BRAISED PORK SHOULDER ✦ CRANBERRY HERB STUFFING ROASTED PORTOBELLOS
SPICY BUTTERMILK FRIED CHICKEN ✦ BEER-BRINED TURKEY BREAST

sugar-glazed sweet potatoes *serves 6 to 8*

My father-in-law makes holiday candied sweet potatoes that could settle in on the dessert table with no questions asked by the buffet grazers. He uses canned sweet potatoes, a ton of butter, even more brown sugar, a low oven, several hours, and a disposable aluminum baking pan. People go wide-eyed at the sweetness, a few sneer at the excessiveness of the ingredients, takers scoop conservative spoonfuls, but none of those potatoes ever turn into leftovers. This recipe is inspired by his. Its more moderate measures favor the natural sweetness of the potatoes themselves and still leave a glossy coating of butter and sugar that balances the savory dominance of holiday tables.

4 tablespoons (½ stick) unsalted butter, melted, plus butter for the baking dish

½ cup packed dark brown sugar

2 tablespoons apple cider or water

1 teaspoon kosher salt

¼ teaspoon freshly ground black pepper (about 20 grinds)

3 pounds sweet potatoes, peeled and cut into 1½-inch chunks

Preheat the oven to 400°F. Butter the insides of a 13 by 9-inch baking dish.

In a large mixing bowl, whisk together the brown sugar, cider, butter, salt, and pepper. Add the potato chunks and fold them in with a large rubber spatula to coat them with the sugar mixture.

Dump the potatoes into the prepared baking dish, scraping everything from the bowl with the spatula. Cover the dish with a large piece of aluminum foil and transfer to the oven. Bake for 15 minutes. Take the dish out of the oven, remove the foil, and fold the potatoes with the spatula to recoat with the sugar mixture that pools on the bottom of the dish. Return the potatoes to the oven, uncovered, and bake for another 45 minutes, taking the potatoes out to stir every 15 minutes (doing so will keep the top layer of potatoes moist and coated with sugar).

After an hour of cooking, the potatoes will be very soft and the sugar liquid will become a thick glaze. Serve from the hot dish or transfer to a smaller serving bowl.

alongside

HONEY-BAKED HAM ✦ RACK OF PORK WITH ORANGE BOURBON SAUCE ✦ CAJUN-SPICED TURKEY
CINNAMON CLOVE SEARED DUCK BREAST ✦ CHICKEN BRAISED WITH RIESLING AND APPLES

roasted butternut and spuds *serves 6 to 8*

The same soft mound of mashed potatoes that has been a staple at the holiday table for as long as you can recall gets a subtle makeover with a mix-in of sweet squash. Roasting the butternut emphasizes its sugars in a way that boiling them can't, and sending both the potatoes and squash through a ricer produces a silky, smooth combination. If you don't have a ricer, use a handheld masher, the paddle attachment on a stand mixer, or electric beaters.

2½ pounds butternut squash, peeled, seeded, and cut into 1½-inch cubes (or 2 pounds or 5 cups peeled, seeded, and cubed)

2 tablespoons extra virgin olive oil

1 teaspoon kosher salt, plus more to taste

2 pounds russet potatoes, peeled and cut into 1-inch-thick chunks

⅓ cup warm heavy cream

3 tablespoons unsalted butter at room temperature

⅛ teaspoon freshly ground black pepper (about 10 grinds), plus more to taste

Preheat the oven to 400°F.

In a large mixing bowl, toss the squash cubes with the olive oil and ¼ teaspoon of the salt. Spread the cubes across a large baking sheet pan and roast for 45 minutes or until tender when poked with a fork. Toss the squash every 15 minutes to avoid overbrowning on any side of the cubes.

While the squash cooks, put the potatoes in a large saucepan (at least 3 quarts) and fill to cover by an inch with cold water. Add ½ teaspoon of the remaining salt, cover the pot, and bring the water to a boil over high heat. When the water boils, turn the heat down to medium, uncover the pot, and simmer the potatoes for 15 to 20 minutes, until they are tender and break apart when poked with a knife or fork. Drain the potatoes and let them dry just slightly while you wait for the squash to finish cooking.

Set the potato pot back on the burner over low heat and add the cream and the butter. Send the potatoes and squash through the ricer into the pot and then mix together by hand until smooth. Season with the remaining ¼ teaspoon of salt and the pepper, or more to taste. If you are using a mixer or beaters instead of a ricer, blend the potatoes and squash for about 30 seconds before adding the cream and butter gradually until you reach the desired consistency. Transfer to a bowl and serve immediately.

alongside

CRANBERRY-GLAZED TURKEY ✦ PAN-SEARED AND ROASTED PEPPER CRUST BEEF TENDERLOIN
ORANGE SPICE PORK LOIN ✦ ROASTED ROSEMARY LEG OF LAMB

BIBLIOGRAPHY

Asbell, Robin. *Big Vegan*. San Francisco: Chronicle Books, 2011.

Bayless, Rick. *Authentic Mexican: Regional Cooking from the Heart of Mexico*. New York: William Morrow Books, 2007.

Cook's Illustrated Magazine. Best American Side Dishes. Brookline, MA: America's Test Kitchen, 2005.

Corriher, Shirley O. *Cookwise*. New York: William Morrow Cookbooks, 1997.

Dornenburg, Andrea, and Karen Page. *Culinary Artistry*. New York: Wiley, 1996.

Dragonwagon, Crescent. *Bean by Bean*. New York: Workman Publishing Company, 2012.

Gutierrez, Sandra. *The New Southern-Latino Table*. Chapel Hill, NC: The University of North Carolina Press, 2011.

Herrick, Holly. *Tart Love*. Layton, UT: Gibbs Smith, 2011.

Levy Beranbaum, Rose. *The Bread Bible*. New York: W.W. Norton and Company, 2003.

McGee, Harold. *On Food and Cooking*. New York: Scribners, 2004.

Nguyen, Andrea. *Into the Vietnamese Kitchen*. Berkeley: Ten Speed Press, 2006.

Scarbrough, Mark, and Bruce Weinstein. *The Ultimate Potato Book*. New York: William Morrow Cookbooks, 2003.

Simmons, Marie. *The Good Egg*. New York: Houghton Mifflin Harcourt, 2006.

Speck, Maria. *Ancient Grains for Modern Meals*. Berkeley: Ten Speed Press, 2011.

Sternman Rule, Cheryl, and Paulette Phlipot. *Ripe*. Philadelphia: Running Press, 2012.

Tyler Herbst, Sharon. *The Food Lover's Companion*. Hauppague, NY: Barron's Educational Series, 2001.

Vetri, Marc, and David Joachim. *Il Viaggio di Vetri*. Berkeley: Ten Speed Press, 2008.

Willis, Virginia. *Bon Appetit, Ya'll*. Berkeley: Ten Speed Press, 2008.

RESOURCES

These are a few of my favorite suppliers, whose products help me make and serve my side dishes. I especially love cookware that doubles as a serving vessel, like enamel cast-iron Dutch ovens or attractive ceramic bakers and pie dishes. A few high-end pieces are worth the investment and will sustain generations of cooking. You can pass those kitchen tools down along with your favorite recipes.

BRANDS

Emile Henry for quality ceramic cookware
www.emilehenryusa.com

Le Creuset for enduring enameled cast-iron cookware
http://cookware.lecreuset.com

Lodge Cast Iron Cookware
www.lodgemfg.com

Staub for durable and elegant enameled cast-iron cookware
www.staubusa.com/

CorningWare for oven-to-table ceramic stoneware
http://www.corningware.com

Oxo for versatile and practical cooking tools
http://www.oxo.com

All-Clad for copper, steal, and aluminum cookware
www.brand.all-clad.com

SPECIALTY DISTRIBUTORS

Williams-Sonoma
www.williams-sonoma.com

Sur La Table
www.surlatable.com

Crate and Barrel
www.crateandbarrel.com

METRIC CONVERSION FORMULAS

To Convert	Multiply
Ounces to grams	Ounces by 28.35
Pounds to kilograms	Pounds by 0.454
Teaspoons to milliliters	Teaspoons by 4.93
Tablespoons to milliliters	Tablespoons by 14.79
Fluid ounces to milliliters	Fluid ounces by 29.57
Cups to milliliters	Cups by 236.59
Cups to liters	Cups by 0.236
Pints to liters	Pints by 0.473
Quarts to liters	Quarts by 0.946
Gallons to liters	Gallons by 3.785
Inches to centimeters	Inches by 2.54

APPROXIMATE METRIC EQUIVALENTS

Volume

¼ teaspoon	1 milliliter
½ teaspoon	2.5 milliliters
¾ teaspoon	4 milliliters
1 teaspoon	5 milliliters
1¼ teaspoons	6 milliliters
1½ teaspoons	7.5 milliliters
1¾ teaspoons	8.5 milliliters
2 teaspoons	10 milliliters
1 tablespoon (½ fluid ounce)	15 milliliters
2 tablespoons (1 fluid ounce)	30 milliliters
¼ cup	60 milliliters
⅓ cup	80 milliliters
½ cup (4 fluid ounces)	120 milliliters
⅔ cup	160 milliliters
¾ cup	180 milliliters
1 cup (8 fluid ounces)	240 milliliters
1¼ cups	300 milliliters
1½ cups (12 fluid ounces)	360 milliliters
1⅔ cups	400 milliliters
2 cups (1 pint)	460 milliliters
3 cups	700 milliliters
4 cups (1 quart)	0.95 liter
1 quart plus ¼ cup	1 liter
4 quarts (1 gallon)	3.8 liters

Weight

¼ ounce	7 grams
½ ounce	14 grams
¾ ounce	21 grams
1 ounce	28 grams
1¼ ounces	35 grams
1½ ounces	42.5 grams
1⅔ ounces	45 grams
2 ounces	57 grams
3 ounces	85 grams
4 ounces (¼ pound)	113 grams
5 ounces	142 grams
6 ounces	170 grams
7 ounces	198 grams
8 ounces (½ pound)	227 grams
16 ounces (1 pound)	454 grams
35.25 ounces (2.2 pounds)	1 kilogram

Length

⅛ inch	3 millimeters
¼ inch	6 millimeters
½ inch	1.25 centimeters
1 inch	2.5 centimeters
2 inches	5 centimeters
2½ inches	6 centimeters
4 inches	10 centimeters
5 inches	13 centimeters
6 inches	15.25 centimeters
12 inches (1 foot)	30 centimeters

Common Ingredients and Their Approximate Equivalents

1 cup uncooked rice = 225 grams

1 cup all-purpose flour = 140 grams

1 stick butter (4 ounces • ½ cup • 8 tablespoons) = 110 grams

1 cup butter (8 ounces • 2 sticks • 16 tablespoons) = 220 grams

1 cup brown sugar, firmly packed = 225 grams

1 cup granulated sugar = 200 grams

Oven Temperatures

To convert Fahrenheit to Celsius, subtract 32 from Fahrenheit, multiply the result by 5, then divide by 9.

Description	Fahrenheit	Celsius	British Gas Mark
Very cool	200°	95°	0
Very cool	225°	110°	¼
Very cool	250°	120°	½
Cool	275°	135°	1
Cool	300°	150°	2
Warm	325°	165°	3
Moderate	350°	175°	4
Moderately hot	375°	190°	5
Fairly hot	400°	200°	6
Hot	425°	220°	7
Very hot	450°	230°	8
Very hot	475°	245°	9

Information compiled from a variety of sources, including *Recipes into Type* by Joan Whitman and Dolores Simon (Newton, MA: Biscuit Books, 2000); *The New Food Lover's Companion* by Sharon Tyler Herbst (Hauppauge, NY: Barron's, 1995); and *Rosemary Brown's Big Kitchen Instruction Book* (Kansas City, MO: Andrews McMeel, 1998).

index